Child Abuse
a study text

A

Child Abuse
a study text

edited by Vida Carver

The Open University Press
Milton Keynes · New York

The Open University Press
12 Cofferidge Close, Stony Stratford
Milton Keynes, MK11 1BY, England

Open University Educational Media Inc.
110 East 59th Street
New York, NY 10022, U.S.A.

First published 1978

Designed by the Educational Development Unit
of Newcastle upon Tyne Polytechnic

Printed by Sydenhams Printers, Poole, Dorset

British Library Cataloguing in Publication Data
Child abuse, a study text
1.   Child advice services
I.   Carver, Vida   II.   Open University
362.7'1   HV713

ISBN 0 335 00231 5

Contents

Introduction

This volume forms part of a planned programme of study. Together with the companion volume, *Child Abuse: a reader and sourcebook*[1] it comprises a closely integrated course on child abuse. The two volumes are not intended to be read consecutively. However, they are closely linked at all points and, in order to follow the course as a student, it is necessary for you to have access to both volumes.

The Reader is made up of articles and other material for which full bibliographical details are given in 'References' on p. 286. The book is referred to in this text as 'the Reader' together with appropriate page references.

In addition to the two printed volumes you will also need for use throughout the course:

1.   an exercise book or large notebook. An A4 sized loose-leaf notebook in a binder is ideal.
2.   a piece of card or strong opaque paper, cut to the same size as this page, for use as a shield when doing 'activities' and as a bookmark.

Two or three other small pieces of card to act as bookmarks in the Reader may also be useful.

The course is divided into twenty-five units grouped into six blocks of four units each, plus a final review unit. Each unit is designed to occupy about two hours of study time. The instructional 'core' of each unit, which guides the student through selected readings, is contained in the present volume. All the essential set readings are in the Reader which constitutes your basic library for the course.

Students vary of course in their overall speed of study, and all will probably find that some units seem longer than others, depending upon their familiarity with the content material. You are advised however to set aside from the beginning regular weekly study periods. Your work on the first unit will give you some idea of your own speed of study. Advice on preparing a study calendar is given at the end of Unit 1.

---

[1] LEE, C. M. (ed.) (1978) *Child Abuse: a reader and sourcebook*, Milton Keynes, The Open University Press.

The teaching methods used are based on those developed in The Open University for correspondence teaching. Some points to note before beginning are:

1. The course was designed by a closely-knit team and is therefore highly integrated. For an overview of the plan you should study the Table of Contents (p. v).
2. To ensure, however, that you have access to a wide range of current research, thought and opinion, each unit in the core text has been contributed by a known, named author, and readings selected for the Reader are drawn in the main from the published works of an even wider field of British and international experts. The facts, insofar as they are known, are presented and you are encouraged to reach your own conclusions.
3. Activities, intended to involve you in tasks that will further your learning, are included in every unit. Activities vary in kind. Some are there to help you memorize important information, but more commonly they aim to stimulate thought by requiring you to analyse readings, compare your views with those of others, formulate conclusions, or suggest practical applications for what you have learned. There are rarely 'right' or 'wrong' answers to an activity – but authors' comments, which draw the threads together and perhaps stimulate further thought, usually follow.

In some important respects, however, this course is very different from the usual Open University course. There are no regular contacts with the Course Team through radio or television, no tutors to evaluate progress, no summer schools or study centres to meet fellow students. However, there is the great advantage that you are able to pace the course at the speed you wish to study it without external factors forcing a timetable. Nevertheless, it is important to establish a firm routine of work. Some students, of course, find no hardship in working alone. There are good reasons, however, on a course of this kind, for coming together from time to time with other students, for mutual support, encouragement and discussion. We suggest two possible methods:

1. *Informal* Find a friend or friends with similar interests and arrange to follow the course simultaneously.
2. *Formal* Form a group, preferably with a more experienced leader, or join a class at a college which has adopted the course as part of its teaching programme.

To assist groups or educational institutions to supplement study in this way the course team has prepared a special 'Teaching Package' which provides additional study and discussion material, tapes and case studies, a guide to further reading, etc. The Package may be ordered only from:

Open University Educational Enterprises,
12 Cofferidge Close,
Stony Stratford,
Milton Keynes MK11 1BY
(Tel: Milton Keynes 566744).

We wish you every success in your studies.

July 1977   The Course Team

Editor's acknowledgements

The development of this course necessarily involved the help and support of a variety of different people and organizations. During the initial stages of the course a consultative conference was held by courtesy of the Council for Educational Technology. Our grateful thanks go to the following organizations:

Association of Directors of Social Services
British Association of Social Workers
Central Midwives Board
Council for the Education and Training of Health Visitors
Council for Educational Technology
Department of Education and Science
Department of Health and Social Security
General Nursing Council
Greater London Council of Social Services
Joint Board of Clinical Nursing Studies
National Association of Chief Educational Welfare Officers
National Children's Bureau
National Society for the Prevention of Cruelty to Children
Royal College of General Practitioners
Royal College of Midwives
Royal College of Nursing

Special thanks also to the staff of the Children's Division of the Department of Health and Social Security.

Particular thanks must go to all those who helped to make possible the writing of Unit 2 – to the police service, and a number of lecturers for their help in making arrangements for the administering of questionnaires, and to all the students and professionals in training who answered our questionnaires and discussed their experience and ideas with us.

We are also indebted to all those who volunteered to study the course prior to its publication. For their helpful comments and suggestions we are grateful to the following:—Jean Ryall (social worker), Lee Fairlie (Pre-School Playgroup Association training and development officer), Colin Leon (general practitioner), Anthea Findlay (teacher), Avril Fendley (health visitor) and Rhoda Cross (woman superintendent, Northumbria Police).

For their help and assistance in obtaining a wide variety of reading material mention must also be made of the library staff of both the Open University and the Newcastle upon Tyne Polytechnic. Special thanks go to Sheila Dale, Keith Harris, Audrey Cook, Ann Ramsay, and Ian Winkworth.

Particular thanks are due to Wynne Brindle, Wendy Doggett and Gerry Bearman at the Open University Copyrights Department; to Sue Dale of Newcastle upon Tyne Polytechnic who designed the book, and to Marsaili Cameron, who copy-edited it.

Finally, the contribution made by the administrative and secretarial staff of both institutions is gratefully acknowledged, in particular thanks to Lesley Brazier, Pat Welch, Patricia Bruce, Stella Fisher and Valerie Hall; and for photocopying facilities to Diana Platt and the staff of the Community and Social Studies Faculty Office, Newcastle upon Tyne Polytechnic.

VC

The makers of the course

The course team

From The Open University

Dr Vida Carver (Joint Course Team Chairman) is Academic Co-ordinator for Courses in Health and Social Welfare in the Post-experience Unit of the Open University. A psychologist, she has published research in the social work and educational fields and is particularly interested in handicap and disadvantage. She was joint chairman (with Phillip Williams) of the Open University team which produced 'The Handicapped Person in the Community' and is currently working on a new course concerned with ageing.

Dr Sue Hurley is presently Senior Counsellor in the North Region of the Open University. Originally trained in biology and biochemistry, her previous work has included lecturing at London University, research in agricultural biochemistry at the University of Illinois and working in Local Authority Adult Education.

Penny Liddiard is a graduate in the Social Sciences with research experience in the field of Social Psychology. She is currently working at the Open University on Health and Social Welfare courses. Before coming to the Open University she worked as a research officer at the Cranfield Institute of Technology.

From Newcastle upon Tyne Polytechnic

Constance Lee (Joint Course Team Chairman) is Principal Lecturer in the Department of Health Studies, Newcastle upon Tyne Polytechnic. A nurse, midwife and health visitor, she has specialised in maternal and child health and has held posts in several countries as a member of the World Health Organization. Her current interests are inter-disciplinary education for the health and social services and information retrieval. She has been concerned with the planning of new courses in Britain and overseas.

Bill Roberts is a senior lecturer in social work at Newcastle upon Tyne Polytechnic, where his particular interest has been residential child care. Before this he was a probation officer and a senior child care officer. He was involved in the Nottingham surveys which provided the raw material for Coates and Silburn's book *Poverty: the forgotten Englishmen*. He spent six months at the National Institute for Social Work, where one of his interests was active methods of teaching.

Richard Fothergill is Head of the Educational Development Unit (PETRAS) at Newcastle upon Tyne Polytechnic. Author of *A challenge for librarians* and *Resource centres in colleges of education*, he was formerly a research fellow with the Council for Educational Technology.

The external assessors

Beryl Day trained as a social worker and has considerable experience in working with families where children are at risk. She joined the NSPCC School of Senior Social Work, where she is Deputy Tutor, in 1964, and teaches on a wide range of specialist courses for social workers and all the helping professions concerned with abused children. Her latest article on the subject was published in *Community Care* on the 16th March 1977.

Margery Taylor is presently Director of Social Services for Redbridge. She has extensive experience of the child care services and prior to her present position was Director of Training for the London Boroughs Training Committee. She has always maintained a broad interest in social work and the social services as a whole but she has a particular interest in the inter-relationship of professions, services and agencies.

The consultants

Dr Winifred Cavenagh, OBE, is Emeritus Professor of Social Administration and Criminology at the University of Birmingham, from which she retired in 1976. Her best known work is *Juvenile Courts, the Child and the Law* (1976). She is a barrister and has had many years' experience as a magistrate in both adult and juvenile courts.

Maurice Chazan, Professor in the Department of Education, University College of Swansea, is mainly concerned with courses in child development and special education and the training of educational psychologists. An educational psychologist himself, Professor Chazan has made a significant contribution to the literature on maladjustment, subnormality, compensatory education and early childhood education. He is currently co-director of a research project funded by the DES on the early education of handicapped children.

Dr Christine Cooper is presently Consultant Paediatrician in the Department of Child Health, University of Newcastle upon Tyne. Prior to this she worked for some years in paediatrics in West Africa and also served on the Houghton-Stockdale Committee whose report in 1972 formed the basis of the 1975 Children Act. A member of the Executive Committee of the Association of British Adoption Agencies, her special interests include neglect and deprivation in child abuse, the adoption of children, the care of children in hospital and behavioural/psycho-social problems of children.

Christine Desborough is Research Fellow in the Department of Social Policy and Social Work at the University of Keele. She was Secretary to the Maria Colwell Committee of Inquiry and is currently working on a study of social communication in relation to child abuse.

Marie-Thérèse Gilbert completed both her general and mental nursing training in the early 1960s. She is presently a qualified clinical teacher in adult behavioural psychotherapy for registered mental nurses. Her main interests are in the treatment of child abuse and child handling problems.

Dr Malcolm Hall is Consultant in Charge of the Emergency and Accident Department at Preston Royal Infirmary, where he has worked since 1961. He has been involved with non-accidental injuries to children since that date and has made a special study of the diagnostic features which enable these children to be distinguished from children who have sustained true accidents. He has published several papers and lectured widely on the subject.

Megan Jobling is a sociologist, whose special interest is the child in society. She worked for the National Children's Bureau, who published her *Helping the Handicapped Children in the Family* and also her recent annotated bibliography, *The Abused Child*. She is at present carrying out a study concerning handicapped children for the Institute for Research into Mental and Multiple Handicap.

Carolyn Okell Jones, formerly Research Officer in the NSPCC's original Battered Child Research Department, is co-author of the account of its work, *At Risk* (Routledge & Kegan Paul, 1976). She continues to be closely concerned with child abuse whilst currently employed at the National Children's Bureau and Bedford College, London University.

Anna Kerr, formerly a child care officer, became a member of the NSPCC Battered Child Research Department in 1970 and is co-author of *At Risk*. In 1972 she became a research social worker at the NSPCC, where her work on child abuse has included some lecturing and supervision of students.

Dr Israel Kolvin, Reader in Child Psychiatry at the University of Newcastle upon Tyne, is Director of the Human Development Unit at the University. He is also Consultant Psychiatrist at the Nuffield Psychology and Psychiatry Unit and he has written extensively on adolescent aggression, psychoses in childhood, and related topics. Currently involved in operational research, his present interests include the later development of children born too soon or too small.

Dr Margaret Lynch is a paediatrician who has worked with abusing families in Newcastle and Oxford for some years. She is now engaged on a two year research project at the Park Hospital for Children on the prediction, prevention, and treatment of child abuse and the follow-up of abused children. She remains actively involved with clinical management.

Dr Catherine Peckham was formerly Senior Lecturer in Paediatric Epidemiology at the Institute of Child Health, London, and Senior Medical Research Officer at the National Children's Bureau. She is now Senior Lecturer in community medicine at Charing Cross Hospital Medical School. Her major interest is in the influence of intra-uterine infection on the child and the impact of medical, social and economic factors on child development.

William Reavley is Principal Clinical Psychologist to the Chichester Health District and is Director of a course training registered mental nurses in behavioural psychotherapy based at Graylingwell Hospital, Chichester. He is interested in environmental influences on behaviour and in the development of behavioural approaches to cover a wide range of problems.

Jacquie Roberts is a research social worker engaged on a two year research project at the Park Hospital for Children, Oxford, on the prediction, prevention and treatment of child abuse and the follow-up of abused children. Her previous experience includes both hospital and community social work. Working closely with Dr Margaret Lynch, she is involved in the treatment of families, both at the Park Hospital and in general practice.

Olive Stevenson is Head of the Department of Social Policy and Social Work at the University of Keele. She was a member of the Maria Colwell Committee of Inquiry and is currently engaged on research into local authority social work, including a study of inter-professional communication in child abuse.

Dr Alfred White Franklin was Physician in charge of the Department of Child Health at Saint Bartholomew's Hospital, London. He is Convenor of the Tunbridge Wells Study Group on Non-accidental Injury to Children. His main interests have been the newborn baby and children with handicaps.

Aims of the course

The course is designed for people who may during their working lives come into contact with children in danger of abuse in their homes, foster-homes or in institutions. It is anticipated that most of those who follow the course will have received, or will be receiving, some professional training in medicine, nursing, therapy, psychology, child care, social or welfare work, teaching, social administration, police work, the law or some related discipline. *The course is not intended as a substitute for professional training in any of these professions and will qualify no-one to take on professional responsibilities for which he is not otherwise qualified.* It is however (fortunately) true that for most practitioners cases of child abuse come relatively infrequently to their notice. The aims of the course are therefore to assist such people to:

1. identify the various types of abuse to which children may be exposed in the context of family dysfunction, with particular reference to non-accidental injury and deprivation;
2. understand something of the roles and attitudes of abusing parents, of the predicament of the child, and of the prognosis for both;
3. understand the professional roles of co-workers and develop improved techniques of effective communication with parents, other workers and the community;
4. identify situations in which preventive action should be taken and know the various forms of action which may be appropriate;
5. recognize symptoms of child abuse and know some of the forms of intervention, management and treatment currently practised, and be able critically to discuss their value and effectiveness;
6. propose measures for the promotion of good child-rearing practices, by the realistic education of potential parents.

Block 1   Introduction to the course

Block 1 sets the scene for all that follows. The first unit discusses aims, objectives and course content, and explains how the course is designed for self-instruction. The three units that follow set 'child abuse' in its context: personal, historical, sociological and conceptual.

Unit 1   A guide to the course
The course team

Objectives

At the end of this unit you should be able to:

1. describe the purpose of the course and its relevance to yourself;
2. outline the range and complexity of the subject, and the variety of professions involved;
3. distinguish the areas in which your thinking and learning need extending;
4. plan the use of the material and design a study calendar.

Have you read the Introduction on p. ix? If not, please read it now. You will not be able to use this unit effectively without the preparation it recommends.

1   A guide to the course

1.1 As you will have seen from the objectives at the head of this page, the purpose of this unit is to help you to use the course in the best way for your individual learning. First you need to understand what the course is about. This unit will answer two fundamental questions about it.

Why has the course been written at all?
How is it put together?

2   Aims and objectives

2.1 Before going any further, please re-read (1) '*Aims of the course*', on page xviii and (2) the unit *objectives*. You will notice that they are couched in rather different terms.

2.2 The unit objectives are very specific in their formulation. They exactly describe four tasks which you should be able to carry out successfully by the time you have finished the unit. Every unit in this course is preceded by a set of objectives. Never skip the objectives. Keep them in mind (or refer back to them) as you work. They will help to guide your study. Work critically. If you think that we have not given you enough information to achieve the objectives you may have to carry your researches further. As you finish each unit, return to the objectives and use them as a checklist to satisfy yourself that you really can now carry out the activities they describe.

In contrast, the aims of the course are concerned with its overall purpose. They are broken down into six themes or topics. These themes are not related to particular blocks or units but recur throughout the course. The structure of the course can best be grasped by studying the 'contents' pages, and will receive further attention in the last section of this unit.

Those who conceived, designed and contributed to the course were concerned that it should be of value not merely as an academic exercise, but should also be of practical benefit to children. The course is aimed primarily, therefore, at people who, through professional or voluntary activity, are likely to become involved in human situations where there is a potential for child abuse.

The material in the course varies greatly. Some is hard clinical data; some reviews recent research; some gives guidance on practical matters; some is conjecture and opinion; and some is about ethics and morals. The common denominator is that every part of it is considered to be relevant and necessary for students who desire to make a contribution to the prevention of child abuse, whether their concern arises from the demands of their professions or from a lay interest in the welfare of children and families.

3   The subject

To understand the aims of the course it is first necessary to gain some impression of the range and complexity of the subject matter. A short *activity* (see *Introduction*, p. x) at this point should help.

A note on activities
Activities are of many different kinds but these guidelines apply to them all:

1   Begin by putting the top of your cardboard shield along the horizontal lines that divide the *end* of the activity from the following comments.
2   Read the instructions right through before beginning the task.
3   Head a page of your notebook with the activity number and *write down*, however roughly, any answers called for. You will often need to refer back to an earlier activity as you work through the course. Note that 'Activity 4.2' means the second activity in the fourth unit.

Activity 1.1

Read 'The Nature of the task' by Alfred White Franklin (1975) in the Reader (p. 42). It is suggested that you read it through quite quickly as you will need to look at it more closely as you work through the unit. Then jot down in your notebook short answers to the following questions:

a. White Franklin uses three different terms for the subject under discussion. What others do you know?

b. When you think of 'child abuse' or 'child battering', what type of injuries or damage do you associate with these terms?

c. What age of child do you think is included in these terms?

Comments

3.2 a. You may have added 'The battered baby syndrome' or 'The battered child syndrome'. These are both terms used for the same condition. The choice of terms is important and will be discussed in Unit 3.

b. Similarly, the symptoms of non-accidental injury will be treated fully in Unit 5 and you should refer back to and supplement your list after studying Unit 5. But did you include – as well as physical injury – deprivation of food, clothing, shelter or other material needs? Did you include children subjected to sexual abuse, fear, nagging, quarrelling, and children kept in isolation?

c. If you have answered 'babies' or 'under two' or 'under five', you have too narrow a view of child abuse. For a variety of reasons, the younger the child the more vulnerable he is, but remember that Maria Colwell was eight when she died, and that much older children can be deprived and abused, particularly emotionally. Adolescents may be physically abused, rejected or exploited.

White Franklin lays emphasis on the importance of preventive action. In later units you will be studying in more detail some of the circumstances which have been found to be associated with deprivation and abuse.

Activity 1.2

List some of the individual characteristics or factors in *adults* and *children* which in your opinion predispose to abuse. Keep your list for revision as necessary as you work through the course. No comments will be given here.

3 White Franklin writes in reference to actual abuse: 'We have to begin somewhere . . . the obvious place of departure is medical'. He also writes: 'If diagnosis is to lead to treatment it cannot be exclusively medical'. Think about these two statements. Apart from medical signs and symptoms, what other 'clues' may lead to a recognition of a family setting where abuse is likely to occur? White Franklin refers to a psychiatric and social approach to diagnosis of the family setting.

Activity 1.3
Make a list of factors *within the family setting* which you think may predispose to child abuse.

Comment

.4 Your list may be very short and is probably subjective. If so, do not worry, you will be able to add to it more critically as you work through the course. This exercise was intended to extend your thinking beyond the abused child in isolation. It is only by grasping something of the complexity of the subject and the range of people involved in every case and by taking the appropriate action, that prevention of non-accidental injury can become a reality.

Activity 1.4
You have already considered briefly the range of abuse to which children may be subjected; you have thought a little about some of the individual and environmental factors which may produce abusing adults. Would you now consider and list professional workers and others who may come in contact with child abuse, or be in some way involved.

Comments

.5 Your list could look something like this:

doctors (including general practitioner, paediatrician, radiologist, casualty officer, pathologist, psychiatrist, epidemiologist)
social workers for statutory or voluntary organizations (including NSPCC)
health visitors
nurses

midwives
police
magistrates
judges
psychologists
sociologists
school teachers
education welfare officers
dentists

3.6 If you look at White Franklin's article again, you will find that he mentions most of those listed above. You have possibly also included playgroup and youth club leaders, solicitors and barristers, probation officers, nursery matrons, child minders, 'neighbours', 'the community', and others.

3.7 In this section we have drawn attention to the wide range of people who may become involved in cases of child abuse, each with a different function but with common aims – to prevent where possible, to diagnose, to treat, and to rehabilitate. This complexity of professional involvement will be the subject of Units 7 and 8. White Franklin's article also briefly mentions conflict of attitudes, and this will be treated further in Units 2, 7 and 18.

4 Course priorities

4.1 You should now be in a similar situation to that of the course team when it began to design this course. You recognize the complexity of the subject, but it is difficult to know where to start in formulating ideas about what should be done about the problem.

4.2 Throughout the course the intention has been to provide information and ideas which students can apply to their own situations. Material has been selected, therefore, on the basis of its value in achieving the aims which will change information into working knowledge.

Activity 1.5
You should by now be in a position to consider how you want to use the course, how you are going to put your knowledge to work. Most students at the beginning of a course, even a short one like this, find that the realization of how much there is to know is daunting and confusing. The way to restore sanity is to provide yourself with a focus and a purpose for your learning. You may find later on that this will

change or expand, but don't worry. It is important to have a focus at the beginning rather than blundering about in a mass of fascinating ideas. It is suggested, therefore, that you read the following questions, which should be equally relevant whether you are a chief constable, a child minder or a parent, and note down the answers to which you can refer from time to time. Some of the answers will raise further questions in your mind; ask and answer these too.

a. What was my interest in beginning this course? (If the answer is rather vague or general, try to pin down one or two fairly specific reasons.)
b. What are the relevant aspects of my own situation? (for example, professional, voluntary, 'social'; resources and powers; colleagues, consultants, guidance; types of situations in which involved; expectations of you by others; expectations of you by self; etc.).
c. What improvements in my activity do I wish to see as a result of following the course?
   (Try to be specific, and to use verbs which suggest action – for example, recognize symptoms earlier; use knowledge of professionals' roles to improve communication; etc.)
d. What sorts of knowledge are required to achieve the above improvements?
e. In what areas do I lack the requisite knowledge?
   (If more than one, list them quantitatively, so that you know those which need 'topping up' and those where there is great ignorance.)
f. What issues do I need to think (or re-think) about?

Comments

3 In this very personal activity no general comments can tell you whether you are 'right' or 'wrong', but here are two hints which should help you still further to clarify your study priorities on the threshold of the course:

a. Re-read and use 'Aims of the course' (p. xviii) to check that you have considered all the major themes the course deals with, that might be relevant to your needs.
b. Use the table of contents (p. v) and mark in on your list the numbers of any units which you think may be particularly relevant to any special learning needs.

5   Self-assessment questions

1 You will have gathered from 'Aims of the course' that the course does not

offer any certification. If you are undertaking it as part of a basic training course, the institution or authorizing body may wish to include it in their general award and testing procedure. However, if you are studying it by yourself, there is no provision for a test. Nevertheless, it is useful for your own satisfaction:

a. to check how well you are doing;
b. to see how much you are remembering;
c. to assess how much you are really understanding.

5.2 The course has been structured carefully, and you should have a good comprehension of one block before you start the next one. To help you check on this, we have provided a set of self-assessment questions (SAQs) at the end of each block of units. Turn to page 46, and have a quick look at those for the first block.

5.3 You will see that the questions are set out on one page, and the answers on another. The questions are of different types: some are of the objective type to which there are definite right and wrong answers; others require a fuller reply, the answer supplied being a minimum list of points that should be included.

5.4 The recommended procedure for tackling the SAQs is as follows:

a. Set aside a minimum of one hour.
b. Read all the questions through and, starting with the one you can deal with most easily, *write* out your answers.
c. Do not refer back to your notes or look back in the text. Answer from memory.
d. Try to answer every question. Even if you find it difficult, have a go at it.
e. When you have finished *all* the questions, turn to the answers on the next page. A suggested number of marks are given against each answer, so give yourself credit and add up your total. You should achieve around the 70–80 per cent level.
f. If there are any that you answered badly, go back to the unit referred to, and go through it again.
g. Be honest with yourself. Nobody else is going to see how well or badly you have done. SAQs have been provided to help you measure your own rate of progress.

6 Planning your study

6.1 Just as there are no external tests, there are also no fixed lesson times. If this is the first time you have undertaken a home study course of this nature in your present environment, you may find some difficulty in organizing your work satisfactorily. The remainder of this unit consists of a series of *suggestions* which may help you. Do adapt and modify them to suit your own learning style.

2   Each unit, together with the relevant sections from the Reader, is designed to take two hours of studying. We suggest you try to do a *minimum* of two units per week, and do not attempt more than one at a session. Allow yourself at least half a day between units, so that you can think over the implications of what you have been studying. Leave at least a day between completing the last unit of a block and tackling the SAQs.

3   You will find it a great help to construct a study calendar which will assist you in organizing your time. A suggested model is given below. In preparing your own, take into account holidays, favourite television programmes, family activities and commitments. Blocking in a reserve time is useful if you over-run on a unit or have an unforeseen interruption.

Day	Time	Block	Unit	SAQs	SAQ mark
Thurs.	7.30 – 9.30	1	2		
Sat.	10.00 – 12.00	(reserve date)			
Mon.	8.00 – 10.00	1	3		
Thurs.	7.30 – 9.30	1	4		
Sat.	10.00 – 12.00	(reserve date)			
Mon.	8.00 – 9.00			Block 1	

Activity 1.6
Draw out your own study calendar. Try to prepare it for the whole course, even if you have to modify it later. Either plan it on a separate sheet of paper or adapt an engagement calendar or diary.

Comments

4   You should have discussed your plan with your family or friends. Their support and commitment to helping you study the course is very important, as they can assist you with encouragement and prevent you from being interrupted unnecessarily. The co-operation of a friend or member of your family can be a very useful sounding board for discussion of some

of the issues raised in the text, even though he or she has no personal or professional knowledge. Personal relationships are most important in understanding and treating child abuse, and you may be able to gain valuable insights from such discussions.

6.5 Finally, a few suggestions for studying the course.

a. Always try to finish a unit at one session. Some units, 7 and 8, 10 and 11, 17–18, 19 and 20, 21–22, are designed as double or linked units, and can be spread over two sessions, but the others should be completed in one. If interruptions or other domestic activities prevent this, try to find an extra period of time before the next session to finish it off.

b. Keep your notes as logically as possible. Start each unit's jottings on a new sheet of paper. Also all the activities should be kept on separate sheets, as later activities refer back to earlier ones and encourage you to amend them.

c. When you begin a unit, make sure you are comfortably settled, with pens, paper, etc. ready, and try to remove from the vicinity any distractions like letters you should have answered. Scan the unit, identifying the pieces you need to find in the Reader, and mark their places in that text ready for instant referral. Note the number of activities, the number of sections and the general shape of the unit. Then get started.

6.6 In both volumes, you will find two types of further reading listed. Those marked 'References' are items specifically linked to the point in the text of the unit or article to which they refer, or are the source of the information summarized or mentioned. Those marked 'Recommended further reading' are other books or articles which add further depth and perspectives in general to the unit you have been studying. If you wish to make use of either type of source, they may be found or ordered at your local library.

6.7 If you want to make use of the further reading opportunities, try to fit them in before starting the next unit, or hold them over to the end of the course. Only if the topic is of very special interest to you would it be advisable to rearrange your study calendar to accommodate these extra items.

Recommended further reading

ROWNTREE, D. (1976) *Learn how to study*, London, Macdonald.
BUZAN, T. (1974) *Use your head*, London, BBC Publications.

Unit 2   Personal attitudes to child abuse
Bill Roberts and Vida Carver

Objectives

After completing this unit you should be able to:

1. list some of the emotions commonly experienced by people on coming into contact with abused children;
2. analyse and come to terms with your own feelings, and be prepared for the ways in which they may affect your judgement in specific cases.

1   Introduction

1   For most of us the subject of child abuse is a highly emotive one. The public interest and outcry which occurs regularly in connection with the more notorious cases of child abuse is fairly conclusive evidence of emotional reaction. Nearer home, think for a moment about your own feelings as you began this course. As well as an academic or practical interest in the subject there were almost certainly underlying emotions: pity, anger, guilt, apprehension, outraged sense of justice – some or all of these, and perhaps others. If you have told others that you are following this course, you may have noticed that almost all of them have fairly strong opinions or feelings about the subject.

2   This unit will examine some of the common feelings which people experience, and their implications. The method which has been adopted to do this is as follows:

a. examination of visual and written material about abused children, and the completion of a questionnaire which helps you to identify your feelings;
b. examination and discussion of the results of 66 such questionnaires, and the implications;
c. examination of your own results in the context of (b) above, and the possible implications for your own learning and practice.

Activity 2.1
If you have little experience of child abuse, you may find this activity stressful. While you are advised to go ahead with it alone, it would be

a good idea to make sure in advance that you have a friend or colleague not far away who will respond if you need to talk through the experience afterwards.

Turn to the colour plates in the Reader and study closely the photographs and captions. Take as long as you like, but do not make notes or read anything else before completing this whole activity.

Next, turn to p. 289 in the Reader and read paragraphs 59 to 67 inclusive of the extract from the inquiry report on L.G. Again, do not make notes. Finally (but not before you have finished looking and reading), turn to Appendix I at the end of this unit, where you will find a questionnaire. Read the notes at the top, and then complete the questionnaire.

2   Common attitudes towards child abuse

2.1   Emotion is a natural and necessary response to many human situations. Psychologists recognize the close link between emotion and motivation. Even the words come from the same root. If we never 'felt an honest emotion', we would be little more than human vegetables, and we would certainly lack understanding of other, more warm-blooded human beings. Cannon's (1945) classical 'emergency theory of the emotions' concep-tualized the physiological changes that take place in states of high emo-tional arousal as 'preparations for supreme effort in flight or fighting'. Most of us have of course been successfully trained from childhood to suppress the full response and usually stand our ground, if timidly, or refrain from hitting out when gripped by emotion, and we may even try to pretend to ourselves that we have not experienced it. But our bodies are not as easily fooled as our minds.

Emergency responses are, however, dangerous guides to cool judgement and wise action. Emotion may act as a filter which screens our sensory and intellectual perception. Thus, we may see only what we expect to see, believe only what we want to believe. (This is well known to psychologists, who call it 'selective perception'.) In connection with this course this effect is doubly important, for it may well operate in two stages. First, it may affect your reception of some of the information which is offered you (and also your perception of it); secondly, it may affect your perception and judgement in real-life situations. Hence objective (2) above. Remember that just as it is no virtue to feel spontaneous pity, neither is it a crime to feel anger. One cannot prevent one's emotions. The important thing is to recognize them honestly and understand them.

2 The questionnaire which you have just completed was previously completed by 66 volunteers. There was a difference, however, in that the volunteers were not asked to read the extract from the report, only to look at the pictures. There were six groups of people: social workers in training, qualified nurses training to be health visitors, police officers in training school during their first year of service, and student teachers. These four groups were selected because they are drawn from some of the professions which it is hoped will make use of this course. Two additional groups were included: students following a course in transport studies; and clerical, administrative and technical personnel. These two groups were included in order to obtain some representation of the 'layman's' response, since by training or occupation they are not directly concerned with social problems.

3 The 66 volunteers are not, of course, necessarily representative of the general population, nor indeed of the professions or occupations they follow. Neither, since the sample was small, have the results any statistical significance. The purpose in using the questionnaire was not to obtain original research data, but to provide a rough and ready general picture of common attitudes towards child abuse to aid you in examining the results of your own questionnaire. We shall, nevertheless, be making some conjectures based on the results of the questionnaire; but they are just that – conjectures to help you in examining your own attitudes, and not statistical proof of general attitudes known to exist.

4 Turn now to Appendix II at the end of this unit, which is a diagrammatic representation of the number of ticks made against each statement by the volunteers. The results are arranged in descending order of frequency of ticking, but the statement numbers and descriptions in the first column correspond with the statements on the questionnaire you have completed.

5 The first thing you will notice is that all the statements on your list were ticked by at least some of the respondents. None of the reactions listed can be considered 'abnormal'.

6 In the Introduction we stated that child abuse is an emotive subject. You may think that the responses in Appendix II bear this out. Nearly half the respondents felt 'deep sorrow', and over half were 'horrified or appalled' at the photographs. Indeed, when the questionnaire was originally piloted the terms used were much milder, and our 'guinea pigs' told us that the language was inadequate to describe the strong feelings which were aroused. Also note that nearly half the respondents were 'anxious or tense or fearful' at being asked to look at the photographs.

2.7 Being more specific, note that a minority (about 35%) felt shame at being a member of a species which does such things to children, and a smaller minority (about 17%) felt disturbed to think that they might be capable of abusing a child. This could be interpreted as meaning that a substantial proportion of the respondents do not themselves identify with abusing adults as fellow human beings, and an even greater proportion (over 80%) do not see themselves as potential abusers of children. Assuming this to be so, what are the implications? One is that unless we can cease to view abusing adults as different from ourselves, as almost an alien sub-species, we shall have great difficulty in taking in the information which suggests the opposite, and consequently equal difficulty in understanding how people come to abuse their children. Understanding is an emotional as well as an intellectual activity, and makes use of sympathy and empathy. Over half the respondents ticked the need for more information about the background of the children in the photographs. In discussion with the respondents the reason for this became clear. It was linked with the fact that most of us see a great difference between an impulsive act of abuse (striking with hand or fist), and a premeditated and continuing one (burning with a cigarette). Perhaps this is because we all experience sudden losses of temper, which might in certain circumstances lead to physical aggression. In other words, we use sympathy to help us to understand such a temporary loss of control. On the other hand, few of us are prepared to admit to ourselves that we have sometimes behaved in premeditatedly hostile ways to others (and even fewer have *never* done so). To understand those who can nurse hostility and plan and sustain a hostile action, we need to have genuine fellow-feeling, the feeling implied by, but sometimes forgotten behind, the professional jargon-word 'empathy'. Search your memory for occasions when you have deliberately hurt (with words or deeds) another person. Don't get off the hook by reminding yourself of how thoroughly he or she deserved it. The exercise will cause you some pain and shame, but remember that these too were probably part of the experience of the abusing mother or father. The need for more information about the backgrounds of those children in the photographs is probably a search for reasons which *we* can understand; that is, reasons that are within our experience. Perhaps the search is doomed to comparative failure unless we can identify more readily with the abusing adult.

Activity 2.2
Conjecturing about the possible meanings of the results is something which you can try for yourself. Try some conjectures of your own, using the diagram in Appendix II. Note down your answers to the following questions before reading on. (Add more questions for yourself if you wish.)

a. The most common response (only four people did not tick it) was, 'I felt pity (or distress, or concern) for the injured children'. Remembering that most of these people are in the 'helping professions', and assuming this to be a very common response, what emphasis would you expect child welfare services to have? And what might they lack?

b. The two next common responses were, 'I felt angry with the individuals who could injure a child in such ways', and, 'I felt that such crimes should not go unpunished'. What are the possible implications for public support for services working with abusing adults? What are the implications for the use of services by abusing adults?

c. 41 per cent of the respondents (most of them professionals, remember) had difficulty in believing that such things could be done knowingly by human beings. How might this affect the detection of child abuse?

d. Some people (perhaps you, too?) ticked answers clearly in conflict with one another, for example, they felt both pity for and punitive towards the abusing adults, or clinically detached and also angry with society. How might such conflicting emotions affect their own behaviour?

Comments

8 These are not 'right answers'. Yours are likely to be as valid.

a. If pity and distress concerning the children is an overriding motivational force, then it might well happen that child welfare services emphasize rescue and protection, and that services are essentially crisis services. What could be lacking could be real attention to the total needs of abused children, the needs of the family, preventive work, research, long-term care, and rehabilitation. This is discussed fully in Unit 23.

b. Anger can be a strongly motivating force. People who feel angry will be more likely to report incidents than those who feel only shame or anxiety. It can also be a means of detachment, or dissociation. Services designed to help, rather than punish, abusing adults might get minimal support because helping lessens detachment, and this is emotionally uncomfortable. The abusing adult is less likely to use a service which he sees as being angry with him and/or punitive towards him. If your action has put you beyond the pale, you may not try to get back in.

c. Inability or unwillingness to believe that ordinary human beings can abuse children could make detection much less likely, particularly in the early stages. If we do not want to believe that a parent is abusing his child, we are more likely to accept an explanation for an injury which our common sense tells us is implausible. Elsewhere in this core text you will find that disbelief is known to be an important factor militating against the detection of child abuse, even amongst medical personnel who are probably best equipped to diagnose an injury as non-accidental.

d.   Conflicting emotions can have a paralysing effect on a person's capacity for consistent action. They are, however, very common. People who have been able to recognize them in themselves are in a stronger position for sorting themselves out before acting than those who only become aware of conflict after the decisions have been made.

2.9   The questionnaire provides some more examples of how our feelings might be affected by our experience. The 66 respondents were asked to give information about age, sex and whether they were, or had been, parents or foster parents. Comparing the responses of different groups is of some interest. For example, 44 per cent of non-parents ticked the 'disbelief' statement as compared with 31 per cent of parents. Perhaps the experience of parenthood makes one more aware of one's own potential for child abuse, and therefore that of others also.

This idea is supported by the response to the statement, 'I felt pity (or distress or concern) for the abusing adults'. 50 per cent of parents ticked this, as compared with 32 per cent of non-parents. Again, perhaps the experience of being a parent makes one more likely to understand the predicament of the abusing parent.

It may not, however, be that simple, for the parents tended also to be older than the rest, so that what we may be seeing is the effect of longer experience of life; that one becomes more tolerant or understanding as one gets older. Comparing age groups, 43 per cent of those under 25 felt a need to be involved in some action to help abused children, as compared with 31 per cent of those over 25. One might argue that what youth lacks in tolerance and understanding it makes up for in enthusiasm for practical action.

3 Understanding your attitudes

3.1   You should now be able to examine the results of your own questionnaire, and do some analysis of it (and yourself). You may find that what you 'feel' about yourself sometimes conflicts with the results of your own questionnaire. If so, and it is quite likely, try to be objective about it.

The questionnaire, if you did it honestly and conscientiously, should provide 'harder' information than the mental picture you commonly carry of your own personality.

Activity 2.3
Examine your own questionnaire and make notes about the following topics, which are meant only as suggestions to start you off. Add your own as appropriate.

a. How do I view child abuse? As a crime, a personal problem, a social problem, a disease? Or what?

b. Do I need to widen my view of it? If so, in what directions?

c. What makes me feel uncomfortable? The helplessness of the abused infant or child? The isolation of the abusing adult? The distaste of physical violence? The thought that abusing adults are fellow human beings? The horror of it all? Or what?

d. If I were to shy away from the uncomfortable areas, to which parts of this course would I pay least attention? (Look at the contents list and note them.) And what situations in practice would I be likely to try to avoid?

2.2 You should now know yourself a little better and it is hoped that you have derived some satisfaction from the experience. If you read over your notes, you should have a practical guide to help you compensate for your own particular feelings, prejudices and values. As far as the course is concerned, you know that you must deliberately devote extra time to those sections listed under (d) above. Also, if and when you find a topic boring, inappropriate to you, or difficult to understand, inquire whether the explanation might be that your feelings are getting in the way of your reason. The notes you have made for this unit should help you to satisfy yourself as to whether this is so, or not.

Finally, in your practice you will know what situations are likely to make you reach for your blinkers, your rosecoloured spectacles, or your shotgun. Forewarned, you can leave them all at home.

You may find that you have some 'delayed reaction' after completing this unit. One way in which this can happen is shown in a letter which one respondent (who had ticked statement 3) very kindly sent us.

'I had a bad nightmare about my dog injuring a puppy the night after filling in the questionnaire. Later my next door roomer told me that she had a bad nightmare too. Obviously the

pictures had more effect than we realized at the time, so I
thought I should tell you.'

If you ticked statement 3 only, perhaps you had better examine your feelings
again. It is easier to face them now with your eyes open than later in the dark.

If you continue to feel disturbed after completing this unit – whether you are
a professional worker in a caring profession or not – talk the problem over
as soon as possible with an experienced professional. Remember, they are
there to help you too.

Appendix I

1. Below is a list of statements made by various people who have looked at the material you have just examined.
2. Think back at the material as honestly as you can, then:
3. In the blank column, *tick* all those items that come near to expressing a reaction of your own. *Omit* any that you did not honestly feel at the time.
4. You may find that you had some reactions that appeared contradictory to others equally honestly experienced. If so, tick both.

1	I felt unable to carry out the instruction to examine the material closely.	
2	I felt anxious (or fearful, or tense, or reluctant) when I first looked at the material.	
3	I felt quite detached and studied the material with clinical objectivity.	
4	I was horrified (or appalled) at the sight of the material.	
5	I had difficulty in comprehending (or believing) that these things could really be done knowingly by human beings.	
6	I experienced feelings of physical nausea (or sickness, or faintness or shock).	
7	I felt guilty, as though in some way personally responsible or involved.	
8	I felt deep sorrow (or I wanted to cry).	
9	I felt angry with the individuals who could injure a child in such ways.	
10	I felt pity (or distress, or concern) for the injured children.	
11	I felt angry with a society in which such things can happen.	
12	I felt disturbed at the thought that I myself might be capable of hurting a child.	
13	I felt pity (or distress or concern) for the abusing adults.	
14	I felt angry with the workers in touch with the families who ought to have prevented the abuse.	

15	I felt that such crimes should not go unpunished.	
16	I felt sympathy or concern for the workers handling these cases.	
17	I felt a need to be involved in some action to help abused children or children at risk.	
18	I felt useless and incapable of reacting constructively.	
19	I felt a strong need for more information about the circumstances of each individual case.	
20	I felt ashamed that such things can be done by human beings.	
21	I felt that some abuses are clearly worse than others and it is unfair to lump them all together.	

Appendix II

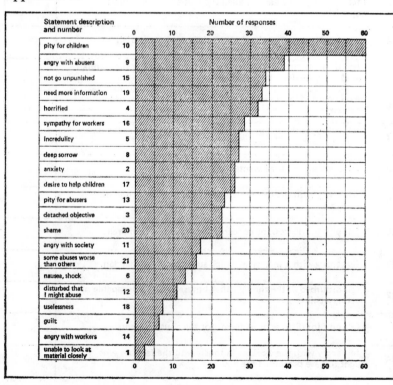

Unit 3 Child abuse: the historical and sociological context

Megan Jobling

Objectives

When you have finished this unit you should be able to:

1. Describe some ways in which society's concept of the child has changed historically;
2. discuss the implications of such changes for standards and methods of 'parenting';
3. give some account of how relationships within the family are affected by social developments;
4. identify the part physical discipline plays in the socialization of children in our culture;
5. explain why the term 'abused child' is now preferred to 'battered baby'.

1 Historical perspectives

.1 Child abuse is nothing new. It is not specific to our particular time or society. There have always been parents who have deliberately injured their own children. For hundreds of years parents have whipped or starved, locked up and thrashed their babies and children. Beatings and mutilations have been recorded from very early times, while from even further back there are myths and legends about infanticide and exposure; many of our fairy stories – which are folk lore rather than tales specially made up for the nursery – have a common theme of abandonment, rejection and physical cruelty to children. Various writers have suggested that child abuse is a primitive form of population control – either by death or by impairment of the child's later mating and reproductive chances. Bakan (1971), for instance, has pointed out how those children who are continuously hurt become unlovable: they cry a lot, become hyper-sensitive to pain, are depressed and destructive and so are unlikely to be loved by anyone. Child abuse is not a new social phenomenon; it has occurred throughout history for a variety of causes. It is society's awareness and concern which is new.

.2 Today's society idealizes the parent-child relationship and emphasizes the 'naturalness' of parenthood, but this is a very recent development. People have not by any means always felt towards children the way we do today. It is always difficult to understand clearly the relationships and the emotions of another time; we tend to attribute our own feelings and values to people of other times and other societies, especially where our central beliefs are concerned. We assume, for example, that in the times of high infant mortality it was because parents cared so much about their children that they cultivated a detachment toward them in sheer self-defence. For us, here and now, to watch and wait for child after child to die in the same family would be agonising heartbreak that would leave terrible scars on both personality and marriage, so we assume that parents then deliberately grew a protective skin. We find it hard to realize that not only physical conditions change over time, but that our whole way of looking at life changes too. We generalize from our own experiences.

1.3 The high infant death rate which persisted until very recently was in part a consequence of the parents' detachment, not the other way around. The quality of mothering is closely linked to infant well-being. Maternal care affects the quality of nutrition and of domestic cleanliness. Maternal empathy can compensate in large degree for lack of knowledge.

1.4 Our image of the child – the way we in today's western society think and feel about children – differs widely from the images held at various points in history. Quite early on, and down through the Greek and Roman ages, there was an awareness of a difference between the world of the child and the world of the adult. Transition between the two was marked by some form of preparatory education or initiation, but by medieval times this had disappeared. By then the concept of childhood as a separate stage of life, with its own psychological nature, simply did not exist. The baby was hardly human, more of a little animal, but the child was a miniature adult.

1.5 The French historian, Aries (1973) has described infancy in medieval society as a period of 'benign indifference', when babies and small children didn't count much emotionally in their parents' lives, but were treated kindly enough. Other writers disagree with his adjective 'benign', claiming that parents deeply resented the mess and demands of babies; although birth itself was a proud event, child-rearing was tedious. Certainly, benign or not, these parents were indifferent to their children's needs or emotions. They thought of them as small, immature adults. As soon as a child could live without constant care, he belonged to adult life. He wore adult clothes and he shared the games and toys, stories, work and sexual jokes of adults. Today we use age as an important definer of role, behaviour and status – our age is part of our individual identity – and we do many things according to our age group; but the turbulent communities of the middle ages lacked this consciousness.

.6 All this is not to say that the children were not loved by their parents – many were. But they were loved in the parents' own way. Children were useful possessions for the family. In wealthier homes, they were important in negotiations for a marriage which could bring wealth and prestige to all members of the family. The child's own feelings and inclinations were very seldom considered. In 1449, for instance, the Paston family were trying to arrange a marriage between their young daughter, Elizabeth, and an elderly widower called Stephen Scrope, but Elizabeth was proving difficult (Gairdner, 1900). In a letter to her husband away from home on a business trip, Elizabeth's mother described the rough domestic discipline she was using to persuade Elizabeth to consent.

> And she hath since Easter the most part been beaten once in
> the week or twice, or sometimes twice in one day, and her
> head broken in two or three places . . . she was never in so
> great sorrow as she is nowadays. . . .

Elizabeth, who must have had a staunch, unconventional spirit for those days, eventually gave in and married Stephen. This same Stephen Scrope had earlier in life been pressed for money and had sold his small daughter's wardship to a knight. He wrote of that incident, 'For very need I was fain to sell a little daughter I have for much less that I should have done'. It was the low payment he regretted, rather than the necessity for the transaction.

.7 Parents saw their children as useful bargaining counters who could bring money to the family, or as another pair of hands to help earn the family's living. It was taken for granted that very young children worked – apprenticeships began as early as seven – and the younger the better. The belief in the social value of child labour was to continue for a very long time. Daniel Defoe (1728) wrote enthusiastically of children of four who could earn their own living. It did not entirely disappear under the pressures of the factory system. In 1876 an Assistant Factory Inspector said of Devon parents that there were still some who thought 'they brought children into the world to no purpose, if they (did) not become contributors to the family purse as soon as they (could) hold a lace pillow, or shuffle a lace stick'.

.8 Very gradually the pattern of indifference to children and the lack of compassion for the state of childhood began to change from the sixteenth century onwards. The child's sweetness, simplicity and quaint sayings became a source of amusement and relaxation for the adult – so much so that by the seventeenth century writers were complaining that children were being spoiled. This change was more noticeable among the upper and middle classes; the traditional indifference persisted until comparatively modern times among many poorer and more rural families.

1.9 The growing fondness for and consequent interest in the child, although still lacking any true empathy, began to be expressed in attempts at psychological understanding and in solicitude for his moral well-being. Now the child was seen as a fragile creature of God who needed to be both safeguarded and reformed. The Puritan concern with salvation reinforced this view and there developed a new, double image of the child as both innocent and evil. At much the same time as Rousseau in France was comparing the innocent child with the 'noble savage', Susanna Wesley, the influential mother of the great religious leader, John Wesley, was also writing:

> Break their wills betimes; begin this great work before they
> can run alone, before they can speak plain, or perhaps speak
> at all . . . conquer their stubbornness; break the will, if you
> would not damn the child. . . . Therefore (1) Let a child,
> from a year old, be taught to do this, (2) Let him have
> nothing he cries for; absolutely nothing, great or small; else
> you undo your own work. (3) At all events, from that age,
> make him do as he is bid, if you whip him ten times running
> to effect it. . . . Break his will now, and his soul will live,
> and he will probably bless you to all eternity.   (Wesley, 1872)

1.10 In fact, one side of the image, the stress on natural simplicity, was in part a form of social criticism. The latter decades of the eighteenth century in England saw the emergence of the new-style capitalist industrialism which was to change the face of Britain. Already many men and women were disturbed by the quickening tempo and restrictive mechanization of life and this concern was given expression and reinforced by the poems and songs of the Romantic poets, notably Blake and Wordsworth, which emphasized the spiritual and emotional qualities of life. The Romantic Movement in England had been stimulated and influenced by the writings of the French Enlightenment Movement and picked up and developed Rousseau's theme of the innocence of childhood. (You will probably be able to think of other, much more recent, social developments which have similarly changed our attitudes and values.)

1.11 Popularized into the angel child full of innocent pranks, the image carried through Victorian times. Socialization came to be achieved by threats and guilt; whipping began to go out of style and punishment by dark cupboards and isolation came in. Then a series of nineteenth-century detailed 'baby biographies' (including one by the evolutionist Charles Darwin) helped to legitimize the study of the child and give it a scientific value, and towards the end of the century various psychological studies were published. Freud's revelations of the importance of early experiences heightened interest in child development and psychology, while the various approaches now being followed in sociology, anthropology and psychology provided a new picture of man, nature and society, which transformed perspectives and attitudes. Increasingly the child came to be valued for himself alone – as an individual personality with personal needs and a temperament which required thoughtful care and cultivation. The concept of the child had changed radically; childhood was now recognized as an important stage of man's development.

2 However, even although the emotional development of society has resulted in changed attitudes to the child with higher emphasis on love and understanding, it is important to remember that the phenomenon of the culture-lag means pockets of tradition may persist for generations. A shift toward higher material standards is not automatically accompanied by a shift toward 'advanced' attitudes.

2 The child in the family

.1 The rapid industrialization of the past 150 years brought enormous changes in our way of life, and these changes in turn brought about others – economic, social and emotional – many of them with profound effects upon the family.

.2 The separation of kinship from other aspects of life, widening literacy, the spread of democratic ideas, factory and agricultural legislation – all these contributed to the ferment of social concern which led to gradual improvements in the position of the poor, and of women and children. At the turn of the century, while writers like Booth and Rowntree were describing how desperately the submerged third of the poor lived, the country was shocked by the discovery of the poor health of young army recruits and attention began to focus on society's treatment of the young. Practical measures (milk, clinics, school meals) were slowly implemented and at the same time there was increasing interest in the importance of the family as a socializing agent. Two world wars, with social disruption and population swings, heightened awareness of the importance of the bonds between child and family, but it seemed that the pattern of family life was changing, affecting the quality of relationships of its members, both with each other and with society. (When thinking about the family and industrialization, do not assume that in modern society all families are nuclear, and that in the past all families were large, extended kin groups. 'The classical family of Western nostalgia' – that happy life on the farm where lots of kinfolk and their children live in a big, rambling house – has been described by sociologist W. J. Goode (1970) as a myth. The nuclear family form predominated in Western Europe and America long before the industrial revolution.)

2.3 During the wars and inter-war periods relationships within the home had become more intense, and those between the home and the community much more tenuous. Less social regulation of the family by the community and loss of the help inherent in a more collective way of life common to small communities meant child-rearing was more private – and also more tense. An American six-culture study reported by Lambert (1971) found that the more mother-substitutes were available, the warmer and more stable the mother was in interacting with the child. Increased knowledge of child development and psychology led to heightened concern for the quality of parent-child relationships; it also led to higher standards and expectations of parenthood. Thought of as a woman's crowning achievement and as a man's proof of masculinity, parenthood was expected to bring happy self-fulfilment to all married couples. A few years later, parenthood was expected to be all this and fun, too. A new concept of parenthood had come into being.

2.4 At the same time, socialization of children was still very much by physical discipline. Society's practice had not caught up with society's knowledge. ' . . . to be aware of this,' say Steele and Pollock (1968), 'one has only to look and listen to the parent-child interactions at the playground and the supermarket. . . . The amount of yelling, scolding, slapping, punching, hitting and yanking acted out by parents on very small children is almost shocking'. In a nationwide American study, Gil (1970) found the majority of people viewed the infliction of physical injury on children as 'an almost normal occurrence' in the course of caring for a child. And, nearer home, John and Elizabeth Newson (1968) found 97 per cent of Nottingham small children were hit – 7 per cent every day. (The British Isles, incidentally, is the only part of Europe where corporal punishment in schools is still permitted by law.)

2.5 In such a culturally sanctioned tradition, impatience is easily expressed roughly, or even violently. And there is always the problem of physical punishment escalating – each beating must be harder than the last if it is to impress. You may find it instructive to consider the difficulties inherent in the situation of those West Indian families who, as part of their strongly nineteenth-century culture, have brought with them to this country a Victorian severity of discipline but have left behind the grandmothers and aunts who eased the burden for both mother and child. Compounded by zeal for conforming 'good' behaviour, poverty and the associated exhaustion and depression, the mother's ability to distinguish between discipline and harshness may easily on occasions blur.

Not every culture socializes its children by physical means. Some modern American Indian tribes are shocked at the white man's habit of beating children into compliance; gentle and permissive with tiny children (they will, if necessary, remove a prized object rather than the child), they use public shaming with the older ones. East Asians are more inclined to use verbal scolding; one child-rearing text widely read in the USSR favours temporary withdrawal of love. (You may, perhaps, have reservations about the emotional consequences of all forms of child-rearing.) Physical discipline however, is still the basis on which western societies rely to socialize children, and the degree to which physical force is used varies widely. Although there has been a great deal of research on the needs of children, few of those who read and accept its findings appreciate the extent to which these needs are met or even understood by some members of the same society.

Only in the last twenty years have we become aware of this gap – aware that too much has been taken for granted. The economic and social developments which have improved our standards of living – and helped to form our image of child and parent – have also brought varying degrees of new strains and stresses. Expectations by no means always match up to reality, but society for some time was in a state of wish-fulfilment, assuming that, because parenthood could be enriching and fun, it was – for everyone.

Activity 3.1
Turn now to the extracts from Gil (1970), *Violence against children*, in the Reader, p. 48.

The first two sections are concerned mainly with socio-economic factors associated with child abuse which will receive further attention in Unit 9. Please pay particular attention now to the sections headed, 'Culturally sanctioned use of physical force in child rearing' and 'Difference in child rearing patterns among social strata and ethnic groups'.

You will note that Gil's survey covered all cases in the United States in the two years 1967 and 1968 that *fell within a given definition of child abuse*. Cases falling within the definition amounted to a little more than 60 per cent of all reported cases of child abuse. Re-read the definition, which is given in the introductory note to the extracts, then write short answers to the following questions.

a.   In the light of your reading, how would you expect that the survey findings may have been biased by limiting the definition to physical abuse?

b. In the first paragraph of 'Culturally sanctioned use of physical force in child rearing', Gil suggests eight ways in which 'professional experts' in America may encourage the use of physical force in child rearing, and five institutional settings in which abuse may take place. List these, then try to recall, for each, examples from your own experience of 'encouragement' and 'institutional approval' which might tend towards abuse in this country.

c. Read closely Gil's discussion of 'Difference in child-rearing patterns among social strata and ethnic groups'. What conclusion would you draw about the cause of abuse in any individual case?

Comments

2.8 a. The last paragraph of the extract would seem to suggest that the exclusion of verbal and psychological abuse from the definition may have produced an underestimate of the incidence of ill-treatment in middle-class families. Child abuse is not limited to any one social class, though predominant modes of abuse may differ.

b. Without knowledge of your examples, no comment can be made!

c. You probably decided that it would be futile to look for a *single* cause, and important to examine *all* possible causative factors in any individual case.

2.9 Some changing attitudes can be traced in some of the legislation of the last fifty years.

2.10 The concept of the child as not merely a miniature adult is demonstrated by the Children and Young Persons Act, 1933. This act set up separate juvenile courts and emphasized that in either care or criminal proceedings the court's first duty was to the welfare of the juvenile.

2.11 The Children Act, 1948, is interesting because of the provision that children could be received into care by arrangement between parents and local authority, without stigmatizing court proceedings. This recognized that there are circumstances in which parents need not be considered to blame if unable to care satisfactorily for their children. A number of other provisions demonstrate the 'good parent' expectation of a local authority towards a child in care. It is expected that the child should have a good and reasonable life, rather than the bare minimum that can be afforded from the crumbs which drop from the ratepayers' tables. For the first time, in an act of parliament, the reference is to 'a' child, not simply to children in general and, in Section 12, a duty is enforced on local authorities to exercise '*their* powers with respect to *him* so as to further *his* best interests and afford *him* opportunity for the proper development of *his* character and abilities'.

2 In 1963, the Children and Young Persons Act raised the age of criminal responsibility from eight to ten, showing, some would argue, a more realistic attitude towards our moral expectations of children. Another important provision enabled local authorities to use resources (including money) to promote the welfare of the child. The 1948 and 1963 Act together show a change in emphasis from removing children from bad parents, to helping parents to provide better care for children.

3 One part (not yet in force) of the Children and Young Persons Act, 1969, will remove all distinction between civil and criminal proceedings in juvenile courts for children up to the age of 14. One idea behind the act is that the court's purpose is to help children in trouble, whatever the symptoms, and that to distinguish between children charged with criminal offences and those before the court as being in need of care is pointless. In support of this view is, for example, the fact that the majority of girls in approved schools, prior to 1969, were there as being in need of care and protection, not because they had committed a criminal offence.

4 The 1969 Act also provides for raising the age of prosecution (when in effect), progressively, from ten to fourteen. The act has proved to be controversial, but when one examines it not in isolation, but in the context of even the few pieces of legislation noted in this section, there is an argument for considering the act not as breaking new ground, but as merely continuing trends which have existed for forty years or so.

3 The battered child syndrome

1 Revelation of the extent and seriousness of deliberate, physical ill-treatment of children by parents is a story with its prelude in the nineteenth century. From the late 1800s, doctors in both Europe and the United States had been puzzled by certain bony malformations in small children, sometimes appearing in every child of a family, and had suggested various rare hereditary diseases. For instance, West (1888) published a paper entitled, 'Acute periosteal swellings in several young infants of the same family, probably rachitic in nature'.

> A child, aged five weeks, was brought by its mother, with the
> statement that its left arm had 'dropped'. A swelling . . .
> occupied the middle third of the shaft of the left humerus . . .
> similar swellings were found on the right humerus and on
> the left femur. There were some slight bruises on the ribs . . .

The patient was the fifth child . . . Of the other children the eldest was similarly affected at the age of a week . . . The third and also the fourth . . . were both affected . . . The second case was seen in a child of the brother of the previous children. It was a girl infant aged three weeks and had developed a swelling of the left humerus a week before being seen . . . This patient was the fourth child. The first . . . had been well always. The second . . . had had both arms and legs affected in the same way at the same age. . . .

3.2 But it was not until 1946 that John Caffey, a specialist in paediatric radiology in the United States, suspected that these cases of multiple fractures of the long bones of infants in various stages of healing were injuries and not caused by disease. He did not, however, attempt to identify their origin. Other radiologists supported his theory and, although Silverman (1953) suggested that such fractures were due to parental carelessness, it was left to Woolley and Evans (1955) to attribute these injuries in babies and small children to deliberate acts by their parents or by those caring for them. The evidence which was becoming available through the post-war improvement of radiological techniques was forcing doctors to realise that – despite general assumptions to the contrary – there were still a number of parents who had neither the ability nor the understanding necessary for safe child-rearing. During the late fifties in the United States several medical authors published conclusions similar to Woolley and Evans.

3.3 Then, in 1962, Dr Henry C. Kempe, a paediatrician at the University of Colorado Medical School, gave a speech at a meeting of the American Academy of Pediatrics in which he coined the new and emotive term, 'the battered child syndrome'. He described a study which he and several colleagues had made of child abuse incidents reported by 71 hospitals and 77 district attorneys from all over the United States. Many of the 749 children involved had either died or suffered serious injury and Dr Kempe claimed that physical abuse by parents or caretakers was a major cause of death and maiming in children.

3.4 The speech, published in the *Journal of the American Medical Association* (Kempe, 1962) evoked general interest and concern, and the terms 'battered child' and 'battered baby' gained wide currency. Dr Kempe's recommendation that reporting of all incidents should be made law was widely acted upon and by 1967 every state in the United States had passed legislation requiring or recommending reporting. Throughout the sixties, social workers and doctors in the United States studied the characteristics of abused children and their parents, publishing their findings in various professional journals.

.5 In Britain, interest was aroused in 1963 when Griffiths and Moynihan published an article on the battered child syndrome. Two years later Cameron and his colleagues (1966) published a summary of what was then known on the subject and the British Paediatric Association circulated a memorandum alerting doctors to the syndrome.

.6 Although Kempe had always stressed that abuse of children covered a wide spectrum, ranging from emotional rejection through physical neglect (which included 'failure-to-thrive' and the more severe deprivation-dwarfism syndrome) to the infliction of severe injuries, the term 'battered baby' became associated in the minds of many in this country with specific characteristics. There grew up the image of a tiny baby repeatedly beaten by parents who yet – between such violent episodes – appeared deeply concerned for his well-being.

.7 Kempe and his colleagues had early reported some such instances of abuse; their bizarre nature guaranteed publicity and memorability – particularly among those who may not have read or did not appreciate Kempe's attempt to draw attention to the overall extent of parental ill-treatment. 'Battering' incidents make up only a minor proportion of child abuse but for some time in this country attention was focused on the parental personality characteristics associated with these particular cases, and so gave rise to a belief that all parents who injured their children could be helped by therapeutic case-work alone.

8 Kempe deliberately used the phrase, 'the battered child syndrome', for its shock value and he now considers that it has outlived its usefulness. Attention was focused on too narrow a segment of the problem of parental ill-treatment and wider issues – such as the pressures, sanctions and practices of today's society – were largely overlooked by those working on the problem. Although various terms are used, Kempe and most United States doctors now talk about 'the abused child'. In this country, the rather clumsy 'non-accidental injuries' is used by the Department of Health and Social Security, but the terms 'child abuse' and 'the abused child' have always been in common use among professional workers here.

9 Study after study, both here and abroad, has shown that the overwhelming majority of abusing parents are ignorant of elementary facts of child rearing (see abstracts in Jobling's bibliography, *The abused child*, 1976). Treatment now has to include instruction in child care. But many non-abusing families need help as well. Parentcraft does not come naturally:

skills have to be explained and learned; children's needs have to be understood. Modern parenthood is an arduous and responsible task, not made easier by confusion between the demanding reality and the romantic image. It is to be hoped that the concern growing in many fields at society's paucity of preparation for parenthood will be expressed in action.

3.10 As a conclusion to this unit, you may like to ask yourself whether we have a national fantasy of life within the family – and in particular of motherhood. . . .

Recommended further reading

JOBLING, M. (1976) *The abused child – an annotated bibliography*, National Children's Bureau.
BRONFENBRENNER, U. (1974) *Two worlds of childhood* Harmondsworth, Penguin.

Unit 4 'Normal' and 'abnormal' parent–child relations within the context of the course
Christine Cooper

Objectives

When you have worked through this unit you should be able to:

1. list the basic needs of infants and explain their significance for the child;
2. list the emotional needs of developing children and explain their significance for the child;
3. describe the ways these needs are commonly met during 'normal parenting' as this term is used in the course;
4. list and describe some of the factors that may damage the development of normal parent–child relationships;
5. list and describe some important features of abusive environments and discuss their possible long-term effects upon children.

1 Normal parent–child development

.1 Parenthood is a developing process extending over decades. The human infant is the most immature and dependent newborn of all species and remains relatively dependent for longer than the young of other species. The infant would perish without a caring adult, and so *mothering has to do with survival of the race* as well as of the individual child. It is a biological and hormonally regulated function. A mother's built-in drive to protect and nurture her baby forms the basis for the child's early emotional experiences which develop and mature in this reciprocal relationship with the mother. Although mothering is rooted in physiological states, the mother's instinctual drives are modified by social attitudes, dependent on the cultural setting, and a wide range of behaviours is seen in different cultures especially in later childhood. In infancy, however, most mammalian societies provide for a group or family structure which ensures closeness between mother and infant in the early months and years of life.

.2 The biological roots of fatherhood are shown to lie in the instinctual drive for survival. The rise in the birth rate in times of war as well as letters from husbands at the battle front confirm this. Religious rites and customs in most societies give expression to man's need to survive through a child of his own sex and, even in western societies, sons tend to be preferred.

33

The father's traditional role as provider and protector is being challenged in many families and societies today.

1.3   The changing role of the family in society and of a father or a mother within the family is leading to much conflict and confusion in the twentieth century. In industrial nations women have become more educated, housework is done speedily by machines, much food is bought already prepared or cooked, birth control means fewer children are born, and so women are freed from household tasks and are available in the work force. They enjoy forays outside the family, as well as the money they earn, which makes them more independent of their husbands. At the same time, fathers are becoming more involved in helping with family tasks and with young children, a role exclusively reserved for women in most societies until the last few decades. There is a tendency to denigrate the mother's important role with her small children, and an over emphasis on physical care, especially on diet and hygiene, has led to relative neglect of the child's psychological and emotional needs.

1.4   Pregnancy is more often planned and children are fewer and more widely spaced, the marked decrease in infant and child mortality and morbidity ensuring that parents expect to rear to maturity the children they bear. Material wellbeing receives much emphasis and in western societies there is an expectation of greater comfort in the home with running hot water, central heating, bathrooms and lavatories, carpets and other comforts once considered luxuries. Most homes, however poor, have a television set. The intrusion of television into peoples' lives probably reduces the time for family interaction, conversation at meal-times, jokes, arguments, games and discussions and this may impair the closeness and involvement of one individual with another in many families today. Material comforts may be increasing but is there a parallel decrease in warm, understanding relationships or interaction between parents and children? If so, does it matter?

1.5   The newborn infant's basic needs are for:

| food | warmth | comfort | company |
| sleep | grooming | movement | |

The mother's role is to study each infant she bears so that she can recognize and respond to his signals, not at her own speed and rhythm but by adapting her actions to the child's. Newborns vary in degrees of irritability and placidity, just as mothers do, but the more in tune a mother is with her infant's needs, the more likely is it that they will adapt to each other and find a settled routine of feeding, wakefulness and sleep by the end of the second month, if not before.

6 The human mother's motherliness is more independent of preformed instinctual patterns than is the case in other species, leaving her freer to adapt to her baby; but socio-cultural traditions may limit her actions. Her skills are tested anew with each of her offspring as well as at each developmental stage as the child matures. The child's innate behaviour is sometimes modified by intrauterine events, or by drugs, anoxia or trauma during delivery, causing him to be more or less alert and responsive, for example, or more or less irritable. The mother's ability to respond appropriately depends on many factors including socio-cultural influences and on learned models of mothering, especially on the tender loving care she received in infancy and childhood. There is increasing evidence that separating her from her newborn in the early weeks after delivery, and especially in the early hours, damages in subtle ways her perception, her empathy and her ability to become engrossed in and to interpret the needs of her infant. There is an increased tendency for sleep and feeding problems to occur (and, later on, elimination difficulties and other behaviour disturbances) when such early separation of mother and newborn or young baby has taken place.

7 Anna Freud, describing the importance of early child development and nurturing, points out that 'all advantages of a later family life may be wasted on a child who has lacked a warm and satisfying mother relationship in the first instance. . . . In this earliest partnership the demands are all on one side (the infant's), while the obligations are all on the other side (the mother's). . . . If she proves a gratifying and accommodating provider for his pressing needs, he begins to love, not only his experiences of wish fulfilment, but her person. Thereby the infant's original state of self-centredness is changed into an attitude of emotional interest in his environment, and he becomes capable of loving, first the mother and – after her – the father and other important figures in his external world . . . the relationship of a mother to her infant is an exacting one.'

8 That parenthood is a developmental process which unfolds and matures alongside the development of the child or children is a very important concept. Preparation for the important role of motherhood was once acquired in large families by experience during childhood. Research has shown that training, together with adequate preparation for childbirth, can increase the mother's effectiveness and understanding of her labours, promoting spontaneous delivery. Fathers are now encouraged to participate in the labour room too and this enhances the parents' attachment to the newborn child and their willingness to be fully involved with his welfare in the next few weeks, and so on to the years ahead.

9 The important ingredient of parental behaviour for the young infant, as

well as for the older child, is *'motherliness'* – the tenderness, gentleness and empathy with the baby, the mother giving without restraint and the ability to value the infant more than herself. This quality is not confined to women, or even to parents but is a human characteristic, and fathers often show it in abundance. There is rhythm and timing in the mother's actions which fit in with the infant's needs, and the mother varies her behaviour according to the child's response. Periods of fatigue, anxiety and frustration enter into many early relationships between parents and baby but parents help each other out, and sometimes need assistance from other relations or from friends in the early weeks. Characteristic behaviour between parents and young children are holding, rocking and cuddling; fondling, stroking and grooming; eye to eye gazing, smiling, talking to the baby, encouraging hand play with the parent's face, hair, breast or ornaments, and later with toys. The talking is by encouraging and promoting remarks rather than by demands or orders, and as soon as the baby vocalizes, at two months of age, long, peaceful interactions take place several times a day with the voices echoing each other as the parent promotes increasingly elaborate vocalization from the child. Sheer delight in each other is obvious to an observer during these and other interactions. Excessive crying in the early weeks or feeding problems may interfere in some degree with the reciprocal relationship and may stem from some anxiety in the mothering situation, or from other causes. As the child matures, the mature mother does not expect more than the child can achieve but gently encourages and stimulates his progress by delight and verbalized praise as each new skill is learnt.

1.10 Parents may be temporarily disturbed by marked displays of independence and negativism in the second year, but where understanding and gentleness constitute the predominant approach, together with letting the baby learn control at his own pace, development without undue stress is promoted. Parents need to understand that certain 'tiresome' stages are normal. Their willingness to give time, patience and understanding to their child's upbringing, and not to rush him ahead beyond his capacity, is rewarded by fewer problems in feeding, behaviour, sleep, elimination or in general development.

Activity 4.1
Before reading further, list from memory in your notebook the seven basic needs of the newborn infant mentioned in this unit.

Comment

You can check your list of 'needs' from para. 1.5 above.

Activity 4.2

Now read Kellmer Pringle (1974), 'The needs of children', in the Reader, p. 26. This paper defines four 'basic emotional needs' of the developing child. As you read, list these and consider for each to what extent (a) it may be satisfied simply by continuing the techniques of mothering developed in satisfying 'newborn' needs and (b) what new mothering techniques may be necessary to meet fully each need of the developing child.

Comments

2 The best way to check your work on Activity 4.2 involves another 'activity' which you cannot undertake during this study period. At the earliest opportunity, however, you should try to visit a family where there is a 'new' baby, less than two-months-old, preferably in the early evening. It is not enough simply to recall and analyse your own parental behaviour, if you happen to be a parent. Styles in parenting vary considerably even within the normal range. Take with you (or commit to memory) your list of first needs. Observe quietly each episode related to one of the seven basic needs and at the first opportunity note down for each incident:

a. how the child signalled his need (or the parent anticipated it);
b. how the parent responded to the need;
c. how the child indicated satisfaction or dissatisfaction

Note failures to respond as well as 'good' responses, and consider how the 'score' on each relates to your overall assessment of the success of the relationship.

3 Later, find an opportunity for similarly observing the interactions of a parent with an older (say a four or five year old) child, using both lists of needs as your base. If you are not on visiting terms with any families containing young children you can carry out this second exercise at least by sitting quietly in a children's playground for an hour some warm afternoon.

4 A wide range of motherliness is seen in young mothers. Some will succeed, even with an irritable and difficult baby, and even when separations occur.

Others easily become tense and anxious and feel at sea with the infant, not knowing how to respond to make him comfortable. The mother's lack of self-confidence may grow into a sense of failure, as conflicting advice from friends or professionals, fatigue, lack of support and understanding from her husband and family combine with her own inexperience and contribute to her anxiety and frustration with her crying young infant. A tense mother usually has an irritable baby. Her own neurotic needs from early childhood conflicts, now buried in her unconscious, may interfere with her mood and responsiveness to her baby. The first child is always 'an experiment' for parents, who gain confidence with their success in child rearing as the months go by.

2 The rejecting mother

2.1 There is not one type of rejecting mother, there are many. No child is wholly loved, and the mother's exacting role sometimes leads to impatience or shouting even at perfectly normal behaviour. When relationships are generally good, such outbursts are part of the variety of the child's environment to which he will adapt as long as they are infrequent. Rejection in spite of devotion is a concept described by Anna Freud. The mother provides satisfaction for her child but is present when he experiences discomfort or pain. It is not reasonable to expect that the child will associate her person only with his pleasures. She becomes the symbol of both pain and pleasure. The nearer she is to the child the more convincingly will both roles be thrust upon her. Paradoxically enough, the most devoted mother may, in this way, seem for the child to be the most rejecting, anyhow for a time.

2.2 A mother who enters parenthood unwillingly may lack feeling and empathy with her child, although most will adapt and love the child as the weeks pass. Discord with her husband whom she feels her child resembles, unreadiness yet to embark on parenting and, in some women, a masculine identification may all be reasons for indifference in the mother's attitudes. If separated from her young infant, as we have seen above (para. 1.6), the mother may lose her attachment, which is somehow bound up with the infant's helplessness, and fail to provide warm mothering thereafter.

2.3 If a mother is emotionally taxed by family illness, husband problems, social or financial burdens, or the birth of a new baby, she may temporarily withdraw her concern and affection for the child while still mechanically caring for him. Such episodes are upsetting for the child who may halt or regress in his development but when warm mothering is restored his progress is again promoted. There are women who gain much gratification and enjoyment from pregnancy and perhaps lactation too, also from caring for a helpless infant. Birth control is not effectively used or desired and as the next pregnancy starts the child becomes increasingly neglected. These women can't cope with responsibility to growing and developing individuals, due to their own immature personality structures. They have been arrested in emotional development before they can integrate the image of the good-enough-mother into their own personalities. Other women are apathetic about their infants and use emotional distance to protect themselves from the guilt and shame at their own destructive impulses. They often train the eldest child from four or five years old to look after the baby or toddlers and so avoid making decisions for the children after infancy.

Many women can't permit themselves the regression to a primitive bodily state that lactation and physical care of the child's body implies. Anxious distancing from the infant depletes such women's source of motherliness producing guilt and frustration at their inability to live up to their biological functions with natural intuitive ease. Mothers relive with their children memory traces of their own childhood and may become over-solicitous, over-indulgent, or over-protective or perfectionist with their offspring in an attempt to undo the harm or alleviate the guilt which alienation from the infant has engendered.

4 The consistently indifferent, cold mother has usually lacked mothering herself. She may have too many children. She makes no effort to time her attentions to the baby's needs or responses, and will disturb his sleep or his play, and will often neglect his loud calls for food or comfort. She gives him little holding, fondling, talking to or play. Such a child is often thin and small, and always slow in development. He lacks the lively and joyful responses of an affectionately cared-for child.

5 A vacillating mother who alternately rejects and is possessive with her child provides an inconsistent atmosphere in which the child is bewildered and produces disturbing behavioural patterns. Other mothers with psychotic delusions may include the baby in their fantasy and, until treated, neglect or reject him.

6 Parents vary in their ability to respond to the different developmental stages and some become less understanding or involved as the child goes through stages and behaviour which arouse old childhood conflicts of their own. The parents' relationship to the developing child shakes their own personalities to their foundations. They reject when they are defending their own repressions, and accept when the child's behaviour meets with secret wishes or fantasies of their own.

3 Characteristic behaviours of parents who abuse young children

3.1 *The abusive parent's basic attitude* towards infants and children is the conviction, largely unconscious, that *children exist to satisfy parental needs.* When children do not satisfy these needs they should be physically punished to make them behave well.

3.2 *The parents make excessive demands on their young infants and children and at too early an age for the child to be able to respond. His own needs are disregarded and when he cries for hunger or discomfort he may be cared for at one time, neglected at another and hurt at another. To such children the world is not predictable and they are unable to develop trust or self confidence, and may waste a lot of energy in hypervigilance to try to keep themselves safe.*

3.3 The child's limited ability and helplessness are not recognized and ever-increasing demands are made on him for compliant behaviour and prompt obedience. No mistakes are allowed in learning new skills, and the child is expected to comfort the parents when they feel distress and tension. This role reversal is a pervasive feature of abusing families. There is parental distortion of reality and misperception of the infant. Parents may say of a month-old infant: 'I had just put a clean nappy on him and he wet it again just to annoy me'. Recently a six-week-old baby, taken to Blackpool by his teenage parents to 'see the lights' cried a lot and failed to 'appreciate' the lights and was then severely injured.

The injuries usually occur during care-taking episodes such as feeding, bathing or changing the nappy. Crying or messy behaviour 'on purpose' may spark off the violent attack. The technical part of feeding and care is well or even obsessionally carried out on the baby by many such parents, but the gentle, warm interactions, with cuddling, kissing, vocalizing and laughter, take place little if at all.

3.4 All parents enjoy the rewarding behaviour of a responsive smiling infant but, at times of puzzling crying or restlessness, normal parents can still be patient and comforting. Aggravated at times by a difficult child, they sensibly leave him alone for a spell to see if he will settle, they go to have a cup of tea and a cigarette, and perhaps discuss the difficulty with each other or telephone a friend. By this time the child may have quietened but, if not, their tension has lessened and he may respond to their next attempt at comforting.

3.5 Abusing parents find it hard when they cannot comfort the infant. They feel the baby is rebuking them for bad parenting and they tend to keep on fussing over him instead of going away for a spell when they know he is fed, dry, and warm. When attempts to quieten him fail, and perhaps when he is interrupting others' activities and TV viewing, the violent impulsive outburst occurs.

.6 On talking to the grandparents as well as to the parents it is often very clear that excessive demands have been made on the parents when young and often on their parents too. And so the tendency to abuse passes down through many generations. Tender, patient mothering in the parents' early life has been missed, and they have a pervasive sense of not being cared for, or cared about.

.7 Failure of the spouse to become involved in caring for the child is a common difficulty, usually the father being indifferent to the child, and often to the mother. He expects her to cook for him, clean the house and care for the kids, and in return he goes out drinking in the evenings after his meal, increasing his wife's loneliness and isolation. In the case of abusing fathers (and sometimes of mothers, too), alcohol may be a factor in the assault.

.8 Clinging and demanding behaviour by abused children should not mislead the observer into thinking all is well. Children *are* excessively clinging when they are afraid or are not getting adequate satisfactory and understanding parenting. Young children have an inbuilt urge for attachment behaviour in order to elicit more mothering and, although it may not bring warm care, it is all this particular child knows.

.9 The NSPCC School of Social Work has found recently some evidence that the characteristics of parents who abuse school-age children are in some respects different from those who abuse infants, and developing research may alert us to new problems in parenting.

.0 With older children, continued verbal as well as physical abuse eventually convinces them they *are* bad. The psychiatrist R. J. Laing composed a poem about this which is a very moving description of the child's feelings, leading to lack of basic trust and low self-esteem:

My mother does not love me,
I feel bad,
I feel bad because she does not love me,
I am bad because I feel bad,
I feel bad because I am bad,
I am bad because she does not love me,
She does not love me because I am bad.

4   The abusive environment

4.1   It is not the injuries themselves, unless they are severe, that cause the most damage to abused children. It is the total environment in which they are reared. Clearly there are wide variations, and no generalizations can be made, but the environment usually contains some of the following features:

coldness and indifference:

i.   to the child's basic needs
ii.   to the child's affectional needs

constant demands for advanced performance, and critical, hostile attitudes to failure;
cruel punishments (not all involving physical pain);
unpredictable or chaotic environment;
sexual abuse;
physical ill-treatment.

4.2   Coldness and indifference

Many young women and men are quite unprepared for the exacting task of parenting a baby or toddler and lack the emotional resources for a full commitment to the child. Lack of help and emotional support from her husband accentuates a wife's distress. Many mothers have this problem to some degree but later overcome it. Other women do not understand the immediacy of the needs of young children and, from the baby's viewpoint, care is spasmodic and his distress from hunger, a dirty nappy, cold, loneliness, or minor illnesses often goes unrelieved, creating anxiety and tension in the child, and a vicious circle of crying and distress. Eventually there may be lack of concern *even for the child's basic needs*, which go unrecognized and so unmet. The baby may be left for long periods in the cot or pram, often with a bottle in his mouth. He is unstimulated and fails to grow and develop properly, becoming delayed in locomotion and speech in particular. The *affectional needs* of the child including

affectionate physical contact	understanding
praise	stimulation
encouragement	talking and playing

may also be disregarded and there is an unnatural lack of concern.

4.3   Constant demands for advanced performance and critical hostile attitudes to failure

The unrealistic demands and expectations of these parents for their child's performance is sometimes hard to believe. A child of one month was bruised and the limbs fractured for not holding her legs still when the nappy was being changed. As the children grow up, verbal hostility haunts them in the form of:

ridicule	frightening
sarcasm	threatening
shaming	tantalizing
belittling	broken promises.

These attitudes do not help children to grow and develop with trust and self-confidence. Instead there may be irreparable damage to their self-esteem.

4 Cruel punishments
These are very worrying because they leave no visible scars yet cause untold suffering and misery, and often permanent damage to the child's character. Children may be locked in cold, dark cupboards or basements, or given excessively heavy tasks. The six-year-old Maria Colwell was made to carry bags of coal up a steep hill until the coal merchant protested. Food and drink may be withheld, or they may be made to eat excreta or other foul material; their favourite animals or toys may be destroyed; they may be tied up for long periods, or be left for hours alone in the house. Many other punishments, some bizarre, may be employed. Siblings may be incited to be unkind to the child. When schoolchildren are affected, the teacher may notice periods of unhappiness, moodiness or preoccupation and these symptoms should cause an enquiry to be made.

5 Unpredictable or chaotic environment
There may be changing consorts, repeated moving of house, or schools and peer groups, and total lack of any regularity in household routine. Feeding and sleep rhythms are not developed and much mental energy is used up by the child foraging for food, warmth and general care so that little remains over for exploring the world of formal learning. The child learns to fend for himself, developing entirely self-centred attitudes, 'I care for nobody, no, not I, and nobody cares for me'.

6 Sexual abuse
This is much commoner than has been realized up to now. It may occur within the family or outside it, where it is often condoned or ignored by parents. Research on the best ways to diagnose and to treat it is still in its infancy.

7 Physical ill-treatment
This is last on the list and is often the least important part of the environment, since the psychological abuse may be much more pervasive and

damaging. Since some injuries can kill or maim the child, physical ill-treatment must always be a cause for deep concern, but at the present time we concentrate far too much on physical injuries and not nearly enough on the damage from the total environment: that is, the damage to normal growth and development which falls into the following categories:

a. *intellectual,* the capacity to learn and adapt to the environment;
b. *emotional,* the ability to form relationships;
c. *social,* the capacity for self-care and independent living and also for contributing to society in work, leisure activities and friendliness;
d. *moral,* by which is meant the child's conscience;
e. *physical,* which is associated with growth and developing skills.

Activity 4.3
This activity should be carried out *after* you have completed the checking exercise for Activity 4.2, paras 1.12–1.13. Re-read the interactional episodes you have recorded and for two from each age group re-write the scenario stating:

a. how the child behaved and what needs he was expressing;
b. how you would expect an insecure or rejecting parent to respond;
c. the child's likely response to the parents' behaviour.

> *Example:*
> a. Child proudly brings mother a 'pie' made from sand (needs: for praise and encouragement);
> b. Mother knocks it out of her hand, saying 'I don't want that filthy stuff on *my* clothes, thank *you*!';
> c. Child turns his back, sits in sand and kicks it morosely with his his heels. (For long-term effects, see paras. 4.2 and 4.3.)

You can then check back with section 4 and match each of the behaviour patterns you have described to its possible long-term effects if frequently repeated.

Recommended further reading

COOPER, J. D. (1974) 'Dimensions of parenthood', in Department of Health and Social Security *The family in society: preparation for parenthood,* London, HMSO.
ANTHONY, E. J. and BENEDEK, T. (1970) *Parenthood – its psychology and psychopathology,* Boston, Little, Brown.

MAHLER, M. S., PINE, F., BERGMAN, A. (1975) *The psychological birth of the human infant: symbiosis and individuation*, London, Hutchinson.

RICHARDS, M. P. M. (1974) *The integration of the child into a social world.* Cambridge, Cambridge University Press.

SHERIDAN, M. (1973) *Children's developmental progress: the stycar sequences.* Windsor, NFER.

SMITH, S. M. (1975) 'Psychiatric, psychological and social characteristics of the parents in the battered child syndrome', in *The battered child syndrome*, London, Butterworth.

Self-assessment questions (Block 1)
Richard Fothergill

1 a. Who first coined the phrase 'the battered child syndrome' in 1962?
   b. In which country does he work?
   c. Which of the following characteristics did he include in his definition of the syndrome?

      i. physical abuse
      ii. physical neglect
      iii. emotional rejection
      iv. dwarfism syndrome

2 Write down three aims of workers in the field of child abuse.

3 Which of the following professions and trades are *unlikely* to come into contact or be involved with cases of child abuse?

   social workers, dentists, nursery matrons, grocers, police, sociologists, opticians, milkmen, playgroup leaders, university lecturers.

4 a. According to Gil, nationalities or groups of people treat their children in different ways to exercise discipline. Associate the groups in the left-hand column with the different treatments in the other.

      A. British   a. temporary withdrawal of love
      B. Russians   b. remove a prized object
      C. East Asians   c. permit beating at school
      D. American Indians   d. use verbal scolding

   b. For what reasons may child abuse be defined differently in other countries?

5 Several instances have been given of attitudes towards, and treatment of children in the past. Write down two examples with the approximate period when they were common.

6 M. Kellmer Pringle listed four basic emotional needs of children which have to be met for a child to grow to mature adulthood. Can you list these?

7 Can you describe some of the probable characteristics of a child whose mother is cold, indifferent and weak in her maternal behaviour?

8 a. From the responses to the short questionnaire in Unit 2, it is clear that some people react to child abuse with anger. If such people are employed as workers, what might be the effects on the service provided?

   b. The older members of the sample who answered the questionnaire were more sympathetic to the parents. Can you give the two suggested reasons for this?

9 a. There were eight statements in the attitudes study that were ticked by at least 40 per cent of the respondents. Write down as many of them as you can.

   b. Write a description of your own response as you feel now.

Answers to self-assessment questions (Block 1)

1   a.   Dr H. C. Kempe   (1 mark)
     b.   America   (1 mark)
     c.   All of them   (2 marks)
    Total: 4 marks (ref: Unit 3)

2   1 mark for each of any 3 of the following:
    to prevent; to diagnose; to treat; to rehabilitate.
    Total: 3 marks (ref: Unit 1)

3   If you answered 'none', then award yourself 2 marks. Any member of the community is likely to notice likely cases or circumstances.
    Total: 2 marks (ref: Unit 1)

4   a.   Ac, Ba, Cd, Db   (1 mark each)
    Total: 4 marks

     b.   Since there are cultural differences in what is considered to be reasonable treatment for children, there will be differences in what is considered to be unreasonable or abusive treatment.   (1 mark)

       What is considered abusive in a culture is anything which seems alien to its own child-rearing norms. For example, American Indians might think ordinary corporal punishment abusive.   (1 mark)

       Abusive treatment is quite likely to be excessive use of a culturally normal method of upbringing (for example, too much physical punishment in Britain.   (1 mark)

    Total: 3 marks (ref: Unit 3)

5   Child-rearing considered messy, tedious, unpleasant – medieval;
    Children treated as possessions – eighteenth and nineteenth centuries;
    Physical punishment to persuade into arranged marriages – fifteenth century;
    Child labour – up to nineteenth century;
    'Breaking the will' – nineteenth century;
    Dark cupboards and isolation as punishment – nineteenth century

    Award yourself 1 mark for the example and 1 for the period.

    Total: 4 marks (ref: Unit 3)

    You may like to consider current attitudes and treatment in the light of these examples.

The need for love and security; for new experiences; for praise and recognition; for responsibility.   (1 mark each)

Total: 4 marks (ref: Unit 4)

Award yourself 1 mark for any 4 of the following points.

The child is often thin, small, slow in development; lacks liveliness, lacks joyful responses; appears bewildered; shows disturbing behavioural patterns.

Total: 4 marks (ref: Unit 4)

a. Award yourself 1 mark for any 4 of the following points.

Services may emphasize rescue and protection, i.e. be crisis services. They may lack attention to the total needs of the family and the abused children, to preventive work, research, long-term care and rehabilitation. Too much anger can inhibit the ability to help.

Total: 4 marks (ref: Unit 2)

b. They were more likely to be parents themselves.   (1 mark)
With age usually comes greater tolerance and understanding.
(1 mark)

Total: 2 marks (ref: Unit 2)

a. Award yourself 1 mark for any 6 of the following.

40 per cent and over of the sample felt: pity for the children; angry with the abusers; such crimes should not go unpunished; the need for more information about the circumstances; horrified at the sight of the pictures; sympathy for the workers; incredulity that these things could happen; deep sorrow.

Total: 6 marks (ref: Unit 2)

b. There are no marks for this part. Check your response with that which you made when doing Unit 2. If you have changed your attitude since then, try to think out some of the reasons for this.

Maximum marks: 40

Score 20 (50 per cent) or less – not nearly good enough.
Score 30 (75 per cent) – a fair pass.
Score 36 (90 per cent) or more – very good.

Block 2   Recognition and diagnosis: a multi-disciplinary approach

Every professional worker in touch with children needs to know how to recognize abuse and may have a part to play in its diagnosis. In Units 5 and 6 a paediatrician and a psychiatrist detail the common signs and symptoms of abuse from their respective viewpoints. Unit 7 outlines the roles and functions of other professional workers and Unit 8 focuses in particular on the need for all workers to pool their knowledge to ensure early detection and diagnosis.

Unit 5 Symptoms, signs and diagnosis of physical abuse

Christine Cooper

Objectives

On completing this unit you should be able to:

1. list, describe and recognize some of the most commonly occurring symptoms and signs of physical abuse.
2. list, describe and recognize some of the most commonly occurring symptoms and signs of the 'failure to thrive' syndrome.
3. list and explain the six studies that should precede full diagnosis.

1 Introduction

1.1 We can distinguish the physical signs of child abuse by being alert and carefully studying every injury in early childhood. Even minor problems such as squashed fingers may not be the innocent accident at first described and, while the significance of many such injuries is still missed, far more are now being recognized even than five to ten years ago. Such injuries must be seen as signals of severe family problems which urgently need attention and help in order to relieve the family stress and improve the safety and nuturing quality of the home for the child.

1.2 The severity of the injuries is no guide to the danger to the child's life and health. The injuries are often of different ages and there is commonly delay in reporting them. If injuries are present on both sides of the body, this should alert the doctor since bumps and falls usually produce accidents on only one side.

1.3 The importance of child abuse in the older child has been overlooked until recently, as we have expected older children to tell some responsible adult about their plight. The Maria Colwell case sadly revealed that children may be afraid to tell, however old they are. Sometimes children do indicate the aggressor and this may be a helpful lead in to the family.

1.4 Although most battered children come from disorganized families with many social problems, some do not. The importance of recognizing child abuse in well educated or affluent families must constantly be remembered. The parents may show more ingenuity in falsifying the history but in fact they *are* anxious to receive help of some kind or another.

5 Normally parents do not allow their young children to get injured and they make a great deal of fuss when accidents do happen, blame themselves and are only too ready to discuss matters with a doctor or nurse, in contrast to the parents of abused children who tend to be evasive and vague, may disappear before the doctor can talk to them and are generally less in evidence when their children are injured.

6 *Skin signs are present in over 90 per cent of all abused children.* Learning to read these skin signs, particularly the bruises, lacerations, wheals and scars and the burns and scalds, as set out in sections 2 and 3 below, is important for all workers concerned with children.

7 There are two main types of signs in the child. First come the physical injuries of various degrees of severity. Secondly, there are signs of failure to thrive, physically and mentally. In some cases injuries also occur in these undersized children.

2 Physical injuries

.1 The following types of injuries are seen alone or in combination:

bruises, lacerations, wheals and scars;
burns and scalds;
fractures and joint injuries;
brain and eye injuries;
internal injuries to abdomen or chest;
poisoning;
sudden infant death ('cot death syndrome');
drowning;
sexual abuse.

.2 **Bruising**
This may occur anywhere on the body, is sometimes severe but may be very slight indeed. Often bruises of different ages are seen. When the face, mouth, ear or side of the head are affected in a baby or young child the situation is dangerous, as the brain may soon be involved. Normally parents do not chastize children by hitting the face or head. Typical bruise patterns are described here. Asterisks in this paragraph and in paragraphs 2.3 to 2.6 will be explained later in the text.

—*a bruised cheek** in a baby or toddler is hardly ever due to a natural accident. The cheek is protected by a bony margin of the cheekbone and the jaw and in normal injuries these become bruised rather than the soft tissue of the cheek.

—*a black eye* is very suspect since the toddler's ordinary fall on a flat surface rarely causes one. Black eyes are due to violence from a round object fitting into the orbit but not small enough to injure the eyeball. Two black eyes are diagnostic in the absence of a fractured nose or of blood tracking down from the forehead, or, exceptionally, a rare disease.

—*bruising around the mouth and lips or a torn frenulum* of the upper lip or more rarely of the tongue are important signs and the mouth should always be carefully inspected. A torn frenulum hardly ever occurs in ordinary accidents.

—*finger tip bruises* occur on the face*, usually with the thumb mark on one side and the finger marks on the other from forcibly holding or pressing down the face of a crying child on the floor or other firm surface. Finger tip bruises are also seen on the trunk when a baby is firmly grasped and shaken.* Often the parent's arms tire, he or she rests a while, the infant slips a little and, on renewed shaking, another set of marks occurs higher up. The thumb marks may be on the back and finger marks on the front or vice versa. Sometimes karate-type finger bruises are seen on the trunk, limbs or face. Finger tip bruises are small, round or oval, flush with the skin surface and with intact skin over them.

—*grasp marks* occur on the limbs from forcibly holding the child down or from grabbing him violently and sometimes from swinging him by a limb.

—*a bite mark* from the adult human is a round or oval mark and often has a gap at each side.* It may look like two crescents and the diameter is about 1.5 inches. Haemorrhagic areas and sometimes broken skin may be seen from the individual teeth and later on the haemorrhage becomes a bruise. The identity of the person responsible can be detected by forensic techniques.

—*an outline of weapons* used to strike the child may be seen.* These are commonly fingers, fists, stick or belt but other instruments may be used. As the object strikes the skin, blood is violently forced out of the surface capillaries to the neighbouring area where it bursts the tiny capillaries, leaving the weapon's outline etched in red. The centre remains white and the shape of the weapon is clearly seen. If it occurs over a flexure, for example, the back of the knee, the pattern may not be understood until the limb is flexed into the position it was in when the injury occurred. Assaults with the flat of the hand leave parallel intradermal haemorrhages about 0.5 inch apart. They may occur on the face and on other areas of the body.

—*subcutaneous bruising* produces a lump under the skin and indicates that considerable force was used. It usually results from hard contact injuries. With a fall on a hard surface, like a concrete path, the integrity of the overlying skin may be disturbed but not with a fall onto softer surfaces like carpets.

—*pinpoint haemorrhages* on the face, around the ears or anywhere on the body are particularly common in babies and toddlers. Rough handling of an infant may produce them. Forcible compression of the chest or neck also produces them on the head, face or in the whites of the eyes. The 'purple ear' from pinpoint haemorrhages on the ear lobe or in front or behind it is an important sign and is hardly ever present in natural injuries.

—*bizarre marking* may arise due to imprinting the skin from pressure through coarse weave cloth, hitting with the bristles of a brush or a variety of other unusual objects.

—*crescentic marks* of finger nails may be seen for several hours after the neck or the limb or trunk of a baby or child has been violently grasped. They are an important sign because they never occur with ordinary gentle handling of a child.

.3 Lacerations or scars

—*scratches*. These may be caused by finger nails and appear as linear parallel lesions, varying somewhat in width and depth and usually deeper and wider at the beginning. They sometimes show heaping up of the cuticle at the end of the scratch. Scratch marks may be muddled up with bruises in an uncontrolled assault on the child. Sometimes scratches are caused by an older child either in play or during a jealous attack.

—*incisions*. Sometimes a clean wound or scar is seen in an odd situation often with a story that another child did it with a knife when in fact the parent inflicted it with a razor blade or other weapon. Occasionally a child arriving with fresh non-accidental injuries is seen to have old scars, especially around head and face. Incisional injuries should not occur on any child since it is the parents' task to protect children from such injuries, although occasional cut fingers may be true accidents.

.4 Burns and scalds

These may be very difficult to distinguish from accidental thermal injuries although the parents' manner and other injuries suggesting a non-accidental cause may arouse suspicion. A history that the child 'backed into the bars of a fire' or that the burn was due to 'a spark flying out of the fire' is particularly suspect. An accurate and detailed history is essential, and vagueness by the parents is characteristic of abuse. Previous burns to the child or siblings also should arouse suspicion. Cigarette burns* are a fairly common symptom of abuse.

—*Fire burns* can arise from forcibly holding a child near a fire as punishment or more rarely from putting a limb or the buttocks on the bars of an electric fire or on a cooker, radiator, hot fireguard, etc. Characteristic markings from these objects or from hot pokers may be seen. Toddlers soon learn to be wary of hot objects and are seldom the subject of accidental fire burns unless clothing catches alight, a rare accident these days.

—*scalds* are even more difficult to be certain about and in a disordered family carelessness can cause small splashes with hot liquid. A detailed history together with very careful inspection of the injury may reveal some discrepancies in non-accidental cases. Scalds on the back only do not occur when toddlers pull over hot liquid from a table. A cup of hot liquid thrown at a child may cause upward splash marks which at once should arouse suspicion.

—*dunking injuries* occur when a hand or foot or the flexed buttocks are dipped into very hot water. They leave a tidal mark which should be carefully looked for. Boiling water poured onto a child standing on a flat surface spares the soles of the feet except where water could trickle round to the instep or beneath the wriggling toes.*

2.5 Fractures and joint injuries

Ordinary fractures across a bone may occur in non-accidental injuries and show the typical signs of severe pain, loss of function, swelling and displacement. Only the history and the attitudes of the parents will then suggest the diagnosis unless other suggestive injuries are present. In babies and young children, however, there are some very typical fractures which occur in cases of abuse. These may be unsuspected on ordinary examination and only revealed by X-rays. Fractures of several different ages may be present. They may not show on the first X-ray if the injury is recent, and may need a second series of films taken two weeks later. This is because the injured gristly non-opaque parts of the bone heal by forming new bone which eventually shows on the X-ray.

—*injuries** to (a) the periosteum, which is the outer layer of bone, or (b) the ends of the long bones in the limbs (i.e. the metaphysis or epiphysis) are common when infants' and young children's limbs are roughly yanked or twisted and these show very typical signs on the X-rays or re-X-rays. These injuries very rarely occur in any other condition.

—*rib fractures* too may be unexpectedly seen on the films and are often of several different ages.

—*swollen joints* and apparent sprain are rarely caused naturally in young children. X-ray and re-X-rays are needed before the typical signs can be excluded and a careful search for bruising or other small signs of rough handling should be made.

Brain and eye injuries

Violently shaking a baby can cause haemorrhage around the brain from tearing of tiny veins coursing from the skull bones to the membranes covering the brain. A deceleration injury from banging the baby, head first, onto a soft surface such as a mattress or padded chair may result in the same type of injury. A large blood clot (subdural haematoma)* may form at once, making the baby severely ill and needing immediate treatment to prevent death. In less violent episodes slight oozing of blood occurs and the clot or haematoma forms slowly over days. Later on, other fluid seeps into the blood clot which slowly expands, causing irritability, vomiting, drowsiness and an enlarging head. Haemorrhages into the backs of the eyes are usually present in this condition and may lead to visual defects later. Removal of small blood clots may lead to recovery and apparent well-being, but many of these children show later problems of clumsiness, learning difficulty, visual defects, fits or personality disorders.

—*other forms of head injury* result from a blow to the head or flinging the child against a wall or other hard surface. The skull may fracture and a soft lump be felt over the fractured area. This is due to bleeding at the fracture site into the outer covering of the skull. Occasionally a scalp bruise may be seen over it. In the case of a baby, bruises from grasp marks or pinpoint haemorrhages should be carefully looked for as well as periosteal and metaphyseal injuries as they are often present with subdural haematomata.

—*signs of brain damage,* with drowsiness, deviation of the eyes, fits, transient or major paralyses, may also occur, and injury to the head and brain is the commonest cause of death in child abuse.

Activity 5.1

List from memory as many as you can of the typical signs of physical abuse described in 2.2, 2.3, 2.4, 2.5 and 2.6. Check and complete your list by referring back to the numbered paragraphs. Then turn to Hull (1974) in the Reader, pp. 62–7 and to the colour plates and identify as many of the signs as possible from the illustrations. Jot down illustration numbers for future identification.

Comment

For every asterisk in the paragraphs referred to in Activity 5.1 you should be able to find a corresponding illustration in the Reader.

2.8 Internal injuries

The second commonest cause of death is injuries within the abdomen, a torn liver, spleen or kidney or a ruptured intestine. These can be present without any sign of bruising to the abdominal wall. The signs are pain, restlessness, fever, vomiting and an ill child who usually has other signs of injury.

—Occasionally *crushing injuries of the chest* damage the heart or lungs or their coverings, usually also with fractured ribs. There is difficulty in breathing and pain; the child is ill and usually has some signs of bruising elsewhere.

2.9 Poisoning

When children are alleged to have swallowed pills, medicines or household fluids one may suspect that the story given is false but this is often hard to prove. Toddlers usually only take a small amount of pills or fluid and no serious harm results. Where severe symptoms of poisoning occur the exact history should be carefully explored. Previous injuries to the child or his siblings, as well as the parents' personality and social problems, must be carefully studied.

Example 1
A nurse brought her year-old son to hospital in the early hours of the morning saying he was breathing very fast and perhaps had pneumonia. He was very ill and panting and was also very thin with the remains of a black eye and some small old bruising around his lips and chin. Investigation revealed severe aspirin poisoning and he very nearly died. This was an example of the scapegoated child – his twin brother was robust and healthy. The false history given by the mother, a nurse, is important, as it was she who had poisoned her son.

2.10 Sudden infant death ('cot death syndrome')

It is now realized that the cot death syndrome occurs much more often in families with similar problems to those of child abuse cases, or to their relatives, while a smaller number of cases occurs in families giving excellent and loving care to the baby. It is difficult to distinguish between the cot death syndrome and suffocation on post mortem examination, and a few families are known where a parent has suffocated several children before it was realized what was happening. A very careful history has to be taken and studied and the numerous social problems common to these families taken into account in order not to miss those cases due to abuse.

Example 2
A 22-month-old Pakistani girl was admitted, very ill, with what looked like pneumonia but was found to be severe aspirin

poisoning. Owing to language problems it was hard to find out how she was poisoned but the father insisted that his wife had given only 2 or 3 junior aspirins daily for teething. This was hard to disprove. Reluctantly, after consultations with social services, the child was eventually allowed home. A month later another girl was born to the family and when the health visitor paid her first call on the newborn she found the infant cold and wasted and the elder one with two black eyes and sundry bruising. Both were admitted and did well, but the local authority lawyer did not feel there was enough evidence to take to court. After a period of convalescence the parents took the children home. Two weeks later the infant was in the post mortem room, said to have been found dead in her cot, though well two hours earlier. Without making enquiries the forensic pathologist signed up the child as a 'cot death'. Ten days later the toddler was also in the post mortem room with the same story. This time her temperature was far too low and indicated that she had been dead some hours. In any case she was too old, at 2½, for the cot death syndrome. The actual cause of death has not been established in these children but it is thought that they were either smothered or poisoned by some rare substance since investigations for common poisons were negative.

11 Drowning

It is now being realized that drowning is sometimes not the accident it is reported to be. The child may have been pushed into the pond. Secondly, some mothers may leave a young baby in the bath alone while they go to answer the door or telephone and, returning, find the infant under the water. This is an attempt, often unconscious, to destroy a baby who is making too many demands on a disturbed and immature mother. Thirdly, some parents punish their children by pushing their faces under water, a very cruel and frightening thing to do to a child.

12 Sexual abuse

This is more common than has been realized, occurring as incest within the family or as various sexual practices and perversons in the neighbourhood of the family. It is important to be aware that some children are the victims of such abuse and to be alert to the need to recognize it. Doctors should include an inspection of the anus and vulva in their routine examination of children with injuries.

3   The failure to thrive syndrome

3.1   This is also called deprivational dwarfism, the maternal rejection syndrome, and other similar titles. In order to grow and develop normally, children need not only food but also loving care and concern, stimulation through play and talking, praise and encouragement. Where the child falls short of any of these needs either his growth or his development, usually both, will suffer. In this context, growth is an increase in size whereas development is an increase in function. It is important to consider development of the five systems described in Unit 4, section 4.7, all interrelated, but capable of being assessed separately. If one system is retarded it is usual for the other to be affected also.

3.2 Poor growth

A significant number of children or their siblings are investigated in hospital for failure to thrive and no organic cause is found. Some have non-accidental injuries as well. Sometimes physical neglect and nutritional deprivation are obvious, and at other times not. These children do well in hospital with ordinary ward care, a situation where no well-cared for child should do better than at home. After discharge to their families they usually fail to continue their improvement. It is important to chart the weight, height and head circumference of all children at risk for poor nurturing, and indeed in all families growth charts help parents understand the child's progress. Because of the rapid growth in the first there years of life, failure to thrive due to neglect and emotional deprivation is most easily detected at that age especially when growth charts are kept regularly.

Activity 5.2

Study the following two examples of children who 'failed to thrive'. As you read the case histories, compare the children's records (dark lines) with those of the normal child's development on the charts. There is a complete set of developmental charts in the Reader, beginning on p. 296.

Example 1 John N.

5 years.	Referred to paediatric clinic for asthma. Disturbed home. Child in convalescent home for three months and gained weight.
$5\frac{1}{2}$ years.	Returned home and slow gain for the next five months, then stationary weight for $1\frac{1}{2}$ years until $7\frac{1}{2}$ years.
$7\frac{1}{2}$ years.	To special school as day boy. Slow gain in weight and some improvement for eight months.
$8\frac{1}{4}$ years.	Much trouble with asthma and with family problems. Gradual weight loss.
$8\frac{3}{4}$ years.	Became boarding pupil at the same school. Immediate rapid gain in weight, 1 st. in 5 months.

9¼ years. Social services suggested a trial at home for weekends and holidays. Weight loss half a stone in the next three months.

9½ years. Fully resident at boarding school again and immediate rapid weight gain.

10 years. Care order in court since family problems persisted. Child in children's home for holidays and visits his family when he chooses.

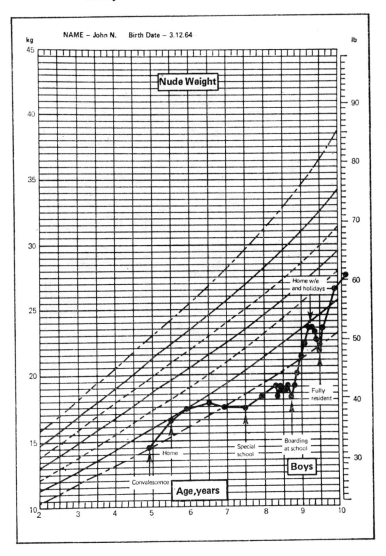

Example 2 Paul C.

Middle of three boys from Social Class 5 family. Gained weight adequately first seven months and then parents' marriage broke up after weeks of severe discord.

13 months.   Seen at child health clinic having had stationary weight for previous six months, together with

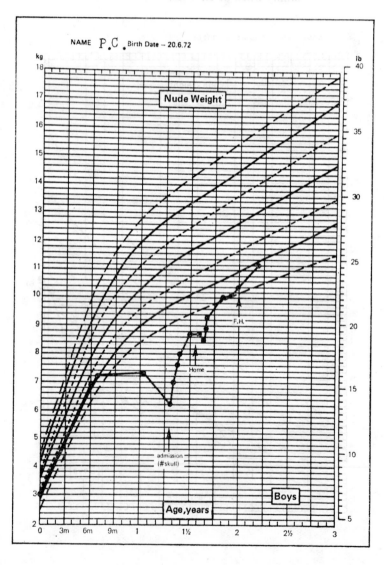

NAME P.C. Birth Date – 20.6.72

Nude Weight

F.H.

Home

admission (#skull)

Boys

Age, years

some bronchitis. Clinic doctor thought poor weight due to bronchitis but, in fact, it was too severe to be wholly due to this and needed investigation. The health visitor was asked to call to help the mother but the mother refused entry to health visitor and social worker.

16 months. Neighbour called health visitor and asked her to rescue the child as the neighbour thought the child would die otherwise. Admitted immediately to hospital. Extremely wasted, miserable, unable to sit up. Immediate improvement and gained 6 lb. in 6 weeks.

18 months. Trial at home with further loss of weight.

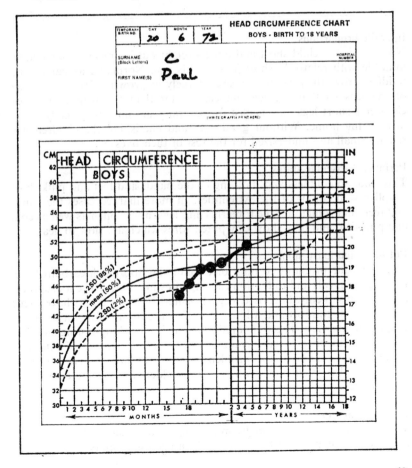

19½ months. Returned to hospital. Immediate gain in weight and sent for convalescence while further plans made.

2 years. Care order in the juvenile court and fostered (FH on chart). Since then thriving and well.

Note: Head circumference chart shows rapid increase in skull circumference from 16 to 20 months during rapid weight gain. Thereafter normal curve on skull chart.

Look now at the developmental charts and at the Denver Developmental Screening Test in the Reader, p. 308, and familiarize yourself with these useful tools for the detection of abnormal development.

3.3 Infantile proportions
Not only is the child short and under-weight but his proportions remain infantile with relatively short legs for his age. Normally, as babies and toddlers grow, their height increases, largely by growth of the long bones of the legs so that the legs increase faster than the trunk. Deprived children's short legs may persist for several years until they really thrive in a loving home. Without good care and cherishing the children will remain small and undersized for the rest of their lives.

3.4 Peripheral vascular status
This leads to coldness and mottling of the hands and feet and pinkish or purplish skin colour of the extremities. In more marked cases the hands and feet, and sometimes the forearms and legs, are swollen as well as cold and purplish, and may show tiny pitted sores which are slow to heal.

3.5 Pot belly and loose stools
These are due probably to poor diet containing too much carbohydrate, to irregular meals and to tension causing intestinal hurry. The loose stools are often mistakenly diagnosed as gastroenteritis. Many adults have vague abdominal discomfort and a loose stool from tension before an examination or an interview. These children's tension is more long-lasting and they often seem to have malabsorption from the rapid passage of intestinal contents. This adds to the problems of growth failure. Their general posture is also often poor with round shoulders and an increase in the lumbar curve of the spine.

3.6 Poor skin and dry sparse hair
The skin care is poor especially in the nappy area leading to excoriation and much discomfort. Elsewhere small injuries and spots often become

infected and are slow to heal. Multiple minor injuries of the face may be present from lack of protection and concern or from inflicted injury. Cigarette burns and other inflicted injuries may be present.

The hair is dry and sparse, partly from dirt and poor care but also from the general nutritional and physical debility. Areas of alopecia (bald patches) may occur spontaneously, or from hair pulling in frustration by the child or as an act of aggression by the parent.

7 Perverted appetite
A voracious appetite is often reported by the parents and this makes them very angry with the child. There may also be scavenging from gutters and dustbins, drinking from lavatories and other perverted eating habits. These probably stem from hunger and inadequate and unpredictable meals, but become an emotional comfort syndrome. Gorging and gulping food may continue for many months after the child is rescued. He often becomes fat from overeating, but later a curb can be put on this by loving caretakers.

8 Behaviour
Commonly these children are cared for indifferently in a home with many problems, including several of the following: overcrowding, poverty, unemployment, criminality, subnormal mentality, marital discord, illegitimacy and low birth weight. The children have often been cared for by a series of people, neighbours, relatives or others. They are unable to form warm attachments because of all the changing care and caretakers they have had. They often become overactive, promiscuous in their relationships, mischievous, lacking in control, disobedient, prone to rages and tantrums, accident-prone and retarded in speech, personal skills and general understanding of things and people.

9 When placed in a loving atmosphere the child becomes affection-seeking and at first this is shallow and promiscuous. He is also attention-seeking at first and really needs a great deal of extra stimulation, activities and play, at a younger level than his true age, to make up the deficits in his previous experience. In a children's home these attitudes will persist if there is constantly changing staff and lack of true parenting. In a secure, patient and loving foster home where the child is placed at an early age and can stay, sounder and more long-lasting attachments will gradually form.

10 Learning problems at school and periods of difficult behaviour including stealing, lying and aggressiveness towards other children are frequently found. With understanding help behaviour problems will resolve satisfactorily, but the learning problems may be more long-lasting.

3.11 **Inertia and catatonia**
While many of these rejected children are naughty, demanding and over-active, some are the opposite and withdrawn into a state of inertia and apathy. Only the eyes are alert. The child cannot play, and often remains a thin, cold little waif, standing still for an hour or two on end. His mother may complain that he defies her, or stares at her and refuses to move. In extreme cases *flexibilitas cerea* (catatonia) is present, so that if the child's limbs are put in an awkward position he leaves them there for minutes or longer whereas a normal child puts them down in a matter of seconds.

3.12 This state of malfunction between mother and child is seldom remediable when it reaches this stage and nearly always direct placement in an under-standing foster home is needed. The foster home has to have particular qualities to help the child to live through a difficult stage lasting many months while he begins to adjust to loving care and control.

Activity 5.3
a. List the characteristics of growth in the 'failure to thrive' child.
b. List some other characteristics of the syndrome of deprivational dwarfism.
c. List (i) the qualities you would look for in foster parents for a child with this syndrome, and (ii) the points you would need to stress in preparing them to receive him or her.

Comment

3.13 Your answers to these questions should now be reviewed while re-reading section 3 above.

4 Summary of the physical findings in child abuse

4.1 Typically the abused child is a baby or toddler (although children of school age are also vulnerable), often from a disturbed home, with small almost insignificant bruises, spots or scratches of different ages and especially on the cheek, face, eyes, mouth or round the ear. Cigarette burns, bite marks or unsuspected fractures are common. More serious injuries also occur. Repeated injuries to the child or siblings should alert medical, social or educational workers of the need for intervention. Stunting of growth, delayed development, speech problems, overactivity and uncontrolled behaviour are frequently present. Severe failure to thrive with vascular stasis, pot belly and withdrawal is a less common but very serious disorder.

2   If a regular check on growth, using charts, and on development in the five systems, are maintained at the child health clinic for all children, particularly those at risk for nurturing problems, an early diagnosis can be made. The provision of extra help, support and instruction for the mother, or a day nursery placement for some hours a week often makes for better progress, but such children should be kept continuously under review.

5   Diagnosis

1   When the physical signs on the child arouse suspicion of abuse or when the history of the injury does not fit the findings, the child should be seen in a paediatric department by the consultant paediatrician or registrar and usually admitted for investigation. X-rays, photographs, blood tests to exclude bleeding disorders, growth and developmental assessment with charts, and a study of parent/child relationships should begin at once. A team approach to the psychosocial study of the family should be initiated immediately by linking up with medical, nursing, educational and social work staff in the community.

2   The *quality of the parent/child relationship* may give clues to the problems at home. The *behaviour of the child in hospital* is sometimes the first clue to the fact that the child is being abused. A passive child who does not object to blood tests and other examinations should concern the staff and lead to further studies.

3   The appearance of *frozen watchfulness* (see also Plates 3 and 4 in the Reader), with the child having an overalert eye to eye contact with those who approach him and usually a tense immobility until he feels the contact will be a friendly one is an important alerting sign. Fear of one or other parent may be seen, but beware of the 'false love' syndrome in which an abused child is apparently friendly with the parent who abuses him and tries to keep the parent amiable. Many succeed for most of the time and various degrees of attachments may be seen in children who are physically abused. Where neglect and deprivation exist, and the child has progressed to the stage of inertia, virtually no communication exists between the parent and child.

4   The diagnosis is eventually reached by carefully considering all the interrelated factors after the following six studies have been carried out:

    a.   appraisal of the child's injuries, X-rays, blood tests, etc;

    b.   a detailed study of the history of the injuries and whether it fits the findings on the child;

c. an assessment of his growth and development;

d. the history of the child's health and his care and progress since birth;

e. a study of the parents' backgrounds, their attitudes to the injuries, to the child and to each other and their family;

f. an assessment of the social circumstances and problems of the family.

5.5 If the injuries are not compatible with the explanation given and the parents' background and attitudes are typically those of abusing parents then the immediate diagnosis of abuse is almost certain. The more complete family diagnosis takes several days or weeks to establish and must be thoroughly assessed before treatment and management is planned.

5.6 More difficult cases are those where abuse is strongly suspected but denied and where the injuries themselves could have arisen accidentally. Usually the parents' own history is that of deprivation and disturbance and if on balance abuse seems likely appropriate steps should be taken immediately to protect the child and help the family.

Activity 5.4
List the studies necessary before the diagnosis is eventually reached, and check with paragraphs 5.4 above.

5.7 Inexperienced professional people may not find it easy at first to differentiate genuinely accidental injuries from those due to carelessness, neglect or abuse. For one thing, even true accidents often follow some environmental stress leading to a breakdown of the parents' usual protective behaviour. For another, most abused children have not had the benefit of being gently taught to be thoughtful and careful in climbing and play. Thirdly, many such children are less skilful and agile than normal because they have been discouraged or prevented from running about, climbing and practising motor skills. Fourthly, some abused children live in very disorganized households and such children become overactive, careless and disorganized themselves.

5.8 For these four reasons abused children may be especially prone to accidents of all kinds, as well as abuse. Where parents appear unable to protect children from repeated accidents and injuries, a thorough appraisal of the family situation and assistance to the child and the parents are essential.

5.9 When inflicted injury is suspected, routine studies as described above (5.1 to 5.4) and carried out by the doctors in conjunction with the health visitor, social worker, teacher where appropriate and sometimes others will leave very few grey areas. A full discussion in a case conference by all who know the family usually helps to give a clearer picture of the child's and the family's situation. A full family diagnosis must include a full study on:

a. the child;
b. the parents;
c. the family.

It is important to think first of the child himself, his injuries, his growth, development, health, learning capacity, behaviour and family relationships.

Next, each parent should be studied, his or her own background, features of his or her childhood and adolescence with special reference to any neglect or deprivation he or she may have suffered, the work record, relationship with own family and friends and strengths and weaknesses of personality and temperament.

Then the marriage should be studied and the satisfactions and disappointments each partner experiences, how they communicate, how they handle stress or solve major disagreements.

The siblings need special attention and assessment, too. They may be suffering abuse as well or they may feel guilty, depressed or helpless at the sufferings of the abused child, and fearful for themselves. Other family members should also be studied, and how they provide support in or aggravate situations of stress.

Finally, the family as a whole should be looked at, both within its intimate circle and also how it functions in the neighbourhood and community. Are its members worried by debts, overcrowding, unemployment or too many young children? Do they have fun? Are there supportive friends or neighbours? Do they use the health and community services appropriately? How is the family seen in the neighbourhood?

This may seem an elaborate ritual for a child with minor injuries but the high death rate from abuse and the even higher rate of permanent disability from brain or eye injuries and damage to the personality make it essential to investigate thoroughly. A baby with a 'trivial' cheek bruise at eight weeks was dying with brain haemorrhages the next time he was seen at four months. Any non-accidental injury is the signal of family stress and it is this which is even more damaging to the child than the injury.

69

5.16 After the family study, if we ask ourselves Kempe's (1971) five questions the grey area will be reduced to a very insignificant proportion:

a. *How do the parents see the child?* Typically abusing parents see him as naughty, demanding and difficult or as dull, stupid and unrewarding.

b. *What do they expect of his development?* Abusing parents have unreal expectations of performance in their children and their ideas often seem incredible, so totally unreal are they. When the child fails to live up to these demands he may be physically abused, in addition to the belittling and verbal abuse so pervasive in these homes.

c. *How were the parents brought up?* Sometimes their own abusing family life is dramatically described, but at others the damaging influences have been subtle and concealed but none the less harmful.

d. *Was there a crisis?* The actual attack is usually the parent's response to annoying behaviour from the child such as persistent crying or messing with food, excreta or adult possessions. A domestic crisis major or minor may have occurred as well.

e. *Have the parents a lifeline?* Normally parents support each other over problems or difficulties with their children as well as having other family members or friends to turn to in times of stress. Abusive parents, on the other hand, are typically isolated people without friends or any support to call on when tired, overwrought or under severe stress.

5.17 The family study usually takes place with the child in hospital. Whenever possible, parents should be living in or visiting several hours daily. The medical and nursing staff in their day-to-day contacts with the family have to be aware of the need to understand all these family and personal problems. Each day new insights are gained and should be shared with the senior ward staff and then with members of the community team. A true respect and compassion for the parents and their overwhelming problems must be engendered by the paediatrician and ward sister. This should promote a proper regard for confidentiality. It is crucial in these days of the explosion of knowledge about child abuse to pay great attention to the need to limit discussions to staff immediately involved.

Unit 6 Psychiatric factors and the abused child

Israel Kolvin

Objectives

At the end of this unit you will be able to:

1. give some account of Erikson's theory of personality development, as a framework for understanding the abused child's reactions to parents and other adults;
2. list some of the reactions which have been observed in some abused children;
3. state what is meant by 'coping mechanisms' and discuss their secondary effects;
4. state and illustrate what is meant by the 'vicious circle phenomenon';
5. list some of the behavioural anomalies that may emerge at different stages of development;
6. state what is meant by 'the psychodiagnostic formulation', and explain why this is preferred in clinical practice to 'diagnostic labelling';

1 Relevant personality theory

Introduction
Erikson (1963) came to feel that social hurdles encountered and dealt with successfully during the course of development were of crucial importance for healthy personality development. He outlines a progression of psychosocial stages each with its own developmental hurdles which the child has to overcome. How well children overcome such hurdles of human relationships may determine how they will subsequently view the world and themselves and cope with new problems as they meet them. The clinical plausibility of Erikson's theory makes the schema an attractive one for understanding and indeed making some sense out of the abused child's reactions. For such purposes Erikson's theory needs to be supplemented by themes derived from attachment theory as outlined by Bowlby.

Comments on attachment and its functions
The human infant characteristically develops an attachment to a single adult, usually the mother. Such an attachment can be defined as 'an affectional bond between two individuals that endures through time . . . and serves to join them emotionally'. (Kennell, Voos and Klaus, 1976).

These are powerful bonds which are supplemented by secondary bonds with the father. The important preparatory steps in the child's attachment to the mother and mother to child are covered in Units 4 and 25 of the course. The child has to grow and mature both physically and mentally within the environment provided by interaction with his parents. Maternal or child illness or other causes of stress in the neonatal period may give rise to disturbances in mothering which hamper the development of affectional bonds. Some workers emphasize the crucial importance of extended contact between not only mothers and infants (Kennell *et al.*, 1974) but also fathers and infants during the early months of life, suggesting that this is a sensitive period for developing mothering skills and also fathering skills (Greenberg *et al.*, 1973). By a sensitive period it is implied that if such skills are not learnt during the early months in relation to a particular infant they will be more difficult, but not impossible, to acquire later. Bowlby (1969) advances the view that during the evolution of man the prime function of attachment was survival in terms of protection from predators. Appleton (1976) considers that the other important functions were to keep the child close to a food source and to provide a fertile environment for cognitive and social learning.

Activity 6.1
Turn now to the Reader, p. 15 and read the extracts from Erikson (1959). Some students may find this difficult. If you are one of these, read it through once and refer to it again as you work through the unit when its significance should become clearer.

Comments

1.3 In his complete paper Erikson describes eight stages of development, but for the purpose of this course the first three are the most important.

a. *Basic trust versus mistrust*
In infancy where there is an adequate affectional bond between the child and the mother or mother surrogate and where the mothering care is satisfactory, consistent and sensitive to the child's individual needs, life becomes a predictable series of experiences. In such circumstances the infant develops a sense of trust in his environment and himself. People can be trusted and the home becomes a pleasant and rewarding experience; the child is therefore motivated to take an interest in it, he explores it and attempts communication. Hence in relation to this developmental hurdle the major achievement is a sense of trust. If the infant does not clear this hurdle then the personality will be founded on mistrust rather than achievement.

b. *Autonomy versus shame and doubt*
This stage occurs in late infancy. It is the stage for achieving a balance between cooperativeness and wilfulness in the child's relationships with adults and in the exploration of his environment. It is a stage for the parents to encourage wisely, to guide and limit behaviour, with the major achievement being a freedom of expression, a sense of autonomy and a reasonable attitude to authority. However, if there is harsh or inconsistent disapproval the child may develop an excessive sense of shame and doubt which constitutes the major defect at this stage.

c. *Initiative versus guilt*
Early childhood is the stage of considerable independence of movement and rapid expansion of language. The advantages of language and locomotion enable the child to expand his imagination towards the selection of social goals and to persevere in achieving them. The achievement is initiative in social relationships. It is during this stage of initiative that the conscience becomes established. The child begins to feel guilt for unacceptable deeds, and even for thoughts and for deeds which no one has witnessed. If the primitive conscience is overburdened by the adult at this stage, the major defect is an inordinate sense of guilt.

4 Before leaving Erikson's theory of personality development, carry out a short exercise to confirm that you have understood it. Erikson defined an epigenetic principle (Reader, p. 15) and from this principle he employed an epigenetic diagram to demonstrate the stages in development of personality.

Activity 6.2
Draw a diagram to illustrate the relationships of the three stages of development as described by Erikson, which occur between the first and the fifth years.

Comment
5 Compare your diagram with that on p. 16. If you have not understood what you have drawn, read again pp. 15–17.

2 Watching the abused child

1 Information is accumulating about the behaviour of the abused child.

Sources are from parents, residential social workers who have taken over parental functions, from systematic clinical assessments, including interview and observation and from research. It is interesting to note that the most valuable descriptions have emerged from systematic clinical assessments in a department where great emphasis is laid on observation of the child's behaviour. The most dramatic, but not necessarily constant set of responses consists of the silence or hypervigilance displayed by these children. The characteristic feature of this syndrome consists of an expression of frozen watchfulness (Ounsted, 1972; see Plate 3 in the Reader). The accompanying features consist of a wariness of adults, the tendency not to smile freely and spontaneously, nor to chatter easily in the presence of adults. Indeed, it would seem that the customary expansive natural curiosity and exploratory behaviour of the child in the late infancy stage becomes blunted. In the light of Erikson's theory, as outlined above, such behaviour is not surprising. The child is being reared in an unfavourable, hostile and unpredictable environment. Such an environment is likely to generate a basic sense of distrust, together with anxiety about child–adult interaction. This unfavourable climate has usually been present from the very early stages of infancy in the case of child abuse and hence constitutes one symptomatic instance of a range of behavioural reactions to the child.

2.2 Abnormal behaviour as coping mechanisms

The pattern of behaviour as described in para. 2.1 can also be understood as a series of techniques which the child has learnt to help him to adapt to and cope with this hostile and dangerous environment in order to survive (Martin and Rodeheffer, 1976). The behaviour patterns thus learned can be described as 'coping mechanisms'. The personality development of the child may be arrested or distorted by the hostile environment and the techniques used by the child to cope with abnormal stresses may inhibit natural exploration and play, learning of social relationships and cognitive development. Another 'coping mechanism' is recognized when the child learns to become sensitive to the needs and moods of the unpredictable and often psychologically unstable adults in his environment. The child anticipates the needs of adults and comforts them, thus reversing the usual role of young child and adult; this 'role reversal' is described by Martin (1972).

3 Characteristics identified by the parents

3.1 It is also interesting how often parents appear to identify negative characteristics in the young child (Ounsted, Oppenheimer and Lindsay, 1974). Such descriptions include: 'too clinging', 'too aggressive', 'too defiant' and 'too disobedient'. Parents who describe their children in this way frequently have unrealistic expectations of the child. It is not unreasonable to suggest that these parents are displaying a lack of sensitivity and empathy when giving such negative descriptions and when holding high expectations. Physical and psychological factors within the parents constitute the most plausible explanation for such distortions of perception. On the other hand, factors within the child which might provoke aggressive responses on the parents' behalf have to be borne in mind. Such factors include temperamental irritability present in some children from birth (Thomas, Chess and Birch, 1968).

2   When attempting to make an assessment of the child's vulnerability to physical and psychological abuse, a number of factors have to be considered. In assessing some psychological reactions, the vicious circle of the child's behavioural response to his unfavourable home environment has to be taken into account. Other factors are the child's basic temperament and personality, whether there is a history of ill-health or slow development, to which may be added some assessment of his use of 'coping mechanisms'. Other features described by the parents are that these children were not easy to cuddle, were often retarded in speech and communicated poorly with the parents.

Activity 6.3   Illustrating the vicious circle

a.   From paragraphs 3.1 and 3.2 select one characteristic of a child.
b.   Imagine a personality trait or need in a parent which is likely to conflict with (a) above.
c.   Copy the diagram below and enter (a) and (b) in the appropriate boxes.
d.   Complete the steps in the circle, by describing the parent's or the child's response, using as many steps as you require.

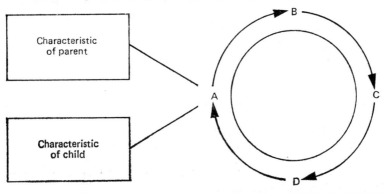

Comment

3.3 Two examples of a vicious circle are given below. Compare yours with these.

Note that in each example the child's characteristic is one which 'attacks' the parent's credibility. This increases anxiety in the parent who is thus less able to respond to the child's need. The child redoubles his effort and further increases parental stress and so on.

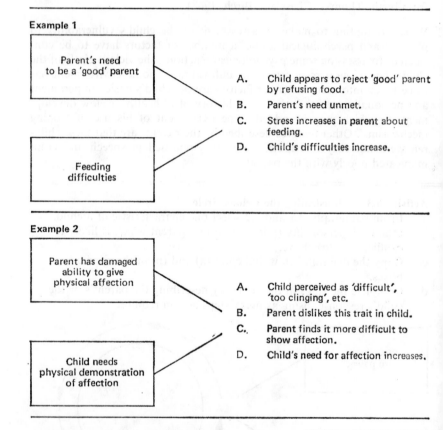

Example 1

Parent's need to be a 'good' parent

Feeding difficulties

A. Child appears to reject 'good' parent by refusing food.
B. Parent's need unmet.
C. Stress increases in parent about feeding.
D. Child's difficulties increase.

Example 2

Parent has damaged ability to give physical affection

Child needs physical demonstration of affection

A. Child perceived as 'difficult', 'too clinging', etc.
B. Parent dislikes this trait in child.
C. Parent finds it more difficult to show affection.
D. Child's need for affection increases.

3.4 Abnormal reactions highlighted during interview

Karen Peterson (1973), from her psychiatric interviews with abused children, describes a sense of helplessness, hopelessness and worthlessness, together with a sense of inadequacy, shame and guilt. It is interesting again to note how such accounts are in accord with the major personality defects outlined by Erikson as a consequence of not dealing adequately with the emotional development hurdles.

5 **Different types of behaviour in relation to different stages of development**
Another way of classifying the children's behaviour is in terms of the abnormalities that occur at the different developmental stages. In early infancy (first year of life), apathy or irritability, excessive crying, feeding and sleeping difficulties, poor cuddliness, delays in motor and social development and communications have been described. Towards the end of this stage, abused children tend to show less anxiety when separated from their parents than do children coming from more favourable homes. They also show the wariness and watchfulness of the environment. In later infancy (approximately one to three years), sleep problems are commonly described and the other main features are a tendency towards apathy and a poor response to novelty, little interest in play and a passive acceptance of direction by adults. This is in contrast to the typical two-year-old negativism which is characteristic of the toddler at this stage of development.

6 In intelligence testing, a great variety of performance is demonstrated, variations in IQ being recorded from one day to the next. Delay in speech and poor communication are particularly evident. At subsequent stages of development, a wide variety of features have been described at psychiatric assessment, the most common being a poor ability to relate to adults with a sense of confidence and acceptance (Helfer, McKinney and Kempe, 1976). A variety of other reactions have been described: that these children tend to be unduly compliant, sometimes passively aggressive, sometimes negativistic (for example, the child might show a quiet and steadfast refusal of food or an apparent indifference to parental affection, or may be indifferent to praise or blame). Many observers have emphasized the child's lack of exploratory behaviour as well as a poor interest in and ability to play. At later stages of development, difficulties in expressing feelings are often present, together with a poor self-image. Poor educational progress has often been noted. While passivity and compliance has usually been emphasized, some of these children may additionally or alternatively display aggressive streaks.

4   Is there a child behavioural syndrome specific to child abuse?

1 If there were identifiable behavioural syndromes specific to abused children, then the young child population could be screened to identify them, rather than seek risk factors in the families. Unfortunately, there is

no constant identifiable picture and the closest to identifying a behavioural reaction specific to an abusive or potentially abusive environment is the frozen watchfulness described in para. 2.1. However, the frequency of its emergence in such circumstances is not yet known, nor how reliably it can be identified, nor in what other circumstances it occurs. There is, in fact, no constant picture.

4.2 The psychodiagnostic formulation

In clinical child psychiatry, the exercise of diagnostic labelling is considered far less useful than the wider exercise of advancing a psychological diagnostic formulation. This in essence consists of an individualized theory advanced to explain the behaviour that the particular child exhibits on the basis of (a) factors intrinsic to him such as personality, intellectual and physical development, and (b) factors extrinsic to him which consist of current and previous life experience in the home, school and community.

4.3 This diagnostic formulation can be undertaken at various levels. Irrespective of whether it is undertaken by the psychiatrist or the social worker, the corner stone of the diagnostic formulation is the social history. A first-level formulation can be derived on the basis of the information contained in this history, which is a reasonable understanding of the nature of the problem and its origins. The history includes an account of the problem, the physical and emotional development of the child; his social functioning in relation to children and adults within and without the family; current and previous social and psychological stresses; his educational functioning and, finally, family and social data.

4.4 The second-level formulation is based on two sources of information – namely, social history and psychiatric interview – and hence is likely to constitute a more sensitive and valid representation of the problem. The third level is based on the previous information together with that available for psychological assessment. This assessment may include a number of different standardized tests to evaluate cognitive and personality deviations, including learning difficulties, and is generally considered the most sophisticated level attained at the end of the investigative stage. However, a definitive formulation may only be achieved later, after the onset of treatment, when information crucial to an understanding of the problem has emerged (Kolvin and Scott, 1977).

4.5 In few conditions is the psychodiagnostic formulation more appropriate and necessary than in child abuse. It takes into consideration social factors, family dynamics and parental psychiatric factors (the ingredients of the critical path analysis explained in Units 10 and 11). It includes factors within the child in its attempt to provide a plausible explanatory theory for the course of events that leads to child abuse, together with an understanding of the abused child's behaviour, his reactions, growth and development. Within the broad environmental patterns described in previous units and in terms of behaviour as described in this unit, there is considerable individual variation. Hence only an individualized psycho-diagnostic formulation can draw sensitively a reasonably accurate picture in the individual case.

Unit 7 Roles and functions of the various professions in the recognition and diagnosis of child abuse (1)

Constance Lee and Bill Roberts

Units 7 and 8 are linked units.

Objectives

At the end of Units 7 and 8 you will be able to:

1. define your own attitude to personal responsibility in initiating action to prevent or to minimize child abuse;
2. identify the appropriate professionals to whom to communicate information and/or from whom to seek advice;
3. state both the primary duties of and the limitations imposed by membership of your own profession;
4. define (in broad terms) the primary duties, the limitations and the probable attitudes of members of some other professions likely to be involved in cases of child abuse;
5. given the case material supplied in text and Reader, pick out the isolated signs and symptoms of abuse presented to different professionals in the L.G. case, and explain their significance when collected together;
6. list the main types of appropriate action that can be taken in cases of suspected child abuse.

1 Introduction

1.1 If you have worked through the first six units including the associated reading and the activities, you will have an overall grasp of the subject of child abuse as it affects the child, the family and the professional worker.

1.2 The aim of Units 7 and 8 is to move from the general to the specific, and to focus attention on the individual worker's role in the prevention and management of suspected child abuse. Appropriate professional action is dependent upon the correct interpretation and use of information received by the worker. The writers of Units 7 and 8 recognize the close relationship between insight and performance and for this reason the objectives for the two units have been combined. Unit 7 discusses some of the problems; Unit 8 suggests practical measures.

2   Personal and professional responsibility

1   **Individual or professional?   A discussion.**
A professional worker has certain advantages as well as limitations. There is, for example, the support which comes from being a member of an established group with its recognized training and code of practice. But there is also the possibility of being so bound by professional 'set' (the cluster of professional ideas, attitudes and methods) that individual response is in danger of being lost. Every professional worker has to come to terms with this conflict in his professional and personal life, but when he becomes a member of a team an understanding of the conflicts of other professionals is necessary also. We would argue that the professional training and socialization of those in whom we are interested in this unit (i.e., health visitors, police officers, social workers, teachers, and so on) has one thing in common. It seeks to capitalize, for the promotion of the professional function, the individual's skills, qualities and values. Normally, the individual's values are reasonably in accord with the values of the profession, or he would not have become a member of the profession. Most doctors believe that healing is a good end in itself; and most members of the police force think that justice and the apprehension of criminals is necessary and proper. It is expected, therefore, that joining one of these professions would enhance personal responsibility, would reinforce some personal values.

2.2   Perhaps this is not always the case in all circumstances. When, for example, a local authority social worker defines part of his client's problem as the failure by that authority to provide a certain service, where does his professional loyalty lie? To the client or to the local authority, his employer? To whom or to what is the doctor being loyal when he allows medical ethics to prevent his telling the police that his patient has admitted battering her child? Later in this unit you will be studying a specimen guide to action by various professions in cases of child abuse. But might there be instances where you have followed the guidelines to the letter; have discharged your professional obligations completely; and the child remains at risk? It may be one of the limitations of the professional that in these circumstances the profession is no longer able to help, and the individual must rely on his sense of personal responsibility. Without this, can the most sophisticated code of practice or set of guidelines be the complete answer?

2.3   Before you move on to the next section of this unit, spend a few minutes thinking of the possible limitations of your own profession, in the context of child abuse. These may be functional (e.g., the health visitor has no statutory power to invoke care proceedings); structural (e.g., police

81

officers below a certain rank have no option but to report the facts of an alleged crime for possible prosecution); ethical (e.g., confidentiality to a greater or lesser degree in a number of professions); and so on. In what ways might you overcome these limitations, as a professional and as an individual?

3 Professional roles and functions

In Unit 1 you considered briefly the range of professional workers and others who may become involved with cases of child abuse. This section will look more closely at the complexity of function and relationships within the team which deals with such cases.

3.1 Below is a list of professionals (in no particular order), with brief notes on their powers, duties and specially relevant skills *in the context of child abuse*. These notes are simple and basic and are intended merely to indicate certain role differences between professions. Thus they make no reference, for example, to legal rights and powers enjoyed by individuals *as citizens*, as distinct from as professionals. Legal questions, including citizen's rights and powers, are more fully explored in Unit 13.

a. **Police officers**

Powers To institute criminal proceedings against an adult alleged to have ill treated or neglected a child. (*Note:* convicting an abuser does not, of itself, protect the child). To institute civil proceedings in respect of a child thought to be in need of care or protection. Senior officers have discretion as to whether or not to institute proceedings of either sort. To remove child under a place or safety order, on own initiative.

Duties To prevent and detect crime. To protect life and property.

Skills Police officers may often have information which might suggest a situation of risk: directly, through a complaint about a child; or indirectly, for example, through being called to a domestic disturbance or a neighbours' quarrel. (The role of the police is more fully discussed in Units 17 and 18.)

Comments Investigation of an alleged offence is not necessarily followed by prosecution. In fact, in many cases of child abuse, investigation begins and ends at the case conference. The decision to prosecute is made only after consideration of all the circumstances. Conviction of an abuser may result in an order which will protect that child or any members of the same family, born or unborn (e.g., by a probation order, hospital order or a care order).

b. **Social workers**

Social Services Departments

Powers   To institute civil proceedings in respect of a child thought to be in need of care or control. To obtain, through a justice of the peace, a place of safety order for the removal of a child.

Duties   A statutory duty to investigate all complaints relating to the neglect or ill-treatment of a child. A general duty to promote and safeguard the welfare of children for whom the department has a responsibility.

NSPCC Inspectors

Powers   To institute civil proceedings in respect of a child thought to be in need of care or control. To obtain, through a justice of the peace, a place of safety order for the removal of a child.

Duties   NSPCC Inspectors are required to take action 'to prevent the public and private wrongs of children and the corruption of their morals'; and to take action 'for the enforcement of laws for their protection.' (Quoted from the Royal Charter of the NSPCC.)

Probation officers

Powers   None, but see 'Duties' below.

Duties   None specific, relating to child abuse. To 'advise, assist and befriend' probationers. Expected to report breaches of probation orders to the magistrates, including the committing of further offences.

Other professional social workers

(e.g., hospitals, voluntary agencies, child guidance clinics, residential establishments, day centres, some schools, etc.)

Powers   None, unless employed and authorized by social services department, in which case, as above.

Duties   None specific to child abuse.

Skills
(all social
workers)   Social workers are trained in group community and/or casework and in the mobilization of resources (including the client's own internal resources). An important part of their work is the making of professional relationships with their clients. Their role places them in a good position to recognize the signs of potential risk to a child even when there are no 'facts' suggesting actual abuse. Good relationships cannot be achieved without

establishing trust and one aspect of this is keeping confidentiality. Thus conflicts can arise. ('Confidentiality' is further discussed in Units 17–18.)

c. **Health visitors**

Powers   None specific to child abuse. (Note there is no legal power of entry to visit a child, and no power to examine a child without parental consent. These powers are not given to anyone else, either.)

Duties   To visit all young children to promote their welfare and proper development, and to advise and assist parents to this end.

Skills   Experts in the normal development of children, and can give valuable advice in this field.

d. **Paediatricians**

Powers   None.

Duties   None specific to child abuse.

Skills   Specialists in the medical care and treatment of children. They can arrange exhaustive examination of a child and its parents where child abuse is suspected, and can give expert advice (and testimony, when necessary) concerning the significance of injuries.

e. **Nurses, midwives**

Powers   None.

Duties   None specific.

Skills   They may often gain information or impressions of children and their parents which may be of significance in the context of other circumstances. Nurses may, for example, notice something unusual about the behaviour in hospital of an injured child, or about the interaction between child and parent at visiting times. Midwives in maternity hospitals or ante-natal clinics are in a good position to notice mother's attitudes, feelings, regarding the expected or newly born baby.

f. **Psychiatrists, psychologists (educational and clinical) working from child guidance clinics**

Powers   None.

Duties   None specific to child abuse.

Skills   Experts in the emotional, psychological and intellectual development of children, and in child–parent relationships.

g. **General practitioners**

Powers   None.

Duties   None specific to child abuse.

Skills   Much knowledge of patients additional to medical history and current ailments. Together with the health visitors (who are now commonly attached to general practices) they are in a good position in many instances to diagnose situations of risk. Doctors place a high value on confidentiality in their dealings with patients (this is true also, of course, of paediatricians and psychiatrists, for it is part of medical ethics), and this can cause conflict when child abuse may be a possibility.

h.   **Teachers, playgroup leaders, nursery and residential care matrons**

Powers   None.

Duties   All these workers are held in law to be *in loco parentis* while a child is in their care, and to have the responsibility of any parent not merely to refrain from abuse but also to protect the child and promote his general welfare.

Skills   They are qualified by training and experience to notice deviations from normal development and, like nurses, they often have special opportunities to observe parent–child interactions.

Activity 7.1
Look again at the information given in para. 3.1 above and note any differences in professional or functional approaches, duties, limitations, which might give rise to conflict between a pair of professionals. Make a few notes of how this conflict might produce misunderstanding and/or prejudice.

Comments

3.2   Here are some suggestions which you might have included.

a.   The paediatrician, as an expert in children, might regard the general social worker as an amateur who might do more harm than good.

b.   The health visitor, accustomed to regarding doctors as her professional superiors, might find it difficult to differ with a doctor over the judgement of a risk situation.

c.   All professionals who are expected to maintain some element of confidentiality may find difficulty in sharing information with workers in another profession – and yet criticize others for having the same difficulty.

d.   Perhaps all professionals tend to think of their own activity as central, and others as peripheral; and therefore that information should flow inwards more often than outwards.

4   Communication failure

4.1   A recurring feature in child abuse inquiries is the lack of communication between co-workers. Often a child would be seen to be seriously at risk if all the pieces of information, sometimes insignificant in themselves, had been pooled. The path from misunderstanding to communication failure is discussed below, using two workers, a police officer and a social worker, as an example.

4.2   Stereotypes are commonly used to some degree in everyday life as a sort of social shorthand; a quick but rough-and-ready way of classifying others. It is not unusual for police officers to be stereotyped as punitive authoritarians interested only in convictions; and for social workers to be stereotyped as woolly minded idealists. There are similarly stereotyped and prejudiced views of doctors (who know it all); health visitors (concerned only with clinical cleanliness); psychiatrists (more neurotic than their patients); and so on.

4.3   If stereotyped and prejudiced views are allowed to prevail, communication across professional boundaries can become very difficult. For example, Renvoize (1974) quotes a doctor describing a meeting between co-workers to discuss co-operation in dealing with child abuse. 'The social workers sat on one side of the hall, the police on the other, and we doctors sat in the middle. It was like throwing the fox to the hounds – they yapped at each other over our heads and neither side was prepared to give an inch. Whenever we opened our mouths it seemed to set off one side or the other, so in the end we just shut up and let them get on with it.' (But see also Units 17–18, p. 200, which comment further on Renvoize (1974).)

4.4   Is there any foundation for the stereotypes suggested above? The police, in fact, have no function or power to punish offenders; this is the prerogative of the courts. They are, on the whole, expected to bring offenders before a court, but even here the police have discretion, and in many cases do not prosecute. However, although they have no punishment function, the police must believe in the rightness of law and order, and in the judicial system in general, which includes provisions for punishment. Thus, many police officers may well believe (rightly or wrongly) in the deterrent effect of punishment of offenders. But this is very different from the general 'punitive attitude' suggested by the stereotype.

.5 The social worker has the general function of helping people to resolve, or to come to terms with, a problem. Professionally he is expected to accept his client as he is, for only by doing so can he understand him. He is not expected to judge him (whatever may be his personal feelings about his client's behaviour), for the client must learn to judge his own actions for himself. As a consequence, social workers may well believe (rightly or wrongly) that punishment is ineffective in deterring offenders. But again, this is very different from the general 'woolly minded idealist' suggested by the stereotype.

.6 Although this is simple and generalized, the beginnings of misunderstanding and prejudice can be understood. On the question of punishment, for example, there is a wide difference of professional opinion, honestly held on both sides. If this were recognized as such, little harm would be done, but it is fatally easy to argue from the general to the particular; that because the police function is to bring offenders to account, and because this often leads to punishment of the offender, then most police officers have a punitive attitude. Or, conversely, that because the social work method is not to blame people, but to accept them as they are, then most social workers are helping to lower moral standards, are idealistic and impractical.

7 The difference in approach to child abuse due to professional 'set' can also be discerned. To the police officer, however sympathetic, child abuse is a crime. If he has the discretion not to prosecute, he can exercise it only if he knows about the crime. Since the discretion has been given to him, not the health visitor or the paediatrician, he should be the one to exercise it; therefore he should always be told. He respects the court, whose duty it is to consider not only the facts of the case, but the circumstances and background of the family.

8 To the social worker child abuse is predominantly a social problem. His understanding of behaviour is a causal one. His approach may be one of removing those causative factors. In this analysis, of what relevance is the court? And, if the parent is treated like a criminal, how can the worker establish the trusting relationship which will enable help to be provided? Is it surprising that some social workers and some police officers find it difficult to communicate effectively with each other about a specific case, when their starting positions are so different? The foregoing discussion is not intended to make any value judgements about the respective merits of police officers or social workers, nor is it suggested that these two professions are more in conflict than any other pair.

9 Our complex society has evolved a system in which a number of social

duties have been separated and institutionalized. It has specialists – doctors, police officers, teachers – to meet special social needs. If society expected social workers to function in the same way as police officers, there would not be two distinct occupations. Co-worker communication in child abuse would improve if each understood the other's function, as well as his powers and duties. With understanding, each is more likely to give the other credit for doing his job competently, and trust him to do so, than to consider him incompetent or misguided because he approaches the problem differently. The goal of all those involved with child abuse – professionals and laypeople alike – is the prevention and alleviation of the suffering of the victims (which may include parents under stress). If we remember this, we may more easily accept that there are different methods of achieving the same goal, and that our particular profession probably does not have a monopoly of the only right one.

4.10 **Optional exercise** Highly recommended
When you have completed Unit 7, arrange to meet a member of the profession which you consider to be most antipathetic to your understanding of, and approach to, child abuse. Spend at least half an hour in getting this person to describe and explain his understanding and approach. You may question, ask for reasons, and examples. You may *not* argue, disagree, or refute his explanations by evidence. At the end of this exercise you may still disagree with him, but you will understand his point of view.

5   Guide to professional practice

5.1 Following the issuing of government circulars relating to child abuse and the setting up of area review committees (to be discussed in Units 15 and 16), many local authorities have prepared guidelines for the benefit of workers in their areas. These guidelines vary considerably in detail and quality, but the general aim is the same: to prevent child abuse where possible, or to take appropriate action when it is thought to have occurred. The British Association of Social Workers published a code of practice in *BASW News* on September 4, 1975 but, despite these preventive measures, cases of child abuse continue to occur.

Activity 7.2
Making your own guide for detection and action.

a.   Turn to p. 238 of the Reader and study the extracts from the professional guide on child abuse issued by the City of Coventry. Note that the guide was prepared by the Coventry Area Review

Committee and the courses of action recommended are specific to the services available in Coventry. It is used here as a good example of the kind of procedural plan produced by many local authorities.

b.   Note particularly that each worker (only two examples are given in the extract) is asked to assess the degree of injury or neglect, to rate the degree as 'low suspicion', 'high suspicion' or 'emergency', and to take appropriate action.

c.   Re-read the section which deals with the three risk categories. Make notes of what information may come to you, what incidents you might observe, in your capacity as professional or layperson. (Laypeople particularly may begin to feel that this is 'spying'. If so, do it anyway, and reserve judgement until you have completed this unit.)

d.   When you have completed your notes, re-arrange the items in groups relating to the three degrees of risk. As you continue through the course you will probably need to add further items, or move some from one category to another.

e.   Re-read the sections on action to be taken. Modify these:
   i   by adapting them to your occupation or status; and
   ii   by adapting them to your locality and its resources.
   Add addresses and telephone numbers.

f.   If a guide has been published in your locality, compare this with the one you have compiled for yourself, and combine the best features of both.

If, in compiling your guide you need to make enquiries about local resources which cannot be done during this activity, make them after completing this unit. You will need your completed guide for use in Unit 8.

---

6   Concern or suspicion?   A discussion

Despite the publication of guides and codes of practice, cases of child abuse still occur, and detection still often occurs later rather than sooner. One reason is that most of us dislike feeling suspicious of people.

Some doctors who are close to the problem of child abuse have suggested that a great improvement could be made in early detection if casualty officers considered all children under two brought to hospital with an injury (other than one sustained in a traffic accident) as possible cases of non-accidental injury. It is understandable that many doctors find this idea abhorrent. Their relationship with a patient is one of help and comfort, not one of suspicion. By this stage in the course you may be feeling this yourself. You are discovering that everyday innocent occurrences may be indicators of child abuse, potential or actual. In Units 10 and 11, you will find that an individual's history, not his actions, may be an indicator, and that you are invited to be suspicious.

6.3 If, as human beings, we dislike adopting an attitude of suspicion on what appears on the face of it to be very slender 'evidence', how much more dislike will be natural in those in the 'caring professions'. For a social worker to suspect the client with whom he is building a trusting and meaningful relationship is not only personally unpleasant, but appears professionally paradoxical.

6.4 Much of the difficulty might disappear if we used a word which has more positive connotations than does the word 'suspicion'. That word is 'concern'. If we think of ourselves as being concerned – and for the parent as well as the child, we may feel more positive about it. It might help also if we remind ourselves of the motivation for our concern, which is to prevent a situation which will damage both child and parents, or, failing that, to reduce the damage to a minimum.

6.5 In Unit 2 we noted that the commonest reaction to contact with abused children was pity for them. Our concern before they have been abused will serve them better than our pity afterwards.

Unit 8   Professional roles and functions (2)
Constance Lee and Bill Roberts

1   Introduction

In Unit 7 you were considering in some detail the conflicts and the responsibilities facing the professional worker. The aim of this unit is to help you to begin to communicate with others more purposefully and more effectively.

Activity 8.1
a.   Study the chart, 'The communications problem', and the explanatory paragraph, on p. 292 of the Reader.
b.   If your own group is not represented, draw it in, in the appropriate place. There will be further references to this chart later in the course.

Comments

Although this chart is an over-simplification and there are some important omissions, it does indicate the frightening range of 'bodies' who may become involved with one family. It is not surprising that 'breakdown in communication' has become almost a cliche; it is perhaps more surprising that effective communication ever takes place. A few minutes studying this chart should have convinced you that concise lines of communication are essential, especially where a child's well-being is concerned, but guidelines are useless without human co-operation, and 'communication' is of little value unless the significance of information exchanged is understood. The next activity underlines the latter point.

2   A case study

Activity 8.2
Bearing in mind the problems of communication, would you now read the case study from the 'L.G.' report, paragraphs 5–71, p. 278 in the Reader. You need make no notes at this stage, as you will be returning to it later.

2.1 You have read the tragic story of a little girl, who, despite the efforts of a number of people throughout her life, died in a very unpleasant manner. One of the saddest aspects of this case history is that the family was not unknown or neglected, but that it received a great deal of attention from a number of concerned and caring people over a period of several years. It is easy to be wise after the event; it is easier to see the shortcomings of other professions than to see the inadequacies of one's own. To help you to identify the signs and symptoms leading to abuse and to make the right decision about your own action in such a case, you will be asked in the next activity to work through the case study viewing the evidence 'through the eyes' of one worker.

2.2 The unit writers have studied the case 'through the eyes' of every one of the characters in the drama and a different picture emerges for each as the information they had is considered. You have probably noticed that the worker most involved in this case was the probation officer, which is why this is the worker chosen for the next activity.

2.3 In using real case material for this activity, it is not the intention of the writers to invite criticism of the people who were involved. It is worthwhile reminding ourselves at this point that it is always easier to be wise after the event than when you are involved and acting (as you think) for the best. Real material is used because there is no other way of involving you in a situation in which you are required to decide your response to actual happenings.

Activity 8.3

a. Read again the paragraphs in the case history relating to the probation officer. These are paragraphs 10, 13–17, 19, 22–41, 43–47, 49, 50, 52, 53, 57, 58, 61, 63, 68–70. *Do not read the rest.*

b. Imagine yourself as the probation officer.

c. Note the information given in the relevant paragraphs.

d. Using the guide which you prepared in Unit 7, decide at what point, and why, you would consider the family 'low risk', 'high risk', and 'emergency' and what action you would take at each point. *Note:* The guide you will be using, based as it is on your own notes on the Coventry guidelines, was not available to the workers concerned in the G. case Activity 8.3 is a composite activity, for illustrative purposes. Indeed, some of the lines of action you will recommend might have been inappropriate or impracticable in the G. case – or in cases you may meet yourself. It is always important to be very clear on local conditions and practice.

Comments

Only the main points concerning the probation officer are commented on below.

a. *Paragraphs 10, 13–17, July to October, 1972*
Family known to probation and after care service, mother on probation, history of defrauding DHSS with husband's connivance. Also history of assaults on neighbours. Top priority for rehousing. Conflict between parents, there have been periods of separation. Three children under school age.
Action Mother to report fortnightly. Discussion with other workers about playgroup and housing. Regard as vulnerable family needing supervision and help. Keep records.

b. *Paragraph 19, November 8, 1972*
Injury to L.'s head (2 years, 8 months). Family stress increasing. Mother depressed about own health, housing and neighbours.
Action Concerned about multiple problems. First knowledge of injury to child. Liaise with other workers. Extra vigilance required. Report to senior probation officer and make record. Regard as *low suspicion*.

c. *Paragraphs 22–25, January 16, 1973*
L. regressing, wetting and soiling. Mother appears to be rejecting child, admits smacking her, but feels guilty about it. Playgroup staff report bruising, also have noticed child stumbling. Concern about mother's health.
Action Discussion with health visitor, serious concern. Regard as *high suspicion*. Make arrangements for medical examination of child. Consult NSPCC. Advise senior and record.

d. *Paragraphs 26–40, January 17 to April 25, 1973*
Mother discusses own background and discloses feelings about L. Health visitor noted child unsteady on feet. Further assaults involving neighbours. Beginning to doubt verity of mother's statements. Mother being treated by general practitioner. Following case conference trainee social worker assigned to case (later withdrawn). Further case conference postponed because housing directorate not able to attend. Arrears in rent. Further bruising to L.s face on March 19. Playgroup staff report bruising on March 23. Pressure put upon housing department. 28th March mother admits hitting L., afraid of being 'found out'. Family rehoused, mother reports 'things going well', but that L. had had a bad fall and bumped head on 25th April; asking about nursery places.
Action Despite periods of reduced tension and rehousing, the children, especially L., are at high risk of injury. Ask for case conference urgently. Regard as *high suspicion*. Action as before.

e. *Paragraphs 41, 43–47. May 7 to June 19, 1973*
    Mother rejecting L., asking for child to be removed. Mother not managing, not willing to take L. to child guidance clinic. Relations with officer strained. Mother made own arrangements for two children to go to children's home. Expressing anxiety about possibility of more children, agreed to attend family planning clinic.
    June 8, 1973   Crisis, children back at home because parents cannot afford fees. Mother wants day nursery places. Health visitor not visiting. Social service department transferred papers to new area and closed case. Mother under stress. Discussion with health visitor about free nursery places.
    Action   As before. Conditions of *high suspicion* continue.
f. *Paragraphs 51, 53, 57, 58, 61, 63. August to September 1973*
    Mother failing appointments with probation officer. Conditions 'unbearable': husband drinking and illtreating her, pregnant again, rent arrears of £100. Propose going to Ireland, considering abortion and sterilization. L.'s arm injured and face bruised around eyes. Because of injuries not accepted in nursery, younger child not accepted either. Discussion about pregnancy, general practitioner supports abortion, gynaecologist does not.
    Action   In view of continuing problems, obvious stress, new pregnancy, husband's illtreatment and the latest injury to L. now regard child as being in serious danger. Arrange for the child to be taken to hospital, alert nursing and medical staff about possibility of non-accidental injury. Advise senior of *emergency* and complete records.
g. *Paragraph 68*
    Discussion with health visitor about unused nursery places (unaware that child was dying of injuries in hospital).
h. *Paragraph 69*
    Asked to assist police in inquiries. Visited home to check on safety of other children.

3   Learning practice

3.1 The objectives of Unit 7 and 8 should have been achieved by this point. Now you are invited to test the usefulness of your learning by participating in a paper simulation. The rest of this unit is, therefore, a rather painstaking, but valuable, activity.

Activity 8.4
a.   Prepare a sheet of paper with three column headings:
     i.   Information recorded in the report.

ii.   Other information you might expect to have.

iii.   Comments.

Leave a margin at the left for the date.

b.   Imagine yourself as either a nursery matron, or a general practitioner. If you are either of these, choose the other.

c.   Extract from the L.G. case history in the Reader all the information recorded as known to the person whose role you have chosen. For the nursery matron, the relevant paragraphs are 54, 55, 59, 60.

For the general practitioner, the relevant paragraphs are 5, 7, **11, 13**, 19, 20, **30, 42, 51, 54, 58**. The paragraphs with bold numbers contain information known directly to the general practitioner. The others contain information which implies the general practitioner's involvement (for example, para. 19 records mother attending hospital outpatients' clinic, so the general practitioner was treating her at this period).

Record the date and the information in column 1, in chronological order.

Use column 2 to record information that you might have expected to have, arising from the events or incidents recorded in column 1. Use your imagination, but do not invent without reasonable justification. For example, if the mother tells the doctor she wants an abortion, you might reasonably suppose that you would have asked her why, and there would have been some discussion of family circumstances.

Use column 3 for three purposes:

i.   to comment on the significance of the entries in columns 1 and 2 in terms of potential child abuse;

ii.   to record when you begin to consider the children may be at risk, and to what degree. Use the terms 'low risk', 'high risk' and 'emergency';

iii.   to record what action you would take and its purpose.

When you have completed your record, re-read it and add any comments which you feel appropriate. Then turn to the following pages, where you will find two examples of what you have been asked to do, followed by explanatory comments. Example 1 relates to the nursery matron; example 2 to the general practitioner. When you have completed reading and digesting the appropriate example, read the other one.

Example 1
Information record — Nursery matron

Date	Information recorded in the report	Other information you might expect to have	Comments
6.9.73	Rent arrears. Desire for abortion (no history of L.).	Difficulties in coping with L. Urgent need for nursery places.	Might gain impression of woman under stress.
17.9.73	L. injured and bruised. Mother told to take L. back to GP.	Mother may have given explanation.	Is explanation reasonable for arm injury? Injury and mother's stress might make you uneasy.
18.9.73	Mother presses for L. to return, though still unwell. (Health visitor told of injury).		Might think mother fairly desperate to offload children. *Possible action:* Talk to mother (1) *re* stresses and pressures. If these great, L. may be at fair risk. Let L. and Amanda attend nursery. (2) Tell SSD of your assessment — (3) giving reasons. Talk to senior worker, not duty officer.
25.9.73	Doctor at clinic session finds multiple heavy bruising of three different ages. Asks you to confirm that hospital has seen L. Confirmed: on 17.9		Now consider L. at 'high risk'. *Action:* enlist (4) doctor's support in alerting special unit, if there is one, or SSD. Seek health visitor's advice *re* action. If no support, take the initiative. Follow up to see (5) action being taken.

Comments on Example 1

3.2 Your first column should be very similar to the example, as it is derived from the inquiry report. Your second column may have more or less comment depending upon how you imagined your role as nursery matron.

You may have become uneasy about L. sooner or later than the example shows. You should, however, have considered L. as being at high risk of fairly severe injury by 25.9.73. Even without the evidence of considerable stress on the mother, the clinic doctor's findings are consistent with the classic pattern of repeated injury found in child abuse (see Unit 4).

Note that as a nursery matron you have no specific legal responsibility in the context of child abuse. You are however in *loco parentis*. The motives for any action taken are professional and personal.

Your action may differ from the example, depending upon local conditions and practices assumed, preference for certain agencies, or because a different purpose was intended. Where you have taken action involving another agency, check that the agency is appropriate to your purpose.

Notes on actions in the example:

1. Talking to mother *re* stress. To determine the level of stress and whether it involves the children. If great, then it would be wise to remove the children from mother, or relieve her of some of the stress.
2. Let children attend nursery. The twofold purpose is to keep the children out of harm's way temporarily, and to relieve mother.
3. Tell social services department. To provide intensive help for the mother, or to remove the child temporarily, or both. Insistence on speaking to a senior worker is accepting the reality that recognition of child abuse requires knowledge and experience which the duty officer may not have. It is a safety precaution.
4. Enlist doctor's support, etc. To enlist expert help so that appropriate action can be taken quickly. The NSPCC, the social services department and the police have machinery for securing the removal of the child if this is necessary.
5. Follow up. It is envisaged that your personal sense of responsibility does not allow you to consider your action completed because you have alerted the appropriate agency. As an individual there is nothing in law to prevent you taking the facts to a magistrate and asking for a place of safety order if you feel that appropriate action is not being taken and the child remains unprotected. (See Unit 13.)

Example 2
Information record — General practitioner

Date	Information recorded in the report	Other information you might expect to have	Comments
3.70	L.'s birth.		
by 10.70	L. frequent bronchitis. Both parents being treated for 'nerves'.	How L.'s bronchitis affects caring for her. Effects on family of parents' 'nerves'.	
c.2.71		Beginning of pregnancy. Mother's feelings *re* being pregnant.	Might consider stress in family is considerable. New baby's arrival in Sept. will increase it. *Action:* note own records to raise this with mother at intervals. Advise health visitor and/or antenatal clinic.
9.71	Amanda's birth.		
11.71	Advise mother to live on ground floor. House damp. (Presumably mother frail in some way).		Mother has a baby and 2 other children ages 1½ and over 3. Health not good, house damp. Other worries. *Action:* discuss with health visitor the care of children; is help needed for family?
11.72	Mother has been referred to hospital outpatients' for treatment or tests. Hospital reports no physical illness.		If not physically ill, then what?
12.72	L. to hospital for operation on bladder.	Almost certain that for some time L. has been bed wetting and wetting during day sometimes.	See summary.

Summary	This family has a number of problems and difficulties. Mother, particularly, is under stress. She does not feel well; the house is defective; she has three young children. L. has probably been a 'difficult' child — she has always been 'chesty' (sleepless nights for mother?), and toilet training has been unsatisfactory. Although there has been no suggestion of any ill-treatment of the children, there are present in this family a number of factors which might lead to abuse(1). It is reasonable to consider this a 'low risk' family(2). *Action:* ensure health visitor examines children thoroughly at regular intervals, undressing them, checking weight and height, etc. Advise SSD.

2.73	Tablets prescribed to help mother control temper outbursts (following assault on neighbour). Mother discusses holidays for children.		Does she lose her temper with the children frequently? What is the significance of wanting them to go away for holiday?(3)
5.73	Mother tells of childhood experiences, and reason for deafness (mother cuffing her on head).		You should consider this family at 'high risk' (4). *Action:* increase checks on children by health visitor. Realert SSD. Enter on Risk Register. Ask for case conf.
8.73	L. brought with bruises and black eye. Arrange for hospital X-ray.		*Action:* make direct contact with hospital paediatrician. Call for full examination — full skeletal X-ray — and interview with mother *re* injuries. Call for case conference, to which all agencies invited, including police.
9.73	Mother's request for abortion supported by you on grounds that she cannot stand strain of another child.		Pregnancy is a further stress — esp. as child is unwanted.
9.73	Report from hospital of swollen left arm and healing fracture of right humerus. (L.)		*Action:* as above. If no results, (5) call police.

Comments on Example 2

7 Your column 1 should be similar to the example. You may have much more in column 2, depending upon how much mother might have told you about other things when consulting you on medical matters.

3.8 Summary (after 12.72). You may not have considered the family as at risk as early as this.

1. Some of these factors, which make for difficulties in caring for the children, are discussed in Unit 4. Others will assume more significance for you when you come to Units 10 and 11.
2. Note that by this time the inquiry report records that the health visitor considered the family to be at risk of abusing the children.

3.9 Notes on comments in column 3.

3. There is not necessarily anything sinister in a parent wanting a break from the children – particularly three very young ones. But it is frequently the case that parents seek ways of removing the children from themselves when they fear that they might hurt them, or have already done so.
4. The significance of mother's childhood experiences, and the fact that she was abused herself as a child, will be clearer when you come to Units 10 and 11. Taken together with the incidents of 2.73 and the whole family history since L.'s birth, this latest piece of information is a very serious warning.
5. The purpose is to remove L. to safety temporarily. Irrefutable evidence is not required to obtain a place of safety order, and your professional opinion is likely to be sufficient.

3.10 Finally, note that there is very little information flowing between you (the GP) and other workers, as compared with the probation officer. This fact underlines the importance of the matters discussed in sections 2 and 3 of Unit 7.

4 Record-keeping

The fairly extensive use of charts and flow sheets in this unit should have made you aware of the value of keeping records, and of using them effectively. Vague feelings of unease about a family can turn into near certainty when you read the history of events over a period of time and add up the significant factors. But one can do this only if the incidents have been recorded in a systematic fashion, and if the record is re-read. If this seems too obvious to be worth stating, check the case files in your office to see how easy or difficult it is to obtain useful information quickly.

Self-assessment questions (Block 2)
Richard Fothergill

1 Which of the following symptoms almost undeniably are due to physical abuse?

    a.   two black eyes on a six-month-old child.
    b.   a fractured arm in a year-old child.
    c.   a torn frenulum under the tongue of a three-month-old child.
    d.   scalded feet with no burns on the soles of an eighteen-month-old child.
    e.   a two-year-old who has swallowed several pills.

2 List 6 symptoms that may be observed in the 'failure to thrive' child.

3 According to Erikson's personality theory:

    a.   What is the first advantage a baby gains through normal mothering?
    b.   In late infancy what characteristic is likely to develop in the child who is disciplined harshly and disapprovingly?
    c.   In early childhood what achievement normally develops from expansion of language and movement?

4 In a psychiatric interview, a number of characteristics exhibited by the child should immediately alert the worker to the probability of abuse having taken place. List 4 of these.

5 Define a 'coping mechanism'.

6 Write down those groups of 'workers' from the following list who have the power, either directly or through a justice of the peace, to remove a child under a place of safety order:

police officers, general practitioners, NSPCC inspectors, probation officers, social service departments, paediatricians, psychiatrists.

7 a.   Below is a list of occurrences which may be signs of potential child abuse. Identify the worker who is most likely to note the sign by associating the letter in the left-hand column with the appropriate one in the right-hand one.

| A | Mother strongly resents labour difficulties | a | Paediatrician |
| B | Parents continually disturb neighbours by fighting. | b | Nurse |

C	Husband convicted of assault, leaves prison to join wife and another man's child.	c	Midwife
D	Ten-week-old child is not putting on sufficient weight.	d	Probation officer
E	Child cries when parents visit him in hospital	e	Health visitor
F	Six-month-old child who is constantly sick, has two black eyes.	f	Police officer

b. Write down the names given by the Coventry Area Review Committee to the three categories of reporting when there are warning signs of child abuse.

c. Assign a possible category to each sign listed in the first part of this question.

d. With which of the following groups is it appropriate for the observer of the signs A, B, E and F in the first part of the question to communicate?
General practitioner; social services department; nursing officer/health visitor; police.

Answers to self-assessment questions (Block 2)

1 a, c, d.   (1 mark each)
   Total: 3 marks (ref: Unit 5)

2 1 mark for any 6 of the following.

   Infantile proportions; peripheral vascular stasis; pot belly and loose stools; poor skin and dry sparse hair; perverted appetite; particular behaviour patterns; inertia and catatonia.

   Total: 6 marks (ref: Unit 5)

3 a. Sense of trust.
   b. Excessive sense of shame and doubt.
   c. Initiative in social relationships.   (1 mark for each)

   Total: 3 marks (ref: Unit 6)

4 1 mark for any 4 of the following.

   Frozen watchfulness; sense of helplessness; sense of hopelessness; sense of worthlessness; sense of inadequacy; shame; guilt.

   Total: 4 marks (ref: Unit 6)

5 A series of techniques which the child has learned to help him to adapt to and cope with his hostile and dangerous environment in order to survive.

   Total: 2 marks (ref: Unit 6)

6 Police officers, NSPCC inspectors, social services department.
   (1 mark for each)

   Total: 3 marks (ref: Unit 7)

7 a. Ac, Bf, Cd, De, Eb, Fa.   (1 mark for each)

   Total: 6 marks (ref: Unit 7)

   b. Emergency. High suspicion. Low suspicion.   (1 mark each)

   Total: 3 marks (ref: Unit 7/8)

   c. A. Low suspicion   B. Low suspicion   C. Low suspicion
       D. High suspicion   E. High suspicion   F. Emergency.
       (1 mark each)

   Total: 6 marks (ref: Unit 7/8)

d. A. Health visitor   B. Social services department   E. Health
    visitor   F. All of them.   (1 mark each)

    Note that these may differ according to the guidelines issued by the
    local area review committee.

Total: 4 marks (ref: Unit 7/8)

Maximum marks: 40

Block 3   Predisposing and contributory factors

The first unit in this block is concerned with the epidemiology of child abuse and looks at the environmental factors which are commonly associated with family conflict. It also encourages the student to examine the research literature closely, to recognize the methodological problems that face research workers in the field and to avoid glib conclusions and comparisons. Units 10 and 11 present, with examples, the critical path approach to child abuse, by which the many and varied family stresses that may precipitate abuse can be traced. The last unit of the block encourages students to look closely at the reports of official inquiries into cases where active intervention has failed to avert disaster, and to draw lessons from these for the improvement of their own professional practice.

Unit 9 The family and its environment
Catherine Peckham

Objectives

When you have finished this unit you should be able to:

1. list some of the methodological problems encountered in epidemiological studies of child abuse;
2. describe the results of studies showing that the occurrence of child
   abuse is a complex of several interrelated factors with particular
   stress on the interaction between social pressures on the family and
   physical and mental health;
3. discuss the relevance of society's attitudes to childbirth and child
   rearing to the problem of child abuse.

1 Understanding the literature on child abuse

1.1 During recent years it has become clear that violence within the family
unit is not a rare and exceptional event. In the UK and the United States
both child abuse and wife battering are well recognized forms of family
violence and homicide rates within the family are higher than outside.
This notion of the family as a potential milieu for violence is obviously at
variance with the traditional view of the family. This latter view of an
idealized situation underlies a sense of shock that child abuse can
take place within the family. Studies of child abuse must therefore be
concerned with family patterns of pathology and not restricted to
studies of individuals. Information at the family level is far from complete since few studies have compared non-violent families with violent
families.

1.2 The methodological problems in studying families with abused children
are formidable. It is difficult to be objective about family behaviour and
there are also great problems associated with questioning abusive families
using conventional questionnaires and interviewing methods. Strong
moralistic expectations affecting family roles may influence data reliability
so that questions tend to be answered by giving socially acceptable responses. These social complexities cannot be ignored and the failures of
child abusers cannot be explained simply as the function of innate
defects.

In order to understand more fully and interpret more accurately the numerous articles and studies on child abuse which have appeared in recent years, it is important to appreciate the basic methodological problems encountered in epidemiological studies.

Activity 9.1

The ability to read, understand and evaluate research findings is an important acquisition for any worker in the field of child abuse. The extracts used in connection with this unit will not be 'easy reading' for all students but they cannot be paraphrased without loss of meaning. If you have difficulty, try this method:

a.   Read straight through the difficult passage. Guess at the meaning of unfamiliar terms from their context, but if they don't become clear by the end of the paragraph underline them.
b.   Go back to the beginning, work through paragraph by paragraph, checking in the light of overall arguments, and using a dictionary if you must. Make notes as required by the activity. A few non-dictionary terms will be defined in this text.

Now read the extract from Peckham's 'The dimensions of child abuse' (1974) in the Reader (p. 45). Pick out and list the various methodological problems which make comparison between different types of research study difficult.

Comments

Clearly the *definition* of child abuse is of primary importance. The larger the definition the more cases it encompasses and the higher the incidence rate. In this course we have defined child abuse as including physical and mental abuses and neglect, but do the surveys cover such a wide scope? Does the definition include neglect or mental maltreatment or merely physical injuries and when does a physical injury constitute abuse? The motivation is obviously important as well as the severity of the physical injury.

The local *awareness of the problem* is another important factor. Where the reported incidence is low, this could be due to either the lack of recognition of cases or to different reporting procedures. This point is of particular importance when comparisons are being made between different geographical areas or different periods of time in the same area. There is a widely held assumption that child abuse is on the increase but at the present time this cannot be substantiated since there is no available systematic information on incidence of abuse over time.

1.6 The *incidence rate* (number of new cases recorded over a defined period of time) will also vary according to the age of children included in a given study. In a population of children aged 0 to 5 years the yearly incidence of child abuse is likely to be lower than a population aged 0 to 3 years since there are more vulnerable children in this latter group. Most of the surveys, however, relate only to the 0 to 4 age group and even within this limitation the cases studied tend to be overweighted with children under one year.

1.7 The *socio-economic background* is another important factor relating to the reporting of cases. Children from poorer families who are already in contact with the social services are more likely to be reported than children from well-off families who may attend private doctors. The social structure of the population studied must therefore be considered because this bias may in part account for differing incidence rates in different areas and affect the validity of comparisons.

1.8 Finally, *the population from which the cases are derived* must be taken into account. Hospital-based studies will not necessarily be representative of the population as a whole.

2 Interrelated causative factors in child abuse

2.1 If distinctions are to be made between abusive and non-abusive parents, and causative factors are to be identified, studies must be carried out within social or racial groups, since habits and styles of living differ between different cultures and subcultures. For example, comparisons must be made between poor families recognized by the community as neglectful with poor families recognized as adequate. Only then will it be possible to elucidate ways in which families who neglect their children differ from those who do not.

Activity 9.2
Re-read the first two sections of Gil's article (i.e., 'The families of abused children' and 'The incidence and circumstances surrounding them') entitled 'Violence against children' in the Reader (p. 49). This has already been studied in connection with Unit 3. Pick out and list the family characteristics which are commonly associated with child abuse.

Comments

Your list will probably include the following:

one-parent family
one step-parent
unusual family structure
large number of children in family
low educational attainment of parents
low occupational status of parents
unemployment
low income
marital problems
mental illness
isolation
psychosocial malfunctioning

3 Child abuse is certainly not confined to one social group but you will appreciate from your reading that, as may be expected, it is more common in families under greater stress with fewer resources to cope with these stresses. Families subjected to environmental stresses and strains associated with socio-economic deprivation are more vulnerable and, where there are few supports to cope with those stresses and the parent is psychologically at risk, this may lead to abusive behaviour towards the child. Such families are often large and living in crowded conditions and have few outlets. Living standards and life style have profound effects on the patterns of disease, and morbidity and mortality rates are higher both among children and adults with low socio-economic levels.

4 The modern family tends to be isolated spatially and emotionally and, as a consequence, when a woman with young children is restricted to the home, she lacks social contacts. The effects of this social isolation together with dissatisfaction with housebound activities, may be exacerbated by the demands of young children and result in depression. In women this type of response to family stress tends to be socially and medically acceptable. Studies on child abuse in the United Kingdom have demonstrated that nuclear families with abused children had infrequent or no contact with the extended family and little contact with neighbours and friends. The degree to which this factor is mediated by differential social class patterns is, however, unknown.

5 A recent study of women living in South London (Brown, Bhrolchain and Harris, 1975) showed a disturbingly high rate of psychiatric illness among working-class women with young children at home. These women, it was shown, were more likely than middle-class women to be exposed to such

environmental stresses as poor housing, money and marriage difficulties, etc. Other important factors associated with psychiatric breakdown in a mother following environmental stress were loss of her own mother in childhood, three or more children aged under 14, and lack of an intimate confiding relationship with her husband or boyfriend and lack of full or part-time employment. The first three features were found to be more common in working-class than in middle-class women and, between them, were sufficient to explain the class difference in vulnerability to psychiatric breakdown.

2.6 Naomi Richman (1974) carried out a survey of the health of mothers of children under five years old living in a council housing estate in North London and found that 41 per cent had depressive symptoms of a moderate to severe degree (17 per cent were judged to be suffering from psychiatric illness severe enough to warrant outpatient attendance). The study clearly demonstrated the isolation felt by mothers at home with young children. A depressed mother is often not in a position to consider her child's emotional and physical requirements and recent research shows a high incidence of accidents among children during periods of depression in their mother.

2.7 Baldwin and Oliver (1975) made two studies in north-east Wiltshire of all families in which a child under five years old had been subjected to very severe active physical abuse. One (the 'retrospective study') identified families from cases which had been reported prior to 1971. The second (the 'prospective study') began in 1971 with a programme of intensive discussion with professionals to improve case recognition. The following extract from their report highlights the association between family environment, psychiatric and physical illness and child abuse:

> Large size, youthfulness, instability, and gross excesses of psychiatric and physical illness and disability, and criminality characterized the retrospective series of child abuse families. Clinically, families in the prospective series, although referred at a much higher rate, were similar. So marked were these features that, even in the absence of controls, it is likely that they identify a group of inadequate and unhealthy families to whom severe physical abuse is largely confined . . .

> The frequency of disease in these families is suggestive of clustering of disorders and is reminiscent of Newcombe's finding of greatly increased relative risk in siblings of handicapped and stillborn children for a wide range of conditions, including accidents, poisonings, and violence. This is clearly a subject for detailed study for which a system of linked medical

records depicting the primary and intergenerational family relationships would be necessary. If disease clustering in such families were confirmed and its nature and extent specified, there could be important implications for both medical knowledge and the organization of health and social care. Child abuse appears to be but a manifestation of widespread heterogeneous, and often severe, medical and social pathology affecting virtually the whole family. Multiple disease and the consequent disability may become so overwhelming that the means of coping with the difficulties of living are no longer possible for the adult members. Violent impulsive aggression, shifting dependence on acquaintances and relatives, and deep ambivalence towards health, social welfare and social control agencies on which extraordinary demands are made, become a characteristic way of life.

8 Again the association between family environment and parental psychiatric and physical illness is identified and it is in these families that severe physical abuse is more common. The implications of this are far-reaching and, clearly, child abuse must be regarded as a complex multi-dimensional problem with no one set of causative factors. Poor environmental circumstances can push physical violence in childhood to unacceptable levels and this stress as well as mental and physical disorders appear to be important precursors. However, although a large number of reported cases arise in seriously deprived families, child abuse is not found exclusively in these groups but in all strata of society.

9 The degree to which industrialization affected the functions of the family is not known, but in the twentieth century there has been a diminution in the size of the family and today families are nuclear rather than extended. This is in part due to the mobility of labour and also to the reduction in family size resulting from advances in contraception and higher living standards. As a result more attention has tended to be focused on the individual child, and child rearing has been amplified so that much greater emphasis has been placed on child development and child psychology. Thus, child rearing which was previously the family's prerogative has become the subject of scientific enquiry so that professionals such as paediatricians and social workers are now in a position to be involved with many of the family's functions. In some circumstances this may have eroded parental confidence.

3 Social attitudes to child birth and child rearing

1 The image of the nuclear family as a self-contained unit is no longer valid

since demands and pressures from outside have increased so that the family boundaries have become less clear and the family more open to inspection. Official abuse such as flogging or beating for minor offences is no longer condoned by society and even corporal punishment in schools is under scrutiny, so that child abuse within the family has become not only more apparent but also more important.

3.2 There are strong pressures for parenthood in our society and it is considered a natural and inevitable event that girls will marry and have children. There is less discussion, however, on how to be a good and efficient mother and it is widely assumed that all women are capable of parenthood.

3.3 In the present scientific era a great deal of attention has been paid to pregnancy and childbirth. There is evidence, however, to suggest that many women do not know what to expect in relation to pregnancy, labour, childcare and breastfeeding. Although these areas are fundamental to a mother's relationship with her infant, there is often a lack of experience and understanding of what is involved.

3.4 In a study in South London (Hubert, 1974) which looked at the attitudes of working-class women expecting their first baby, the ineffectiveness of campaigns about contraception were well illustrated. Half the pregnancies were unwanted and birth control was ineffective. There was a lack of communication from clinical hospital staff, most of the parents' information came from their own mothers, and they were not prepared for the birth.

3.5 Society's portrayal of motherhood has been greatly idealized. Girls living in small families only rarely come into contact with newborn infants and the realities of motherhood, and the relative isolation of the family means that young mothers have little concept of what is expected of them. When faced with their newborn infant who requires constant attention and is a disruptive influence on the family, they are often unprepared. Following pregnancy and labour women are often at their lowest ebb and may be depressed, which can only exacerbate the situation, particularly if the pregnancy was unwanted. This underlies the need for adequate preparation for motherhood. This topic receives further attention in Unit 24.

Unit 10 Predisposing factors within the family (1)
Margaret Lynch and Jacquie Roberts

Units 10 and 11 are linked units. The end of Unit 10 makes a' natural break', but nothing will be lost if you spread your workload in a different way over the two study sessions.

Objectives

After completing this unit you should be able to:

1. state what is meant by 'bonding failure' and explain why the concept is considered of central importance in the aetiology of child abuse;
2. list some experiences commonly found in the biographies of abusing parents and explain how they relate to later abusive behaviour;
3. describe some of the social problems often found in abusing families and state what is meant by 'diffuse social problems';
4. outline the part that medical problems may play in the aetiology of child abuse;
5. explain how these various types of problem may interact, and how they can affect the interaction between parent and child.

1 Introduction

.1 This unit is concerned with the problems in the family which predispose to child abuse. It is based on clinical and research experience at the Park Hospital for Children. The hospital has a family unit where the abused child and his family can be admitted for residential assessment and treatment. Over 200 abused children have been known to the hospital. It is from our experience of these children and their families that we have come to see the inflicted injury of a child as a symptom of underlying bonding failure between parents and child. We use the term 'bonding failure' to describe the failure to establish a consistent loving relationship between a child and his parents. When bonding failure occurs it can produce a number of child-rearing problems of which child abuse is an extreme example.

.2 Each case is different and we have learnt that there is never a single cause. In every family it is the result of a complex process which may have begun years or even generations before the child is harmed.

1.3 In each case we need to understand how the parents came to abuse their child and to assess the influence of parental biographies, social circumstances, medical events and the child's development. We have found it helpful to view the process that leads to abuse in the form of a critical path.

Activity 10.1
At this point please read Lynch (1976) 'Child abuse: The critical path' in the Reader (p. 54) which illustrates the process in one family and discusses some of the commonly observed predisposing factors.

1.4 We will now discuss in more detail the factors described in the paper you have just read. We will retain the same framework as the paper, using the headings *parents' biographies*; *social circumstances*; and *medical problems*; and we will add a fourth, *attributes in the child*. Before each of the first three sections you will find an activity requiring you to think through some question or questions suggested by the article before moving on to the discussion.

Activity 10.2
Write short notes in answer to the following.

a. List some of the *types* of childhood experience you would expect might be predictive of abusive behaviour to one's own children in later life, with reasons.
b. How strongly could you rely upon predictions made from such evidence? Again, give reasons.

Keep the notes you make on this activity (and on those that follow) beside you and refer to them from time to time as you read on, comparing your own answers with the text – and amending them if you meet evidence or an argument that convinces you of any mistakes in your own ideas.

---

2 The parents' biographies

2.1 There are a number of factors in the parents' biographies that may increase their potential to abuse. However, when trying to identify these

116

factors, it must be remembered that much of the information is derived from retrospective enquiries into the childhood of battering parents, and we do not yet know how many people with the same childhood experiences have become successful parents. Furthermore, many characteristics found in a sample of abusing parents may simply illustrate the population from which the sample is drawn, rather than differentiate abusers from non-abusers.

2   Nevertheless, there are characteristics shared by many abusing parents regardless of social or ethnic group. For example, it is universally reported that many battering parents have themselves been battered as children. This is often because children suffer emotional damage from abnormal child-rearing patterns of which physical injuries are only a symptom. The emotional disturbance results in an inability to form stable relationships, even with their own children. When such a fragile relationship is put under stress, they subconsciously resort to the kind of parental behaviour to which they were conditioned in their own childhood. Some battering parents will have grown up in homes where communication has been by shouts and blows and are inevitably at great risk of continuing such violent behaviour, both with spouse and children.

.3   We have found that even good-intentioned harsh discipline, like that endured by 'Linda' in the 'Critical path' can affect a parent's ability to care for a small baby. Rigid expectations of 'good behaviour' have been drummed into such parents throughout their childhood and they often find it difficult to understand when a tiny baby does not 'obey' them.

.4   In many cases, the battering parent may not have suffered overt physical violence, but rather emotional abuse or deprivation. We have often found that abusing parents have been separated early in life from one or both parents. Some have spent all their childhood in an institution or in a series of unsuccessful foster placements. They have completely missed the experience of being loved and cared for consistently either by parents or parent substitutes. Even if they have spent their childhood with their natural parents and have suffered no physical abuse, they may have experienced total rejection, which produces an overwhelming feeling of worthlessness. Such a deprived person is unable to give love and demands care and affection from others, even their own small child.

.5   All these adverse childhood experiences produce the same fundamental characteristic in abusing parents, that is, basic mistrust. They have not yet passed the emotional developmental hurdles of childhood which have been conceptualized by Erikson (See Unit 6). They have been unable to establish a balance between trust and mistrust. As they have been constantly let down by those close to them, they don't expect anyone to be consistent and reliable. Their links with their own parents may be very close and dependent, but at the same time full of bitter resentment. The attitude of mistrust is a very difficult one for workers to deal with as the parents expect criticism and rejection. They also tend to resent anyone in authority.

2.6 An unhappy childhood almost invariably leads to difficult adolescence. Again using Erikson's terms, they suffer a 'crisis of identity' or 'role confusion' which they have not resolved years later. A number of battering parents have reacted to this difficult time of adolescence by running away: as teenagers they have fled from home or run from one job to another, failing to make any satisfactory achievements. It is during the adolescence, while running from their problems that abusing parents find each other and 'assortive mating' occurs. People with such disturbed biographies frequently find and are accepted by only those with similar backgrounds. It is inevitable, then, that the parents' difficulties extend into their adult relationships; when an emotionally deprived person chooses a partner with equal problems, neither finds what they need in the other. Almost invariably abusing parents are found to have marital problems. Disturbed and unhappy sexual relationships are common and their attitude to contraception ambivalent. These attitudes and problems seem to be symptomatic of the underlying identity and personality difficulties.

2.7 Marriage and parenthood have often been seen as another form of escape. We have found abusing parents are more likely to embark on parenthood at an early age. When comparing a group of 50 abusing mothers with their controls, we found that 50 per cent had had their first child under the age of 20 compared with only 16 per cent of their controls. Such early parenthood has been reported by many other authors. These immature parents look to the new baby to provide them with the love and care they have missed, but the baby demands more than he can give and the result is disappointment and a failure to understand the baby's needs. So often in abusing parents we see that they expect too much of their child, often expecting him to make up for their own failures.

2.8 In conclusion, then, it is necessary to look for aspects of deprivation, failure to fulfil needs, emotional disturbance and harsh treatment in the biographies of abusing parents. If the picture builds up like that in the critical path of Cindy, then the couple is beginning parenthood with the potential for child-rearing difficulties which could lead to emotional and physical abuse.

3   Social circumstances

Activity 10.3
Treat these questions as you did those in Activity 10.2.

a.   What are some of the social problems commonly observed in high-risk families?

b.   How might such families be distinguished (with reference only to social problems) from the many low-risk families with some of the same problems?

c.   How might a social problem *interact* with a personality problem to exacerbate abusing tendencies? Give an example.

1   Social problems play an important part in the process that leads to child abuse, but these are not necessarily problems caused by poverty and adverse social conditions. The majority of poor families in inadequate housing do not batter their children. Social problems affecting abusing families are usually a direct result of underlying relationship difficulties, and are therefore multiple or diffuse. A wide range of interlocking and long-term difficulties beset the whole family and it is this which differentiates abusers from non-abusers. For example, we find that many abusing parents have needed social work help around the time of their child's birth, but they can be distinguished from the main body of maternity social-work cases because of the 'diffuse' nature of their problems. Most families seeking maternity social-work help have 'defined' social problems which are isolated problems in otherwise stable families. The problems have well-defined limits and, although they are not always easy to solve, (e.g., housing) the solution is apparent. Linda and Robert, from the critical path, provide us with a typical example of a young family with diffuse social problems. The early life experiences of both parents made it difficult for them to form good trusting relationships, and therefore, when they moved abroad, they remained isolated, unable and unwilling to make new friends and become part of the community. Their antagonistic attitude led to rows with their landlord, Robert's problem at work, accumulation of debts, difficulty in finding domestic help and a series of unhappy foster placements for John.

.2   The accumulation of difficulties is so intertwined and diffuse that there appears to be no escape. Often the parents react to such chaos by denying reality. Some build up a fantasy world in which they believe so strongly that others collude. For example, an attractive middle-class wife with a beautifully decorated home, loyal husband, and perfectly dressed children so strongly projected the image of a perfect wife and mother that professionals denied the possibility of abuse, even after she had admitted to inflicting severe injuries on her children. Beneath the facade was a series of interlocking problems which precipitated the abuse. Her hostile relationship with her own parents, financial strain, marital and sexual difficulties were all aggravated by coping with a demanding toddler and persistent tiredness and anaemia following her second pregnancy.

3.3 We have seen that difficulty in making relationships affects all aspects of these people's lives and, therefore, when they become parents, they do not know how to relate and react to their newborn baby. In a recent study we have found that 22 out of a sample of 50 abusing mothers had caused sufficient anxiety about their mothering capacity for the maternity staff to have recorded concern in the notes even before the baby had left the hospital. The irony is that abusing parents often see their baby as the solution to their problems, someone to love them and compensate for their previous disappointments.

4 Medical problems

Activity 10.4

Treat this question as you did those in Activity 10.2.

What are some of the medical problems or deviations commonly found in (a) high-risk parents, (b) high-risk children? In each case, indicate the *way* this problem might operate to increase the likelihood of abuse.

4.1 There is a high incidence of ill-health in abusing families. They have medical problems that need assessment and treatment. This applies to the parents and the siblings as well as to the abused child. Treatment for the abused child and his family must therefore always include medical services.

4.2 Parents need to be in good physical health to cope adequately with the demands of young children. Both major and minor health problems will interfere with the way a parent interacts with the child. A serious illness means much family anxiety, probably hospitalization as an emergency. Parent and child may well be separated for some time. The effect of a serious illness on family life can be dramatic, but because it is obvious, help is usually available. Minor long-term health problems can be even more damaging because they are less easy to identify. Parents may be reluctant to seek medical help, and the social worker may not think to ask in any detail about a client's health. Chronic conditions such as long and painful periods, anaemia, migraine and dental caries can all have a detrimental effect on a person's ability to cope with life. A woman tired from anaemia and in constant pain from dental caries finds it impossible to enjoy a new baby. Treat the cause of her anaemia and persuade her to go to the dentist and the risk to the child may well diminish. In a study which compared abused children with non-abused brothers and sisters, we found that the mother was far more likely to have experienced a complicated pregnancy or to have been ill in the abused child's first year of life than during the same period of the sibling's life. Illness in pregnancy can affect a mother's relationship to her unborn child who may well be resented before he is even born. In other families it is during the strain of a complicated pregnancy that a child is abused for the first time.

3 If the new baby is ill or very premature, mother–child bonding is further jeopardized. Our studies and those of others have shown that abused children are more likely to have required admission to a special care baby unit than unharmed siblings or population controls. It is difficult to feel pride in a bundle of skin and bone connected to a lot of complicated wires and apparatus. Many mothers have said to us, 'She did not seem to belong to me'. Of course parents with a high potential for abuse because of their biographies are particularly vulnerable. They don't trust hospitals and see their inability to produce a large healthy baby as another criticism of themselves as people. The baby who is ill in the first year of life is also at greater risk of abuse. The illness may be a persistent irritating one, like eczema, colic and vomiting or a serious illness requiring hospitalization and therefore likely separation from parents. The most frustrating illnesses are those in which the parents sense that there is a serious problem with a child, but this is as yet unrecognized or undiagnosed by their medical advisers.

4 Both parents and abused child need a thorough and sophisticated psychiatric assessment. Examples of severe mental illness, psychopathy and gross immature personalities are found. About 10 per cent of the parents seen at the Park Hospital have a formal psychiatric illness. Those with a psychosis must be identified; it is often impossible for them to bond or relate to the baby normally. The very act of battering may be part of their delusional system. Not infrequently mentally ill people have married a partner equally disturbed. Removal of a child from such parents is a necessity. Some parents may show evidence of pathological jealousy. By this is meant that one of the parents is irrationally jealous of the other's feelings towards the baby. Most commonly, it is the father who aggressively resents the attention the new baby receives from his wife. The women in abusing families often have a history of suicidal attempts by drug overdose.

4.5 The majority of parents will have complaints of anxiety and/or depression, but this is usually an appropriate response to their domestic and social circumstances. We do not consider that it should be regarded as a psychiatric illness. Obsessionality often features in the personality of both parents which, together with rigidity, makes it difficult for them to adapt to the inevitable mess of having a baby around. Many abusing parents do get referred to psychiatrists and acquire a variety of diagnostic labels. It is, however, more realistic to regard emotional disturbances as yet another facet of their diffuse interpersonal and social problems.

5 Attributes in the child

5.1 When a child is abused, it is a result of the interaction between parent and child. It is therefore to be expected that certain attributes in the child predispose him to be abused. One study referred to in the Lynch article in the Reader compared 25 abused children with their 35 unharmed siblings. By using this internal control group instead of the usual matched controls or population figures, the parents' biographies and personalities remained constant, so highlighting the importance surrounding the children's early lives. The contrast between the abused and their unharmed siblings clearly emerged. Six factors were highly significantly overrepresented in the abused child's biography: abnormal pregnancy, abnormal labour or delivery, neonatal separation, other separations in the first six months, illness in the first year of life, and illness in the mother in the child's first year of life.

5.2 Abusive parents have high unrealistic expectations of their children. Any child who deviates from an accepted or expected 'normal development' puts himself at risk. Some abused children do indeed have very real medical, developmental or behavioural problems that have helped precipitate the abuse. For others the deviation is very minor and would have caused no more than slight anxiety in most families. The clumsy, slow-learning, eneuretic child will compare unfavourably with a quicker, better coordinated, dry sibling. A powerfully developed exploratory drive in a very active child is likely to drive such parents to distraction. The child may merely have been of the 'wrong sex'.

5.3 Most of the events dealt with in this study were concerned with ill-health. Some of the separations, however, occurred not because of illness in the child but for other reasons such as hospitalization of a parent, or placement with relatives or foster parents while domestic crises were sorted out. Any separation between parents and child makes a consistent and trusting relationship more difficult to maintain. So often in these families we see already tenuous parent-child relationships put under additional strain by separation.

6   Summary of Unit 10

The relative importance of the above categories of predisposing factors differs for each case of child abuse. At one extreme, parents may be so disturbed that they would abuse any child, regardless of stress. At the other extreme, we have examples of parents who have had normal secure upbringing but, because of a series of acute medical or social events, are unable to bond to their child and are driven to battering. A thorough knowledge of a critical path leading to the injury of an abused child will confirm the diagnosis. It also forms the essential basis to a treatment plan for the whole family. None of the factors can be used in isolation to predict child abuse. If they are viewed in the context of the total family history they can be used as alerting signals. Many of the factors described bring the family to the notice of doctors, social workers and health visitors and, if further appropriate information is gathered, then the child 'at risk' can be identified. In many families, child-rearing problems have existed for some time before the actual injury was incurred. In babies such as Cindy this is commonly persistent screaming, difficulties with feeding and failure to thrive. In older children problems presenting to the doctor and health visitor include sleeping, eating, soiling and difficult behaviour. It is often the parents' attitude to these problems that gives the clue to the underlying disturbance. Recognition is more difficult when the parent presents with either physical or psychological symptoms. Knowledge of the whole family would help identify those whose real problem is coping with a young family. A better understanding of the process and factors leading to abuse enable us to identify the more explicit signals – the 'open warnings' described in the last section of the Reader article.

Unit 11   Predisposing factors within the family (2)
Margaret Lynch, Jacquie Roberts and Bill Roberts

Objectives

After completing this unit you should be able to:

1.   expand your notes on Unit 10 to include some further problems which might predispose to abuse;
2.   draw up a 'self-advice' guide to the collection of critical path data in real-life situations;
3.   from given data (the biography of a family) produce a critical path analysis which traces the many factors and the interactions between them that may culminate in abusive action.

1   Introduction

1.1   This unit consists of two activities, both intended to help bridge the gap between *knowing* something about family problems and processes that may culminate in child abuse and *being able to use* that knowledge to recommend intervention in appropriate cases and at appropriate times.

1.2   It will be clear to anyone who has studied Unit 10 that many families in which abuse occurs are families which have for a long time been in need of help. It is therefore important to think of the critical path type of analysis as a tool which can be used whenever family stresses are suspected, and to formulate one's goals not in the negative terms implied by the concept of 'prevention' but in a detailed positive programme which aims to improve the family's whole pattern of interaction and quality of life.

2   Activities

Activity 11.1
Read now the extracts from Kempe (1971), 'Paediatric implications of the battered baby syndrome', in the Reader, p. 72. This is a classic paper which merits thorough study. If you have not read it before, we suggest you read it twice and offer two tasks which should help focus attention as you read:

a. Make notes to supplement the notes you made on Unit 10 on factors which may predispose to abuse. Kempe's paper contains several points not covered in Unit 10, and expands on some of those already mentioned.
b. The paper also contains a great deal of valuable and sensitive advice for professional workers who are faced with obtaining family histories and sifting them for reliability. Pick out and list these points as you read. You will need them again for Activity 11.2.

Comments

All the information needed to carry out this activity in full is in the Reader article, so it should not need repeating. If you feel that you have not satisfied your own standards in your replies go back to the article and re-read it yet again!

Activity 11.2

Turn again to the case history of the G. family in the extract from the official report in the Reader, p. 278. Then:

a. Using the model in the Reader article 'The critical path' (p. 55), draw up your own critical path for the Family G.
b. You cannot have missed that in almost every paragraph of the G. history some contact with the health or social services is recorded. Mark with a star any point or points where you think a family history in critical path form might have suggested to workers forms of intervention that might have been really effective in helping this family change direction.

Comments

2 Now turn to the end of this unit and compare your own 'path' with the one you will find there. It is not claimed that this path (made by Bill Roberts) is the perfect and only possible answer to this question. Yours may differ slightly in form, in the words used and perhaps in minor details, but if you find substantial differences you should check back with the text.

3 As with Cindy's family, so with the Family G. it is extremely difficult to find one point where it is possible to say 'this was the crucial episode'.

The picture in each case is of a rising tide of interrelated events which it seems must inevitably overwhelm the family in disaster. Effective intervention at any time must take account of *all* the relevant factors to make it possible to plan treatment for all the individual elements of the diffuse overall problem. To be of value, then, the critical path must record them all.

2.4 Look backwards now from one of your starred points and imagine that the contact at that point has been made by you. Using the notes you made for Activity 11.1, suggest an approach and line of questioning which you think might have been effective in obtaining reliable information from Mrs. G. across the full range of the family's problems.

Recommended further reading

LYNCH, MARGARET A., and ROBERTS, J. (1977) 'Predicting child abuse: signs of bonding failure in the maternity hospital', *British Medical Journal*, **1**, 624–6.

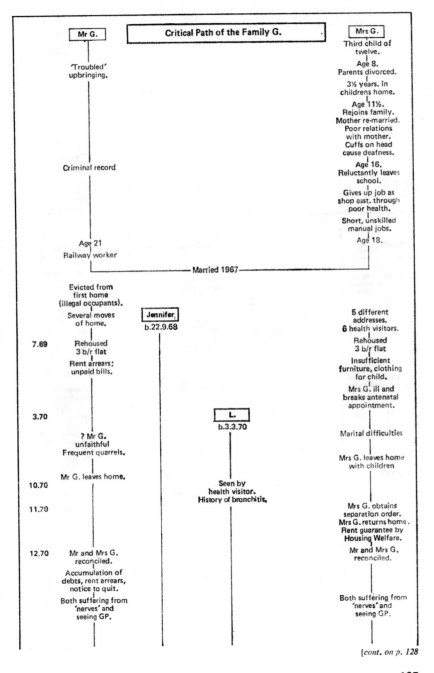

Mr G.

Critical Path of the Family G.

Mrs G.
Third child of
twelve.
Age 8.
Parents divorced.
3½ years. in
childrens home.
Age 11½.
Rejoins family.
Mother re-married.
Poor relations
with mother.
Cuffs on head
cause deafness.
Age 16.
Reluctantly leaves
school.
Gives up job as
shop asst. through
poor health.
Short, unskilled
manual jobs.
Age 18.

'Troubled'
upbringing.

Criminal record

Age 21
Railway worker

————— Married 1967 —————

Evicted from
first home
(illegal occupants).
Several moves
of home.

Jennifer.
b.22.9.68

5 different
addresses.
6 health visitors.
Rehoused
3 b/r flat
Insufficient
furniture, clothing
for child.
Mrs G. ill and
breaks antenatal
appointment.

7.69   Rehoused
3 b/r flat
Rent arrears;
unpaid bills.

3.70   L.
b.3.3.70

Marital difficulties

Mrs G. leaves home
with children

? Mr G.
unfaithful
Frequent quarrels.

Mr G. leaves home.

10.70

Seen by
health visitor.
History of bronchitis.

11.70   Mrs G. obtains
separation order.
Mrs G. returns home.
Rent guarantee by
Housing Welfare.

12.70   Mr and Mrs G.
reconciled.
Accumulation of
debts, rent arrears,
notice to quit.
Both suffering from
'nerves' and
seeing GP.

Mr and Mrs G.
reconciled.

Both suffering from
'nerves' and
seeing GP.

[cont. on p. 128

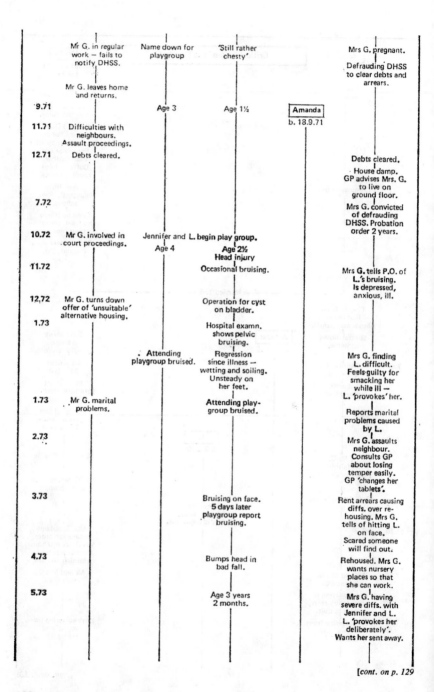

	Mr G. in regular work — fails to notify DHSS.	Name down for playgroup	'Still rather chesty'		Mrs G. pregnant. Defrauding DHSS to clear debts and arrears.
	Mr G. leaves home and returns.				
9.71		Age 3	Age 1½	Amanda b. 18.9.71	
11.71	Difficulties with neighbours. Assault proceedings.				
12.71	Debts cleared.				Debts cleared. House damp. GP advises Mrs. G. to live on ground floor.
7.72					Mrs G. convicted of defrauding DHSS. Probation order 2 years.
10.72	Mr G. involved in court proceedings.	Jennifer and L. begin play group. Age 4	L. begin play group. Age 2½ Head injury		
11.72			Occasional bruising.		Mrs G. tells P.O. of L.'s bruising. Is depressed, anxious, ill.
12.72	Mr G. turns down offer of 'unsuitable' alternative housing.		Operation for cyst on bladder.		
1.73			Hospital examn. shows pelvic bruising.		
		Attending playgroup bruised.	Regression since illness — wetting and soiling. Unsteady on her feet.		Mrs G. finding L. difficult. Feels guilty for smacking her while ill — L. 'provokes' her.
1.73	Mr G. marital problems.		Attending play-group bruised.		Reports marital problems caused by L.
2.73					Mrs G. assaults neighbour. Consults GP about losing temper easily. GP 'changes her tablets'.
3.73			Bruising on face. 5 days later playgroup report bruising.		Rent arrears causing diffs. over re-housing. Mrs G. tells of hitting L. on face. Scared someone will find out.
4.73			Bumps head in bad fall.		Rehoused. Mrs G. wants nursery places so that she can work.
5.73			Age 3 years 2 months.		Mrs G. having severe diffs. with Jennifer and L. L. 'provokes her deliberately'. Wants her sent away.

[cont. on p. 129

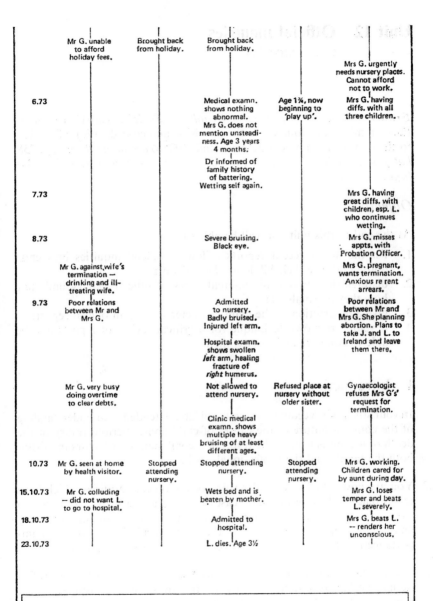

Fig. 1 Critical Path by Bill Roberts on the Family G. from data in the *Report of the Committee of Inquiry into Non-accidental Injury to Children with particular reference to the case of L. G. (1975).* Based on the method developed by Dr C. Ounsted at the Park Hospital, Oxford.

Unit 12　Official inquiries
Constance Lee

Extracts from the Department of Health and Social Security's Report of the Committee of Inquiry into the provision and co-ordination of services to the family of John George Auckland (1975b) *are in the Reader, p. 258, but you are advised to get a copy of the whole report if possible before beginning work on this unit.*

Objectives

At the end of this unit you will be able to:

1. list the major recent reports following official inquiries into child abuse and give their bibliographical detail;
2. distinguish between the different types of official inquiry and state how they came about;
3. give a description of the main characteristics of an official report;
4. develop your own technique for a critical review of reports and be able to compare and discuss them.

1　Introduction

In your study of preceding units you will have extended your understanding of the complex nature of the causes of child abuse. Serious injury or the death of a child is usually the result of a combination of factors involving both the family and the professional workers.

1.2　You are now asked to consider some of the official inquiries which have taken place following dramatic cases of child abuse in recent years. To study such reports objectively and be able to assess the findings critically and, where appropriate, to adopt the recommendations is of great importance for the continuing improvement of professional practice.

1.3　The volume of literature being produced which is relevant to the professional worker is daunting, even to the most avid consumer. Most professionals would agree that reading and interpreting official literature is an essential part of their work and many would admit to a state of perpetual unease that important reports remain unread.

1.4　This unit aims to comment upon the reports of official inquiries into child abuse, and also to offer some help in developing a technique for dealing with a mass of other official literature.

5 Many students of this course will be already well acquainted with the nine official inquiries referred to in this unit and may also have developed a satisfactory system for gaining the maximum information from vast amounts of literature with the minimum of time and effort. If you are one of these you need not spend long on this unit.

2 Official inquiries

1 The aim of every member of a child-care team must be to minimize and, if possible, prevent child abuse. It is worth remembering that resources and much effort are daily put into safeguarding children. Despite these efforts large numbers of children are treated in surgeries and hospitals every year; some die, and some are left with a permanent disability. Of these serious cases a small number become the subject of official inquiries.

2 The nine inquiries to be considered were published between January, 1973 and March, 1977. Full bibliographical details are given on pp. 138 and 139. To make reference easier the reports have been numbered 1 to 9 chronologically and will be referred to by number followed by the name taken from the title. There have been earlier reports about abused children, notably the Monkton report (1945) relating to Denis and Terence O'Neill. The ill-treatment of these children led to an official inquiry (Curtis report, 1945) into the boarding out of children and later to changes in the law. To read just one report into the non-accidental injury of a child is a painful experience. The attempt to read several, one after the other, may be distressing to the uninitiated and it would be advisable to read them gradually. Remember that these are amongst the most dramatic and notorious cases, but such cases have occurred and the serious student of child abuse must regard official inquiries as essential reading.

Activity 12.1
Before reading further, jot down what you think is 'an official inquiry'. How is such an inquiry initiated? How many of the nine recent reports listed on pp. 138 and 139 do you know something about?

Comment
3 If you have read some of the reports; if you have some of them in front

of you, as yet unread; or even if you have so far only looked at the list of titles, you will have seen that the nine reports have in common an inquiry arising from the ill-treatment of a child or children. You would have observed also that three of the reports, No. 2 (Maria Colwell), No. 4 (Auckland), No. 6 (Richard Clark) were prepared for central government departments, two for the Department of Health and Social Security and one for the Scottish Education Department and Social Work Services Group. All three were published by Her Majesty's Stationery Office. The remaining six, No. 1 (Graham Bagnall), No. 3 (Max Piazzani), No. 5 (L.G.), No. 7 (Steven Meurs), No. 8 (Neil Howlett), and No. 9 (Wayne Brewer) were prepared and published by various local authorities.

2.4 What is the difference? Following an inquest or trial arising from the death or serious injury of a child, a local authority might consider it desirable to hold an official inquiry into the services provided. Sometimes the decision is prompted by the comments of a judge, magistrate or coroner, for example, in No. 7 (Meurs) para. 1.02, 'Mr. Justice Willis at the trial of Sandra Meurs expressed the hope that due inquiry would be made as to what he felt to be a lack of liaison between the various public services . . .' (in this case the Norfolk authorities had already agreed to hold an inquiry); and in No. 1 (Graham Bagnall) para. 2, 'The Chairman of the Social Services Committee . . . thought it right . . . to invite a working party . . .'.

2.5 Sometimes a case is of such public concern that a major inquiry is called for. This happened in the cases of Maria Colwell (No. 2), Susan Auckland (No. 4) and Richard Clark (No. 6).

In such cases the appropriate secretary of state appoints a committee. Certain services for the inquiry and costs are provided by central government. The report is then published by HMSO. The purpose of an inquiry is generally (a) to establish what went wrong, and (b) to prevent similar mistakes in the future.

3 Studying technical reports

3.1 Do you find reading official reports a tedious duty to be endured, or do you positively look forward to the publication of some of them? Your attitude might be related to your method of reading. The most satisfactory way of reading most 'ordinary' books is to start at the beginning and read to the end. This is not the most interesting way to read a report. A report is different from a book in a number of ways and in order to gain the maximum from the contents it should be read differently.

2 If you are not well acquainted with reports you will find it helpful to have one or two by you for reference purposes as the various features are discussed. You have already observed that there are two main types of official inquiry. They can be distinguished easily by looking at the covers. You can see also that the subject of the report is stated clearly on the cover. There are no fancy titles but a statement of fact, 'Report of the Committee of Inquiry (or Joint Committee) into . . .'. If the title of the report arouses your interest and you are wondering whether to read it, look first for the 'terms of reference'.

3 'The terms of reference' is part of the official language of reports and, used in this context, the phrase means the brief given to the committee, or the limit set to the scope of an inquiry. Sometimes the terms of reference are precisely stated before an inquiry begins, sometimes the exact wording is decided by the committee early in the proceedings. In a well prepared and presented report the terms of reference are found clearly set out near the beginning. It is worthwhile spending a little time reading and thinking about what is written. Look at No. 4 (Auckland). You will find the 'terms of reference' in paragraph 3 (Reader, p. 258). 'On 23rd April 1975 the Secretary of State appointed us as a Committee to inquire into and report upon the provision and co-ordination of services to the family of John George Auckland by the relevant local authorities and health services and by any other persons or agencies'. Note also that reports are paragraphed and that reference is always made to the paragraph number and not to the page number. This practice will be followed hereafter.

Activity 12.2
Read again the terms of reference in the Auckland report. Underline the key words and ask yourself whether these terms are clear or ambiguous. If you can, compare these terms of reference with some of the other eight reports. You will find them similar, although some are more clearly stated than others. Jot down what you have learnt.

Comment

4 This exercise should have told you when the inquiry was initiated, and by whom; that it was a major inquiry; also what the committee was expected to inquire into and report upon.

3.5 You are now better informed about the purpose of the inquiry, which should add to your interest and aid your critical assessment when you read the report, but you should gather a few more facts before starting to read. Your curiosity should have been aroused on two further points. First, do you know who was the Secretary of State at that time? If not, look at page nine and you will see that she was the Right Honourable Barbara Castle, M.P. Second, you now know what is expected of the committee, so find out who was given this onerous task. The names and qualifications of the committee members and secretary are on page three. The committee is usually a small one. Sometimes extra information is given about the committee and other major contributors. The membership of expert committees is criticized frequently, and there are complaints about inadequate or unequal representation. Sometimes such criticism appears to be justified but more often than not it highlights the critic's ignorance of the way inquiries work. The 'terms of reference' require the committee 'to inquire into . . .'. This inquiry in the official language is known as 'taking the evidence'.

4 The evidence

4.1 Evidence is of two kinds, oral and written. How this evidence is obtained is described in reputable reports. If you read paragraphs 4–9 and Appendices A, B (A and B) C and F of No. 4 (Auckland), you will see that information was obtained from many sources. This should dispel any doubts about the adequacy of small committees. There is one more exercise which, although not essential, is helpful before beginning to read a report, and that is to read any notes about the structure, which are usually in the preface or introduction.

5 The structure of reports

5.1 Reports are usually divided into paragraphed chapters with a summary and recommendations. Sometimes the summary and recommendations are placed at the beginning, more often at the end. In very long reports each chapter or section is summarized. The Auckland inquiry was particularly complex in that, in addition to the large number of services and agencies to be considered in all such investigations, the complicated Auckland family history was especially relevant. The mass of information resulting from inquiries calls for great skill in preparation of the data to present it in an orderly and interesting form. The structure adopted for report No. 4 (Auckland) is described in para. 10 of the report, Reader, p. 260.

Activity 12.3

If possible, you should now read report No. 4 (Auckland) in full, or
read one of the other official inquiries. Sections of Maria Colwell, No. 2
and L.G., No. 5, are in the Reader, pp. 244 and 278. The main comment
in this unit will be restricted to one report, No. 4 (Auckland). As you
read, make full use of the appendices and keep in mind the terms of
reference. If you have time, compare this report with another,
preferably No. 7 (Meurs), and note the differences. Make notes of
your assessment. In particular, think about the following.

a.   Were the terms of reference realistic in relation to the nature of the
     inquiry, and in relation to the resources available to the committee?
b.   Were the terms of reference followed by the committee?
c.   How was the evidence taken?
d.   Was the report easy to follow? If so, why? If not, why not?
e.   In your opinion was the report well written? If yes, why do you
     think so? If not, what was wrong?
f.   Were the findings realistic?
g.   Were the conclusions fair?

Comment

These comments refer only to the Auckland report.

a.   The terms of reference were clear without being inflexible. The words
     'by any other persons or agencies' allow scope for the committee to
     explore other services as might become necessary during the course
     of an inquiry.
b.   Yes. See Chapter 2, paragraphs 12–40.
c.   See Introduction, paragraphs 6–10; also Appendices B (A and B)
     C and F.
d, e, The report is regarded by many as a model of objective inquiry and
f, g. reporting although, like all reports, it has its critics. In an interview
     with Morris (1975), Geoffrey Dunn, director of the social services
     department concerned in the Auckland case, strongly criticized the
     Committee for 'ducking the main issue' in failing to give guidance on
     the moral and social stance which social services departments should
     assume on the question of whether or not a man who has served his
     sentence for killing a child should ever be allowed to have any of his
     children with him for the rest of his life. During the inquiry, the
     British Association of Social Workers (which also submitted evidence)
     arranged for the continuous monitoring of the proceedings by some
     twenty members of its South Yorkshire branch and the comments of

seven of these monitors were later published as a symposium (Berry *et al.*, 1975) in *Social Work Today*. Some of the recurrent themes from critiques of other inquiries echoed in the comments are: the 'legalistic' approach adopted which is felt by witnesses and observers as more relevant to blame placing than truth seeking; insensitivity to the demands of the task in relation to the adequacy of resources; heavy reliance on documentary evidence which has the ironical effect of making those who keep full records subject to closer scrutiny than those who do not; and the selective, superficial and often sensational press and media publicity encouraged by the public conduct of the proceedings.

5.3 The method of commenting after each main section is helpful in keeping track of an involved narrative. Note that the report makes it clear throughout what is factual information and what is the committee's comment upon the services provided. The answers to the last four questions are a matter of personal opinion.

5.4 You have now read at least one official report and sections of others. You have probably recognized similarities in the narratives, relating to (a) abusing adults, (b) professional activity.

Activity 12.4
Make a note of characteristics or events which appear to recur in the narrative of these reports.

Comment

5.5 Your list may look something like this.

Characteristics of parents or caretakers are similar in several reports. The wide range of services and agencies involved with the families concerned. Inadequate reporting. Failures in communication. Failure to recognize and act upon signs and information.

5.6 Before coming to a conclusion about these issues in relation to child abuse, remember that these were all particularly involved cases which lead to official inquiries and that abuse can occur in less dramatic circumstances. Modify your attitude if necessary and try to base your conclusions upon work done in other units and, if possible, upon some of the research which has been referred to.

6 The costs versus benefits of inquiries

Official inquiries are exceedingly expensive in both monetary and human terms. The Maria Colwell public inquiry lasted 41 days, the Auckland inquiry 18 days, and this was only a small part of the total time given by many individuals. Before, during and after an inquiry the stresses on the committee members, the relatives and friends of the families concerned, but particularly on the workers involved are incalculable. After the publication of the report there is further publicity, sometimes 'scapegoating' and the possibility of panic decisions for fear of making similar mistakes.

Against all these 'costs' must be weighed improvements in organization and practice derived from the publicity of failures. Some published reports have had more impact than others. The Maria Colwell inquiry had a profound effect upon the nation generally; the Steven Meurs report caused particular distress to professional workers. In view of many similar findings in the nine reports being considered, what are your views on the possible value of any future inquiries?

Activity 12.5
Make two columns and jot down the 'pros and cons' of an inquiry.
Try to weigh the pros (for example, the development of preventative measures and research, the dissemination of information and improved techniques arising from inquiries, the raising of public awareness) against the cons (for example, the adverse publicity for 'helping' agencies, anxiety aroused in those concerned and anything else you think relevant).
Draw your own conclusions.

Comments

The practice current at the time of writing whereby inquiries may be initiated in different ways, either by the local authority or by the Secretary of State, has been questioned in a discussion paper by the Personal Social Services Council (1976). It is suggested that a number of questions need to be answered in order to formulate publicly known procedures. These include a decision about who can request an inquiry. Where does local responsibility lie? What should the procedures be – and what form of appeal should there be? Staff rights have to be protected, as well as those of consumers.

7 Conclusion

7.1 Obtaining reports

Reports have correct titles but they acquire popular names. Frequently they are named after the chairman. At the time of writing the 'Court Report' (Department of Health and Social Security and Department of Education and Science 1976) is being quoted widely. In the case of official inquiries into child abuse, reports have become known by the name of the child or family. This naming is part of accepted professional jargon and is convenient in discussion with colleagues, but it is incorrect usage in a report, article, bookshop or library where full bibliographical detail must be given. Full details are given in the list at the end of this unit. Some reports quote a series number and some a Command number (preceded by 'Cmd.' or 'Cmnd.'); if one is given it is helpful to quote this also. Local authority publications usually can only be obtained from the authority concerned.

7.2 You should now feel much more 'at home' with official documents. Faced with a pile of unread reports you should be able after a few minutes 'detective work' to sort them into three piles in order of priority.

a. Those you need not read (but at least you have noted the title and terms of reference).
b. Those which you could explore superficially by reading summaries and recommendations.
c. Those essential to your work which should be studied, discussed and perhaps acted upon.

Sound recommendations can sometimes be adopted without waiting for a change in the law.

Recommended further reading

No. 1 SALOP COUNTY COUNCIL (1973) *Inquiry into the circumstances surrounding the death of Graham Bagnall and the role of the County Council's Social Services.*

No. 2 DEPARTMENT OF HEALTH AND SOCIAL SECURITY (1974) *Report of the Committee of Inquiry into the care and supervision provided in relation to Maria Colwell*, London, HMSO. (Extract reprinted in the Reader, pp. 244–57.)

No. 3 ESSEX AREA HEALTH AUTHORITY AND ESSEX COUNTY COUNCIL (1974) *Report of the Joint Committee set up to consider co-ordination of services concerned with non-accidental injury to children. (After the death of Max Piazzani).*

No. 4   DEPARTMENT OF HEALTH AND SOCIAL SECURITY (1975) *Report of the Committee of Inquiry into the provision and co-ordination of services to the family of John George Auckland*, London, HMSO. (Extract reprinted in the Reader, pp. 258–77.)

No. 5   LAMBETH, SOUTHWARK AND LEWISHAM AREA HEALTH AUTHORITY (TEACHING) (1975) *Report of the Joint Committee of Inquiry into non-accidental injury to children with particular reference to the case of Lisa Godfrey*. (Extract reprinted in the Reader, pp. 278–91.)

No. 6   SCOTTISH EDUCATION DEPARTMENT, SOCIAL WORK SERVICES GROUP (1975) *Report of the Committee of Inquiry into the consideration given and steps taken towards securing the welfare of Richard Clark by Perth Town Council and other bodies or persons concerned*, Edinburgh, HMSO.

No. 7   NORFOLK COUNTY COUNCIL AND NORFOLK AREA HEALTH AUTHORITY (1975) *Report of the Review Body appointed to inquire into the case of Steven Meurs*.

No. 8   THE CITY OF BIRMINGHAM DISTRICT COUNCIL AND BIRMINGHAM AREA HEALTH AUTHORITY (1976) *Joint Inquiry arising from the death of Neil Howlett*.

No. 9   SOMERSET AREA REVIEW COMMITTEE (1977) *Report of the review panel appointed by the Somerset Area Review Committee to consider the case of Wayne Brewer*.

Recommended listening

Tape from BBC Radio 4 programme, *Death of a child* (Teaching Package).

Self-assessment questions (Block 3)
Richard Fothergill

1 Write down 4 methodological problems in epidemiological studies of child abuse.

2 Give 2 reasons for using the 'critical path' system.

3 Lynch and Roberts find it helpful to study case histories of abusing families under four main headings. List these.

4 Define the term 'bonding failure'.

5 a. Explain the term 'open warnings', and give two examples.
  b. If you were a doctor seeing a child suffering from an accident, which aspects of behaviour would you look for in every case?

6 Caroline Robinson has brought her four-month-old son, Bernard, to the hospital. She is in tears. As she explains it, Bernard had woken her up yet again. When she put him down, he hit his head on an iron bed post and is bleeding heavily.

  a. Construct a checklist to include at least 8 characteristics commonly appearing in the histories of abusing parents which would help alert you to the possibility that Bernard's injuries may be parent-inflicted.
  b. When Caroline has calmed down, you question her. Write down 5 questions you might ask to help you determine whether she has difficulties in 'mothering'.
  c. List 3 ways in which Caroline might describe the character of Bernard, assuming that she is in fact responsible for his injuries.

7 a. State 3 ways in which an inquiry may be established.
  b. State 2 general purposes of an inquiry.
  c. If you are presented with the report of an official inquiry, list the order in which you would set about reading its various parts.

Answers to self-assessment questions (Block 3)

1   1 mark each for any 4 of the following.

Absence of full reporting; lack of clear definition; different geographical areas; differing standards of medical documentation; variations in age distribution; difficult definition of populations; lack of social or racial group separation.

Total: 4 marks (ref: Unit 9)

2   a.   It helps to analyse the factors and interactions that led to the abuse.
     b.   It provides knowledge as to the most likely points and areas of difficulty at which intervention and help can be given.   (1 mark for each)

Total: 2 marks (ref: Unit 10)

3   Parents' biographies; social circumstances; medical problems; attributes in the child.   (1 mark for each)

Total: 4 marks (ref: Unit 10)

4   The failure to establish a consistent loving relationship between a child and his or her parents.   (1 mark)

Total: 1 mark (ref: Unit 10)

5   a.   'Open warnings' are explicit warnings of damage to the child which precede a severe assault.   (1 mark)

        Examples shown to a doctor could include: bleeding from the mouth; bruising on the cheek; bruising on the buttocks. (1 mark each for any 2 or similar signs)

Total: 3 marks (ref: Unit 10)

     b.   A discrepant, vague or absent history of the injury; delay in seeking medical help; potential for abuse in the family setting. (1 mark for each)

Total: 3 marks (ref: Unit 11)

6   a.   Your biography should contain 8 of the following.   (1 mark for each).

        Mother was battered herself; suffered rejection; has marital problems; suffered illness, mental or other; had difficulty at

142

Bernard's birth; aged under 20 at first child's birth; may have too many children; only parent; step-child; child absent for first months or fostered; unusual family structure; parents of low educational status; parents of low occupational status; unemployment or low income; isolation from own parents, friends, etc.; false concept of motherhood; early medical problems with child.

Total: 8 marks (ref: Units 9, 10, 11)

b. 1 mark each for any 5 questions or similar from the list below.

Does your baby cry a lot?

How do you manage your baby's crying?

Does it upset you when you are unable to stop your baby crying?

How do you feel inside when your baby cries?

Have you been afraid to be alone with your baby?

Does it make you anxious to have someone watch you feed your baby?

Do you ever get the feeling that others are critical of how you feed or take care of your baby?

Do other people understand the problems you have with your child?

How well do you feel your child understands you?

Can he tell when you are upset and does he help?

Total: 5 marks (ref: Unit 11)

c. Common descriptors are: slow; bad; selfish; defiant; hard to discipline.   (1 mark for any 3 or similar descriptions)

Total: 3 marks (ref: Unit 11)

a. Local authority may set it up on its own initiative. A judge, magistrate or coroner may request that one be established. The appropriate Secretary of State may initiate one.   (1 mark for each point)

Total: 3 marks (ref: Unit 12)

b. To establish what went wrong; to avoid similar mistakes in the future.   (1 mark for each)

Total: 2 marks (ref: Unit 12)

c. Award yourself up to 2 marks for your approach. Our
    recommendation is:

    after reading the title, move on to

    a. terms of reference
    b. membership of the committee
    c. any special notes which may be in preface or introduction
    d. summary, recommendations and body of report.

Total: 2 marks (ref: Unit 12)

Maximum marks: 40

Block 4   Crisis intervention

The lesson of earlier blocks was that if the signs of severe family conflict can be recognized early, crisis can often be averted. If a crisis arises, however, prompt and effective action is essential. Unit 13 sets out the legal processes by which a child can be protected or an abusing adult brought to justice. Unit 14 examines the responses of parents to crisis intervention and of the professionals who become involved in the family's conflicts. The last two units deal with the government's guidelines for coping with crisis and the need for clear communication between professionals.

Unit 13   Children and the law
Winifred Cavenagh

Objectives

On completing this unit you should be able to:

1.   Distinguish in cases of child abuse between proceedings brought in a juvenile court and in an adult court in respect of:

   a.   the purpose and focus of the proceedings
   b.   the powers of the respective courts
   c.   the nature of the proceedings.

2.   list the statutory criteria which should be met if it is proposed to seek compulsory powers;

3.   list and describe the various powers invested in the juvenile court and the orders which may be made by it;

4.   draft a report recommending court proceedings from data supplied.

1   Which courts are involved in child abuse cases?

1.1   Legal matters and court proceedings are often strange and confusing to the layman and may be a little frightening as well. The aim of this unit is to clarify some of the more important issues as they may affect students involved in legal proceedings in cases of child abuse. Its scope is set out in the unit objectives above and you are advised to look back at them now if you have not studied them carefully.

1.2   Court proceedings in cases of non-accidental injury may be taken either in the criminal courts or in the juvenile courts, or in some cases in both, depending upon what it is expected and hoped that the proceedings will achieve. It is essential to remember that neither court has any power to initiate proceedings itself. There are, however, a number of important ways in which these courts differ. Some of these are summarized in Table 1.

Activity 13.1
Study Table 1 carefully, reading down the columns first to get a general picture of each type of court. Then read across the rows, comparing

differences at each stage. These differences have important implications for those who feel that it is necessary to obtain compulsory powers in any particular case.

Table 13.1

	Juvenile court	Criminal court
	(Not fewer than 2, not more than 3 magistrates, one where practicable being a woman)	(Magistrate — who must refer more serious cases to crown court for trial by judge and jury)
Access by public	Public excluded	Normally open to public
Proceedings	Civil proceedings	Criminal prosecutions
Brought by	Local authority, NSPCC or police	Police, NSPCC or local authority
Proceedings centre on	The child, *injured or at risk*	The adult *charged with inflicting injury* or with *neglect*
Entitled to legal representation at public expense	(i) The child (ii) Sometimes the parent, at the discretion of the court, in certain unopposed cases	The accused adult only
Evidence	(i) Only necessary for evidence to satisfy the court that, *on a balance of probability,* the situation is as alleged (ii) May include any historical information relevant to the probability of *future abuse*	(i) Must be strong enough to place the matter *beyond* reasonable doubt (ii) Only factual evidence relevant to the *specific charge* admitted
If successful	(i) Court can make an order for *the child's welfare* (ii) Court *cannot* order punishment for the offender	(i) Court can *punish offender* by prison or fine, or place on probation. Court can also give a conditional discharge (ii) Court *cannot* make any order relating to the child

Note: Any member of the public *may* institute criminal proceedings but private prosecutions are very rare. The prosecution must make all investigations and produce all evidence, and is not eligible for legal aid, and costs (which may run into thousands of pounds) are not fully recoverable even if a conviction is obtained.

Then answer the following questions.

a. Could you bring a prosecution against a woman you had seen attempting to suffocate her baby?

b. If the parent in the above case were prosecuted and found guilty of the abuse, what order would the court be likely to make in respect of the child?

c. If neither you nor any other witness had seen the episode described above, but you had evidence in the case history that the parent had similarly endangered the lives of two older children, what legal action (if any) could you recommend?

d. If in the latter case you had decided in favour of the juvenile court, (i) who could bring the proceedings, and (ii) on whose behalf?

e. If in the latter case the proceedings in the juvenile court had been successful, what action would you expect the court to take against the offending parent?

Comments

1.3 Your answers should be:

a. Yes, in theory, and if you were convinced of its necessity. But you would be wiser to take your evidence first to the NSPCC or the police for their official investigation and action;

b. None;

c. Proceedings in the juvenile court;

d. (i) Local authority, NSPCC or police; (ii) the child's;

e. None.

All these answers can be found in Table 13.1 but are examined further below.

2 Statutory criteria for invoking compulsory powers, and taking emergency action

2.1 In crisis intervention it may appear that compulsory powers are necessary. These may be obtained by using the machinery of the law in a variety of possible ways. Whatever course is selected, however, there must be reasonable cause to believe that the child is endangered and that a need for care or control is shown by the child's situation, both present and prospective. The statutory criteria are twofold and relate to both of these aspects. They are that:

a.   *As regards the present situation*
   i.   his proper development is being avoidably prevented or neglected, or his health is being avoidably impaired or neglected, or he is being ill-treated; *or*
   ii. the above condition is probable following a finding in respect of another child who was, or is, in the household; *or*
   iii. it is probable that the conditions set out in paragraph (i) will be satisfied in his case having regard to the fact that a person who has been convicted of an offence mentioned in schedule 1 to the Children and Young Persons Act, 1933 (e.g., neglect, cruelty, etc.) is, or may become, a member of the same household as the child, *or*
   iv. he is exposed to moral danger; *or*
   v.   he is beyond the control of his parents or guardian; *and*

b.   *As regards the prospective situation*   He is in need of care or control which he is unlikely to receive unless the court makes an order in respect of him.

.2   Provided these criteria are met, it is possible in an emergency to obtain compulsory powers *while court proceedings are pending* by:

a.   *Approaching the police*[1]   The police have power to remove a child and detain him in a place of safety *without application to a magistrate* for up to eight days, though his parent or guardian on his behalf may apply for his release; *or*

b.   *Obtaining a Place of Safety Order*   Anyone may apply to a magistrate to remove and detain a child for a period not exceeding twenty-eight days, pending care proceedings; *or*

c.   *Wardship proceedings*   Any person having an interest in a child may, by a simple procedure of issuing a summons, make the child a ward of court. The court can then make orders to protect the welfare of that child if it is satisfied that it is in the child's interest to do so. In cases of extreme urgency such order may be made before the summons is issued.

.3   **Interim Care Order**   It is also possible for the juvenile court to make an interim order committing the juvenile to the care of the local authority for not more than twenty-eight days at a time, at any time during the proceedings in either court. Such orders may be necessary for various reasons, one of which may be that the child is at risk if left in the family

---

[1] The statutory powers of the police are set out in more detail in the Reader, p. 242, *Coventry professional guide on the detection and treatment of child abuse* (last two sections).

home whilst an accused adult is out on bail pending or during criminal proceedings. The juvenile court has no power to hurry the prosecution along but the social services department can express its anxiety about the effect of delays upon the child. Clerks and justices have been instructed by the Home Office to inform the crown court in such cases.

3 Orders which can be made in successful care proceedings

3.1 In cases concerned with child abuse, care proceedings in the juvenile courts are much more common than criminal proceedings so proportionally greater attention will be given in this unit to actions of this kind. The same statutory criteria apply for orders following juvenile court proceedings as for interim orders. We shall deal first with possible outcomes, then with the nature of the proceedings and some of the problems that arise in the present system and, finally, with the preparation and giving of evidence.

3.2 After a care case had been found proved, the local authority social services department makes a full report to the court on the social background of the child and includes any recommendations it wishes to make as to the choice of order if this is not self-evident from what has gone before.

3.3 Orders which can be made in successful care proceedings are as follows, in order of frequency of use.

   a. *The Supervision Order* lasts three years, or less if specified. The local authority social workers usually supervise unless a probation officer is already working with the family. The order can be discharged early on the application of the supervisor or the parent or the juvenile himself. There is a duty on the supervisee to receive visits but no right of entry for the supervisor. The supervision is of a general character.

   b. *The Care Order* gives the local authority powers to override the parents or guardians in the exercise of most of their parental powers and duties. The court has no power to supervise their use, which is entirely a matter for the authority once the order is made. The most usual arrangements made are a community home, a foster home, the use of a hostel, or even the return of the juvenile to his own home. Arrangements are subject to the availability of these facilities. If not discharged earlier the order runs until the juvenile is 18. The local authority must review each juvenile in care at least once in six months. The authority, the parent or guardian or the juvenile himself may apply to the juvenile court for discharge, which may be granted completely or by the substitution of a supervision order.

   c. *Parental Recognisances* may be taken with the parent's consent only (and not exceeding £50, or for more than 3 years) requiring the parent to exercise proper care and control. In practice these orders are only infrequently useful since threats and exhortations, forced or willing promises, social work with the family, including various forms of help on a voluntary basis, have usually already been tried and have failed.

d. *Hospital or Guardianship Orders*　A hospital order may be made in the same case as a care order where it is appropriate and advisable to do so, so that proper care is then ensured on the discharge of the child from hospital.

4 *Appeal from juvenile court*
A right of appeal exists against both finding and order in care proceedings, and against a refusal to discharge a care or supervision order. Notice must be given *by or on behalf of the child* within 21 days, and legal aid may be granted.

Activity 13.2

Table 13.2

	Action or type of order	Who can initiate action?	Effect	Maximum period of duration unless discharged earlier (where applicable)
A. When proceedings pending a. b. c.				
B. During proceedings a.				
C. Following successful proceedings in a juvenile court a. b. c. d.				

The above tasks are to help you test and strengthen your recall of essential information in sections 2 and 3. All the necessary information is included in the text but don't look back until you have tried to complete each task by memory. Then check, and correct if necessary.

a. List the five alternative statutory criteria that refer to the child's *present situation*.
b. State what must also be shown as regards the *prospective situation*.
c. Copy (leaving plenty of space!) and complete Table 13.2.

4 Proceedings in the juvenile court

4.1 **The child is the centre of the proceedings** in the juvenile court. It is the child himself who is eligible to apply for legal aid at public expense. At the time of going to press the parents are not normally eligible, although they usually behave as if the child's lawyer was representing them since they are regarded as acting on the child's behalf. This is a confusing situation since in care cases it is part of the complainant's case that there is a conflict of interest between the child and his parent or guardian. However, the Children Act, 1975, when fully in operation will make it possible for the court to rule in certain cases that the parent or guardian is not to be regarded as acting on behalf of the child and is also to be eligible to apply for legal aid on his own behalf. There is a further provision which will enable the court, in certain cases, to appoint a *guardian ad litem* to look after the interests of the child. At the time of going to press these provisions are only in operation where there is an application for the *discharge* of a supervision or care order and the application is unopposed. In the cases concerned, these changes will do something to safeguard the interests of the child who is too young to give evidence or brief his own lawyer rationally.

4.2 **Exclusion of parent or juvenile during the hearing**   In a civil case in the juvenile court the court can exclude the child whilst part of the evidence (other than to his own character or conduct) is given, though the parent or guardian must then be allowed to remain. It can also exclude the parent or guardian whilst the child gives evidence, though the absent party must later be told the substance of any allegations made against him in his absence so as to have the opportunity of refuting them.

4.3 **Evidence**   Those bringing proceedings must be prepared to produce the evidence to prove the case. It is not the job of the court to find the evidence. This is a matter which calls for careful consideration by social services departments expecting to appear either as witnesses or complaintants. It is also particularly important that the lawyers on either side in a juvenile court case should be familiar with the procedure in care cases. Proving the need for the court to make an order often enables the complainant to bring forward in evidence a great deal of family history. This is admissible evidence in so far as it concerns relevant behaviour as observed by the witness and the conclusions he bases on it and on the personalities involved, in relation to the likelihood of adequate care in the future.

.4 **The local authority in a dual role.** Local authority social workers who are already in a helping relationship with the child or his family may be called as witnesses. In any event, if a supervision or a care order is made it will, in most cases, be the department's social workers who must try to continue or establish a relationship of mutual trust. As the putative aftercare agent, the local authority may feel itself to some extent inhibited in giving the sort of evidence required to prove the case. Moreover, the care proceedings may rest on a conflict of wishes, or of actual interests between the child and the rest of his family, as well as between his own view of his interests and that taken by the authority. The court is concerned with the child himself whose views, if he is able to express them, must be ascertained, and only with his family in their relation to him. In this light it may be seen as affording an extremely important protection to the child against all other parties, be they social service departments or his own family, against whom he sees his interests as in conflict.

.5 **Legal representation in juvenile courts** is too often of poor quality and cases are lost through ignorance on the part of the complainant's lawyer as to what evidence is admissible and even as to the existence of the juvenile court Rules. Expert and specialised legal advice and representation should be available to social services departments on a practical basis, since an up-to-date knowledge of the way the wind is blowing currently in the Appeal Court is a much safer guide to the probable outcome of proceedings than an academic reading of the relevant act.

Activity 13.3

Read now the following two papers in the Reader:

a. Jackson (1975) 'Court procedures in child abuse' (p. 162). This paper, which offers a layperson's approach to court proceedings, re-summarizes some of the issues covered in sections 1 to 3 and is useful for revision. If, however, you are satisfied from your self-testing in Activities 13.1 and 13.2 that you have now thoroughly grasped the differences between the courts, and the basic legal issues, skip to his section, 'Giving evidence', on p. 165 of the Reader.

b.   Cavenagh (1975) 'A view from the courts' (p. 156). This paper is primarily concerned with the matters discussed in section 4, and a careful reading should widen and deepen your understanding of these.

5   Preparing and presenting evidence

5.1 It is unlikely that you will be required in any particular case to decide entirely alone when to seek compulsory powers, when court proceedings should be brought, and how to prepare all the evidence. Nevertheless, you should be able to make strong recommendations on all these issues if you hope for a successful outcome from proceedings. The papers you have just read should help you to do so.

5.2 In preparing a report which recommends legal action you will need:

a.   to make a summary of the history of the case as known to you which sets out clearly, but briefly, episode by episode, all the events in that history which can be cited as relevant evidence, excluding vague general impressions and hunches.

b.   to recommend the type of action you consider appropriate, i.e., juvenile court proceedings, adult court proceedings, or both, giving your reasons.

c.   state what outcome you would wish to achieve.

This report would be the basis for your own evidence in court.

5.3 It has probably occurred to you that the 'critical path' studied in Units 10 and 11 could be a valuable tool in analysing your case records.

Activity 13.4

For this activity take the critical path you prepared on the L.G. case as a starting point. Assume the role of one of the workers on that case and

a.   choose the point in the path where you think that you have sufficient evidence to recommend court proceedings.

b.   draft a report (in note form if you are pressed for time) which covers the three points made at 5.2 above.

Your report will, of course, depend upon your choice of role and your personal judgement so no comments can be offered. There is, however, one further step you could take to prepare yourself for a court appearance. Find out from the clerk of the justices at the magistrates' courts whether there are any care cases or cruelty cases set down for hearing in the near future. You will need to obtain permission from the juvenile court justices beforehand (through the clerk) to attend care proceedings, but cruelty cases in the adult court are usually heard in public. There are not many of either type of case since legal action is usually a last resort. You may have to go to your nearest sizeable town to find one.

Recommended further reading

CAVENAGH, W. (1976) *The juvenile court,* Chichester, Barry Rose.

Unit 14 Crisis reactions of parents and professionals to the identification or suspicion of child abuse

Anna Kerr

Objectives

When you have finished this unit, you should be able to:

1. describe some of the ways in which parents react to suspicion or discovery of injury to their children and how they respond to professional intervention in their lives;
2. discuss the difficulties that arise for those who intervene and make suggestions for facing and reducing them.

1 The parental predicament

1.1 When child abuse is suspected or discovered, many different professionals can become involved in a family. The general practitioner, health visitor, a social worker, hospital doctor or the police may be called in, and all start trying to help in their own ways, usually at first by trying to find out what has happened. Parents respond in different ways to such approaches. Their reaction depends on their own past experiences with parents, family, friends and other professionals. Often they have been in care as children. They cannot trust people in this category; they see doctors and social workers as against them, as wanting to catch them out, punish them and remove their children. For the intervening professional, or non-professional, sympathy with the parents' predicament is not enough. Indeed, it may even mislead one into errors of judgement. The relationship you need to form will initially be unwelcome, so you must understand clearly the attitudes and behaviour you may meet.

Activity 14.1
Write a short letter, in your own professional (or personal) role to a parent whom you suspect (either from your own observations, or because the case has been referred to you) of abusing a child. The letter is intended to bring about a meeting between you.

Activity 14.2
Now imagine that you are the parent who has injured the child. Write a brief autobiography (it is important to write it down) including a

156

paragraph on each of the following topics. You may find it useful to stimulate your imagination by looking back at earlier units (6, 9, 10, 11) which deal with predisposing factors, but do not invent a personality too far removed from your own.

a. Imagine an early memory involving a conflict with a parent of 'your' own. How did 'you' as a small child react? Say what you did rather than what you felt (for example, did you lie, scream, run away, sulk, etc?)

b. Describe briefly your present circumstances: your home, your partner's behaviour, your child (how did he or she behave to provoke your ill-treatment)?

c. Now, suppose that you have just received the letter written in Activity 1. Anticipate the interview. What do you expect is going to happen? What will you do?

d. What will you do in the interval before the proposed meeting? How will you act towards your partner, your child, your neighbours? Will you seek help? If yes, where? If no, why not?

Comments

.2 If you have carried through Activity 14.2 successfully you will, however tactful the letter you wrote at 14.1, have imagined only one of a wide range of possible reactions to crisis intervention. You will certainly, however, have sensed the dread of suddenly becoming overwhelmed by powerful and strange people who will invade your life and ask you the most intimate and searching questions about yourself and your family relations and may destroy all the precarious defences you have erected against the repeated stresses you have experienced.

.3 In this situation, most abusive parents feel engulfed and unable to trust the professionals who have become involved in their lives. They respond with open aggression and hostility or by withdrawing from the whole thing into passivity and non-co-operation. Some seem to suffer from a genuine amnesia about their attack on the child, and present a real blankness when questioned.

.4 They may angrily counter all questions and attempts to form a relationship with: 'What the hell are you asking me all these questions for? Are you accusing me of being a child batterer? I don't want you to visit me or come to see me. I know what bloody social workers (or doctors or lawyers or policemen) are like'. Or they may show no apparent sign of distress or feelings: 'I've no idea how the injury happened, I just noticed it one day. No, there's no problem in our family, no, he's always been an easy child, nothing to say, really. You can come and see me if you like but I don't see much point in it'. Both these types of response cover a deep suspicion of people trying to get close to them and a fear of what will happen, of being misunderstood, punished and of having their children removed.

1.5 There are a few parents, and we hope there will be more, who are worried about what is happening to them and have some faith that it might be worth asking for help. They may already have approached someone in a direct or indirect manner (as considered in Units 7 and 8). Their response to the crisis situation is largely determined by how they were handled when they did ask for help. Occasionally, there is an obvious sense of relief that at last someone is taking notice of the urgency of their feelings and they are able to pour out to the right listener what has been happening. 'It makes such a difference to be able to tell you all about it and know that there are other parents who feel the same. You really do have other people who hurt their kids? You must be able to understand me. I thought I was the only one'.

1.6 If it is thought necessary to remove the child from home or keep him in hospital under a place of safety order, the parents may feel their worst fears are being realized. They are being punished and penalized by the very people who claimed they wanted to help. There is generally an intense conflict of feeling involved; sometimes parents say that they feel relieved that the child has been removed and the tension temporarily lifted. Sometimes, however, particularly when they are denying the situation, they will fight the child's removal to the bitter end.

Activity 14.3
Read now two of the extracts from *At risk* (Baher *et al.*, 1976) in the Reader: 'Reaction of parents to court appearances', from the beginning of the extract on p. 167 to the first sub-heading; and 'Parents' reactions to hospital care' on p. 94.

Then check back on your 'autobiography' comparing your 'own behaviour' with that of parents described in the comments and the extracts. How did the activity expand your understanding of their situation?

Finally, look again at your letter (Activity 14.1) and see if you wish to make any changes in it. You might find it helpful to discuss it with an experienced co-professional or a friend. Or even, if you are in touch with one, with a parent who has been in trouble.

2 The professional dilemma

1 A home in which a child has been abused is always a home in conflict. Sometimes the conflict between child and parent(s) is also a reflection of a conflict between parents. One immediate effect of intervention is often to deepen the conflicts. In such a situation all parties (including the child) demand attention and seek allies. The professional worker must face the fact honestly that his sympathies may be drawn in all directions and deliberate attempts will be made by desperate people to manipulate them. A clear distinction must be made, again, between personal feelings and professional roles. A good professional is certainly not someone who has stifled the capacity to respond to human distress. Only if he responds as a full human being can he be sensitive to the range and variety of human needs that surrounds him. In his professional capacity he may have to behave selectively. He cannot expect to be able to convince people in open conflict that he is equally on all their 'sides'. The child's safety is usually held to have first priority, but the worker may antagonize the parents by insisting on the child's removal or by appearing to sympathize with a 'naughty' child, and so slow up the development of a therapeutic relationship with them. Even quite young children, however, are sensitive to the additional stress the family is experiencing. Indeed, in some cases the children may be at greater risk immediately following intervention then they were before: some parents may blame the child for the 'trouble' they find themselves in. The long-term needs of the children are the subject of Unit 23. At the moment of crisis, however, a child also has a need for attention and understanding which may rival that of the parents. The conflict for the professional must be recognized. If he cannot meet all needs it is his professional responsibility to ensure that those he cannot meet are being met by others.

2 Working with abusive parents in the crisis situation can be particularly difficult if the professional involved feels personally disgusted by child abuse. Sympathy and understanding cannot be feigned. Think about this yourself. If you are communicating with a parent who sometimes feels or acts harshly towards his or her child, you need to examine your own feelings and attitudes. Such parents are so sensitively attuned to rejection that they will sense revulsion and criticism when it is not obviously expressed. One cannot help such parents unless one has some kind of real understanding of their feelings and situation. Most parents, or people who work or spend time with small children, will admit, if they can be honest, that they have known anger and harsh feelings towards the children in their care, even if they have not injured them. To be able to say to yourself, 'I know what it feels like at times even if I have never . . .' is a great help in working with battering parents.

2.3 It is of crucial importance how the first contact with the parents is made. If they already have a relationship with a health visitor, general practitioner or social worker, it may be easier for him to discuss the injury with them in a less threatening manner, within the context perhaps of previous conversations about the difficulties of care of the particular child. However, one cannot forget that one is dealing with an injured child; whoever has the difficult task of making the first contact with the parents has to combine sympathetic understanding with a recognition that something serious has happened to the child.

Activity 14.4
Read now the extract from Baher *et al.*, *At risk* (1976), 'After abuse: the social worker's interview' (Reader, p. 70).

Comment

2.4 At this point you may find it helpful to refer back to the analysis of your own attitudes made for Unit 2. It is possible that they may have changed in some respects by now. Consider how they might affect your behaviour in the crisis situation.

3 Inter-professional relations

3.1 The way in which the removal of the children, if necessary, is handled and the whole process leading up to and during the juvenile court hearing are crucial. Some workers in the field consider that a different professional should be responsible for taking and handling the legal side of the case from the primary therapeutic person for the parents.

Activity 14.5
Crisis intervention heightens conflict but also makes explicit conflicts in a family. For the professional worker, too, it is a time of stress since he or she cannot avoid involvement in conflict.

Now read the rest of the extract from *At risk*, 'Reaction of parents to court appearances' on p. 167 of the Reader: that is, the sections on parents' legal representation and the separation of legal and therapeutic roles.

Now, looking back at *all* the extracts from *At risk* you have read, pick out and list as many examples as you can of *types* of conflict illustrated in the readings, under the headings below:

a. Conflicts in the family
b. Conflicts between family members and those outside
c. Conflicts between professional workers
d. List (by role) any examples of professional individuals experiencing *internal* conflicts

Set out in tabular form your analysis using role titles only, followed by a space as below:

a. Conflicts in the family
   i.   Parent(s)   *vs*. Child
   ii.   *vs*.
   etc.

We can regard those conflicts which directly involve family members (a and b) as the primary conflicts and those which involve *only* professional workers, i.e., all under (c) and some under (d), as secondary conflicts. Each secondary conflict is directly related to a primary conflict by the role of the intervening professional who, as the crisis develops, is required, as his or her professional duty to represent the interests of the various members of the family – or of another professional. Now, for each conflict you have identified which concerns *professionals* only, insert in brackets after the professional's role title the family or co-professional interest which each professional represents. In the case of individuals in conflict there will of course be more than one 'interest' represented.

Comments

.2 The purpose of this activity was to help you to think through and make explicit the nature of inter- and intra-professional conflicts. It was probably difficult to do but, as you worked on it, you possibly came to feel that it may be unrealistic to imagine that conflict can be completely eliminated for professional workers closely involved in crisis intervention. As you compare your findings with those that follow, however, you should consider how the stress associated with involvement in crisis intervention may be to some extent relieved by a clear understanding by professionals and between professionals of the representational relationship of their secondary conflicts to the primary conflicts in the family. This principle applies of course to other crisis situations, as when a teacher takes up the interests of a child in her care against one of 'her' parents. Your final list (incorporating both parts of the activity) should look something like the following, although you may have identified other conflicts or interpreted differently occasionally.

a. *Conflicts in the family*
   i.   Mother   *vs.* Father
   ii. Parent(s)   *vs.* Child

b. *Conflicts between family members and those outside*
   i.   Parent(s)   *vs.* Court
   ii.   Parent(s)   *vs.* Hospital staff
   iii. Parent(s)   *vs.* Doctors
   iv.   Parent(s)   *vs.* NSPCC social workers
   v.   Parent(s)   *vs.* DSS social workers
   iv.   Parent(s)   *vs.* 'Own' solicitors

c. *Conflicts between professionals*
   i.   Solicitor[1] (parents) *vs.* Social work agency (child)
   ii.   NSPCC SWs (child) *vs.* DSS SWs (parent(s))
   iii. DDS SW (parent(s)) *vs.* Senior DSS SW (child)

d. *Internal conflicts (professionals)*
   i.   NSPCC SWs (parents *vs.* child)
   ii.   DSS SW (parents *vs.* child [rep. by Senior])
   iii. Solicitor (one)[1] (parents *vs.* child)

3.3 In any case, it is important that the worker who is going to work with the case in the long term should be involved as early as possible. He or she should meet the parents at the earliest point of crisis and should give them as much time as possible in the first few weeks of treatment, offering emotional and practical support during the ordeals of interviews with doctors, court officers, possibly police and during juvenile court appearances. The foundations for a fruitful therapeutic relationship have often been firmly laid during the first few weeks of intense crisis, confusion and suffering for the parents.

Recommended further reading

HALL, M. H. (1974) 'The diagnosis and early management of non-accidental injuries in children', *The Police Surgeon* (October).

---

[1] At some point check with Unit 13 – who is the solicitor *supposed* to represent?

DAVOREN, E. (1968) 'The role of the social workers' in Helfer, R. E. and Kempe, C. H. (eds.) *The battered child*, University of Chicago Press.

POLLOCK, C. and STEELE, B. (1972) 'A therapeutic approach to the parents', in Kempe, C. H., Helfer, R. E. (eds.) *Helping the battered child and his family*, Philadelphia, Lippincott.

OUNSTED, C., OPPENHEIMER, B. and LINDSAY, J. (1974) 'Aspects of bonding failure: psychopathology and psychotherapeutic treatment of families of children, *Developmental Medicine and Child Neurology*, **16**, 4, 447–56.

Unit 15   Government guidelines on child abuse
Christine Desborough

Objectives

After completing this unit you should be able to:

1. explain how the government, through guidelines issued by the DHSS, has sought to influence local policies, practice and procedures in relation to child abuse;
2. summarize the main recommendations made on the structure and functions of (i) area review committees, (ii) case conferences, (iii) registers, and the problem of confidentiality, from the DHSS Circular on Non-Accidental Injury to Children, LASSL (74) 13 April 1974 (and Welsh office circular no. 123/74, Scottish Home and Health Department NHS Circular no. 1975 (Gen) 23 and Northern Ireland Department of Health and Social Services Circular HSS (Gen 1) (1975));[1]
3. trace the development and variations in local practice from the DHSS Circular, LASSL (76) 2 February 1976;
4. state and discuss some of the difficulties and doubts that have arisen in the context of local implementation of government recommendations;
5. collect information about the practices and procedures operating in your own area.

1   Introduction

1.1 In recent years the Department of Health and Social Security has issued several circulars on child abuse and they are the most important, but not the only, means by which the government lays down guidelines for dealing with the problem. Some circulars are designed to disseminate information to promote greater understanding of child abuse. For example, a circular was issued to local authorities, health authorities and voluntary bodies in

---

[1] Throughout this unit the references are to the guidance issued to English and Welsh authorities. Circulars of guidance relating to Scotland and Northern Ireland, with their different organizational arrangements for the provision of health and social services, are available from the Scottish Home and Health Department and the Northern Ireland Department of Health and Social Services.

1975 following a conference organized by the DHSS. This circular made
no recommendations. It merely stated that the proceedings of the conference had been published, continuing

> A copy of the booklet is attached for your information, and
> we particularly hope that you will bring it to the attention of
> those concerned with non-accidental injury or with the training
> of staff who may encounter it.

Other circulars are of a different type in that they *recommend* that certain
things be done, that certain procedures be instituted. Two such circulars
are the subject of this unit. One, issued in 1974, is entitled 'Non-accidental
injury to children', Local Authority Social Services Letter (LASSL) (74)
13, and another, issued in 1976, is entitled 'Non-accidental injury to
children: area review committees', LASSL (76) 2. Extracts from both are
included in the Reader (p. 226) which you should keep open beside you
as you work through the unit. Look at the 1974 memorandum and read
the first paragraph *only*. This indicates the scope of the whole memorandum. Sections (a) and (c) have not been reprinted, as most of the topics
they deal with receive extended treatment in other parts of this course.
Section (b), 'Local organization', contains the first fully formulated
statement of governmental recommendations for a local organizational
framework for dealing with child abuse. Before reading this, attempt
Activity 15.1.

2   Area review committees

Activity 15.1
a.   Circular LASSL (74) 13 strongly recommended the formation of
     area review committees as policy-making bodies for the
     management of cases of child abuse, with regular meetings three
     or four times a year. What useful purposes, in your opinion, can
     such committees serve? What ought they to *do*? The guidelines
     indicate their functions under eleven short headings. As a help to
     study, make your own list before looking at the memorandum.
     Then check against para. 12 of the circular to see what you have
     omitted. If you have included items not on the recommended list,
     consider for each one why it was not included.
b.   Para. 13 recommends that the committee should be at senior level
     and should include representatives from
     i.   Local authority (4 leading offices are named),
     ii.   Health services (15 offices)

iii. Other agencies (3 offices).

Again, construct your own list before checking with the circular.

2.1 If you worked through Activity 15.1 you should by now have a good working knowledge of the government's 1974 proposals on the functions and structure of an area review committee. The second circular, LASSL (76) 2, was issued nearly two years later, by which time a good deal of information had accumulated on how the guidelines had been interpreted locally, and this is summarized in the circular.

Activity 15.2
Read now the extracts from LASSL (76) 2 down to and including para. 14. The paragraphs in italics offer 'further guidance'. As you read, note down points where this guidance is at variance with, or goes beyond, that given in LASSL (74) 13. For each point noted, try to suggest a reason why the initial recommendation now seemed inadequate, i.e. was the fault in the recommendation, or in the localities? If you think it was in the localities, why did they fail to respond?

2.2 Policies devised by area review committees often determine the action to be taken in cases of child abuse, since many have issued detailed procedural handbooks to staff. Individual cases can be discussed or reviewed at full meetings of area review committees but the main focus of their work is on formulating policy and procedures.

3 Case conferences

Activity 15.3
The basic guidelines for case conferences on individual cases are given in LASSL (74) 13 (paragraphs 14, 15 and 16). As in the case of area review committees, a progress report and further guidance is offered in LASSL (76) 2 (paragraphs 26 to 31 inclusive). You will find it an aid to study if you use the same method as for Activity 15.2. Please retain any critical comments for further consideration later.

Clearly, sharing information and decision making is crucial and, following the tales of inadequate communication revealed by committees of inquiry into cases where things have gone wrong, many people have welcomed the case conference as the panacea. However, to translate the broad government recommendations into effective action is not easy. Formal case conferences in which workers from a number of agencies are involved require careful thought and planning to derive maximum benefit from the substantial input of time. To take a few practical examples: how much work do people expect to do before attending a conference? how well prepared are they to present their own observation and assessment? how much, if any, written material is circulated in advance and has it been read and understood by all present? If you have ever attended a case conference, try to recall its composition. How was the list of those present compiled? Were significant other workers missing and, if so, what repercussions did this have? Were the parents there, and, if not, do you think they should have been?

Some of the practical and the more fundamental problems associated with inter-professional communication which can limit the effectiveness of formal arrangements for communication will be explored in Unit 16.

4   Registers

Activity 15.4
Read now: LASSL (74) 13, para. 17, and LASSL (76) 2, paragraphs 16 to 25 inclusive. Then write answers to the following questions:

a.   Based on your close study of para. 23, what additional information would you personally wish to find in a register if you had need to refer to it?
b.   What arrangements for access would be most helpful to you?
c.   In the light of the wide variety in registration systems, would the situation be improved if the reporting of all cases were made mandatory (as in all states of America since 1966) and standard procedures demanded? List reasons for and against this, and formulate a conclusion.

Comments

No 'right' answers can be offered for any of these questions but the following discussion may help you to clarify your own views further.

4.2 Drake (1975) argued:

> I share the view that there should be a statutory obligation to report abuse to the local authority in the same way that it is obligatory to notify certain illnesses and diseases to the health authority; this would relieve the doctor of the responsibility of deciding whether or not he was betraying a patient's confidence and would perhaps lessen delay.

4.3 Others argue that there would be formidable difficulties to overcome – not least, reaching agreement on a definition of the term 'child abuse'! The criteria for placing a name on the register vary widely from area to area. Some registers record the names of children about whom there is 'concern', not necessarily associated with physical risk, while others are narrower in their interpretation of the phrase 'at risk'. Some also have categories (e.g., A, B and C) which distinguish between those considered to be more seriously at risk than others.

4.4 Whatever conclusions you reach on the issue of mandatory registers, it is important that those involved with cases of child abuse are clear as to the criteria for and the implications of a decision to place a name on the register. For example, will the parents have to be told? For the opinion of one 'anonymous battering parent' see 'Consumer's viewpoint' in the Reader, p. 111.

5 Local practice and procedures

5.1 It will be helpful to find out about the practice and procedures adopted in your locality. Some key questions to answer are:

a. who is the chairman and what is the composition of your local area review committee?
b. what are the criteria for placing names on the register?
c. what local guidelines have the area review committee produced for handling cases of child abuse?
d. if you are employed in an agency which deals with cases of child abuse, has the agency produced its own handbook of procedures for staff?

5.2 Much of this information will be available within agencies dealing with cases of child abuse or from area review committees which can be contacted through the local social services department or area health authority.

6   How should the government guide?

There has been criticism of over-reaction to the problem of child abuse and in particular of the time involved in implementing the formal arrangements recommended in the guidelines. The following extracts from an article by Fry (1976) in *Community Care* illustrate the point.

> After all the recent inquiries, soul-searching and circulars,
> another symptom of child abuse – over-reaction – is gaining
> official recognition in social service circles. . . . Directors (of
> social services) have voiced undisguised irritation at the
> ever-increasing complexity of area review committees. . . .
> Over-cautious attitudes to case conferences have also come
> under fire. . . . In a critical reference to one department which
> had consented to three case conferences – each lasting a couple
> of hours – on one child in ten days, he (Jeremy Burns, BASW's
> assistant general secretary) said such procedures had become
> an unsatisfactory substitute for good social work practice. . . .

Clearly governments must achieve a balance between the responsibility to take action in an area of legitimate public concern while not over-interfering with local autonomy. The government guidelines are therefore often, although not always, broad in scope, leaving detailed implementation to local arrangements and professional judgement. It is for you to decide whether you think that the right balance has yet been achieved between a directive and a permissive approach, and, if not, what changes you would suggest.

Further recommended reading

All the government circulars mentioned in this unit merit further study, as well as any local publications you have collected. The circulars are listed in the Reader, p. 224.

Also CASTLE, R. L. (1976) *Case conferences: a cause for concern*, London, NSPCC.

Unit 16 Obtaining and communicating 'good' information

Olive Stevenson

Objectives

After completing this unit you should be able to:

1. distinguish clearly between fact and impression in writing or reading records;
2. assess the usefulness of a piece of recording in relation to *the purpose* for which it has been written;
3. outline some factors you would take into account in *convening* a case conference to ensure its usefulness;
4. outline some factors likely to affect the *process* of a case conference or other committees with which you are familiar;
5. suggest reasons for some of the difficulties in communication which arise within 'welfare' organizations.

1 Introduction

1.1 The previous unit concentrated upon procedures formally recommended by the government to ensure effective communication between professionals in cases of child abuse. Important as such procedures are, they are not the whole of the story. A number of other matters have to be considered if children's well-being is to be safeguarded. A great deal of time is necessarily spent, not in direct contact with the child and his family, but in discussing problems with others and in sharing and recording information where appropriate. There is some feeling at present that such processes have become *too* time-consuming and may reflect excessive anxiety, following a series of well-publicized inquiries. There are also problems of confidentiality, discussed in the DHSS Circular LASSL (76) 2, paragraphs 24 and 25, which you studied in connection with Unit 15. However that may be, there is no way in which children's welfare can be assured without greater attention to aspects of communication than has been given heretofore. This unit, therefore, focuses your mind upon three key aspects of communication:

a. Recording;
b. communications *between* professionals, with especial reference to the case conference;
c. communications *within* agencies.

170

Activity 16.1
Read now the extracts in the Reader, p. 244, from the *Report of the Committee of Inquiry into the care and supervision provided in relation to Maria Colwell* (1974). As you read, make notes under the three headings given above of any points that seem to you of particular importance. Retain these notes for reference as you work through the unit.

---

2 Recording

1 One of the lessons of the Colwell inquiry was the importance of distinguishing in all recording between what we may call 'hard' and 'soft' facts. For example, if a statement is made that a child has gained weight, that can only be a 'hard fact', substantiated by evidence. This is not to say that 'soft facts' are not equally important. For nearly all purposes, the observations and assessment of the worker of the child and his family is a necessary part of the picture which needs to be built up. Thus, one should not shy away from statements like 'the mother *appeared to be* depressed' because one is not psychiatrically trained. It is the distinction which is crucial, provided (as in this case) that the status of the statement as a 'soft' fact, or an individual's impression, is made clear.

2 In writing reports, above all in cases of child abuse where emotions run high, it is also important, as far as it is humanly possible, to avoid using words which carry with them moralizing or over-dramatic overtones. For example, the material conditions and state of the home can be described thus: 'the house was filthy and stank of urine' or 'the house was very dirty and there was a strong smell of urine'. The former is less objective than the latter and reveals the feelings of the worker which, although understandable, are irrelevant to, and possibly distort, the assessment. It is also important to realize that even such a simple statement as 'the house is dirty' is a 'soft fact', unless substantiated by concrete detail. People's standards vary greatly in such matters!

3 Two crucial questions to ask in the preparation of any report are, quite simply, *who* is it for and *what* is it for? There are a number of different people for whom we write reports. The most common are:

a. for ourselves as an aide-memoire;
b. for our seniors to inform them and/or to use as a basis for consultation;

c. for other professionals;
d. for 'legal' purposes, i.e., court proceedings of different kinds.

Rightly, we write them differently, although the distinction between 'hard and soft' facts applies to them all. There is a need to put ourselves imaginatively into the shoes of the reader and to ask: will this person or persons (whoever they may be) get what they need from what we write? Thus, for example, doctors are accustomed to abbreviated recording and are likely to be impatient if social workers adopt a more discursive style. Equally, do workers in health services think whether their medical terminology will be understood by others?

2.4 The preparation of court reports presents some particular difficulties; for example, reports to juvenile courts have not in general been lengthy, it being assumed that magistrates would not wish to be burdened by too much detail. (This has been contrasted with reports presented to the judge in child custody proceedings.) Whether or not the now conventional length and mode of presentation is appropriate is for debate. But it certainly places a heavy burden on the 'presenter' to sift, condense and select in such a way as to present a balanced picture of what is usually a highly complex situation.

2.5 The question 'for whom' leads naturally to 'for what purpose?' The vital distinction here is between recording for clarification of one's views and feelings (either for personal use or sharing with colleagues) and recording 'for evidence'. The latter may, or may not, involve legal process but, in any case of suspected child abuse, there must be documentation in which observations, assessment and action are clearly set down and are distinct from reflections, important as these may be in the process of understanding the situation and communicating with others.

2.6 This raises very difficult and as yet unresolved problems about the status of records when they are used at inquiries. In the Colwell inquiry, records were minutely scrutinized and used by counsel for various parties. It happened that the social work records were fuller than any other and some of the 'reflective discussion' recording was used to apportion blame. You may wish to think further about the implications of this.

Activity 16.2
Assume that you have been called upon to prepare a background report for a case conference about a family in which a child is thought to be at risk. You may use the L.G. or the Maria Colwell case as your point of reference if you wish but you are not required here to write the

report. You should make a list of headings which might also serve as a checklist when writing such reports. It should include all those aspects of the case on which the conference would need to be informed to enable it to reach wise decisions. Refer to your earlier work on the L.G. case in Units 7 and 8, the Maria Colwell report (particularly paragraphs 153 to 165) and your own notes for Activity 16.1 to assist you in deciding how to order the material.

Comments

There is no need for you to have covered every imaginable contingency, but the broad headings should include as a minimum.

a.   In what ways is the child now feared to be 'abused' and by whom? (concrete evidence carefully distinguished from suspicion).

b.   Past history, medical (including birth) and social, of this child.

c.   The family unit now – who it comprises, place of child at risk within it.

d.   Child's behaviour, compared with siblings.

e.   Economic and material circumstances of family.

f.   The parents: health, mental and physical; intelligence, etc. Own family background.

g.   Attitudes of parents to their children, with special reference to child at risk.

h.   Other important people in the family's life, relations and 'officials'.

3   Inter-professional communication

This section will concentrate mainly on the case conference (as distinct from the formal area review committee). Obviously, much communication takes place outside the case conference, but it is useful to focus upon the conference because in many ways it is a microcosm of the wider situation. A group of people come together, with different roles, experience and training to talk about a child or family. All are worried; but their concern may be about different aspects of the problem, as may be their views as to how best to handle it. Anxiety levels are often high and this affects communication, especially as people seek to cope with anxiety in different ways; for example, some talk too much, some go very silent; some want quick action to relieve their own stress, and so on.

In a small research project which the author recently conducted, a number of case conferences were attended by the researchers, and all the participants at six of these conferences were interviewed individually. The object was to assess, through observation and discussion, what factors were most important in a 'successful' conference; that is, one in which participants felt the sharing of information had been meaningful and useful and that the decisions reached (if any) had been satisfactory. Our report is not yet complete, but here are some of the questions to which we addressed ourselves.

a. *Does it make any difference to the participants where the conference is held*, for example, in a school, hospital or the social services department? Initial impressions suggest that, especially for those who customarily work in a particular building, 'going somewhere else' may make for some insecurity. People may also be affected by the associations which the host building has for them. The hospital is the clearest example of this and the doctor's authority may be less challenged if the conference is held there. Indeed, it may even lead to some confusion as to who is actually taking the chair!

b. *Do people understand each other's language*? We all have our 'in-talk' or jargon, understood by our own working group. At a case conference, people come together who are experts in different fields. Medical terminology may be unfamiliar (and it is interesting how few people ask for explanations of terms they do not understand). The use of initials (or nonsense syllables derived from initials) to replace the names of institutions and even small internal committees can be particularly confusing and frustrating to someone not 'in the know'. Social services have legal knowledge and often use their shorthand, with terms such as 'section 1', 'place of safety', and so on. Are the implications understood by others? For example, we learnt from one interviewee that she took it for granted that care proceedings to 'commit' a child must follow if a child had been removed from home 'on a place of safety'. Perhaps most important of all is the extent to which everyone 'hears' the hints or indirect references to aspects of the parents' or the child's background and behaviour which might indicate abuse (for example, failure in the early bonding – see Unit 10). The speaker may assume a common core of knowledge which does not exist.

c. *Do people understand each other's frame of reference?* This is subtler than language: our frames of reference derive from our personal value systems, much affected by training and by the agencies in which we work. This topic was treated in some detail in Units 7 and 8. The crucial example here concerns, quite simply, the value placed upon keeping a child with his own family. In many conferences the possibility of removing a child is present in everybody's mind. What risks are justifiable and unjustifiable are agonizingly real dilemmas. But behind the views expressed lie deep feelings about family life and, frequently, a tension between social workers and 'the rest' because social workers more than others see the consequences for some children of a life in care.

3 You will see that these three dimensions of the case conference can be readily applied to communications outside that situation. There is, however, one key factor peculiar to the case conference: namely **the role of the chairman.** How the chairman plays his part will greatly affect the matters discussed above. For the chairman can do much to facilitate communications. It is a highly skilled task, for which there is need for special training. Firmness is important on two counts. First, to discourage irrelevancy: many people complain of unfocused and rambling discussion. Secondly, it is vital to ensure that all necessary information is extracted. For example, it is perilously easy to concentrate upon one child at the expense of another who may prove to be equally at risk. But the firmness has to be balanced with permissiveness; that is to say, every encouragement must be given to the less forthcoming members to speak. Such elementary matters as ensuring that everyone knows each other's names and roles play a part in this.

4 **The local scene.**   There is no 'blueprint' for successful professional communication in every locality because there is an infinite variety of local circumstances which have to be taken into account. For example, in places where staff are relatively stable, more reliance can be placed on informal communications. In some areas, one professional group may be much more mobile than another, and this creates difficulties. The need is to analyse the local situation and seek to pinpoint its strengths and weaknesses.

5 **The national scene.**   Some problems crop up so frequently as to suggest that they are not the product of local agencies or personalities. Here are three examples.

a.   It is generally said that general practitioners (GPs) are 'poor attenders' at case conferences and related gatherings. GPs in turn protest that meetings fixed in the mornings clash with morning surgeries and it is exceedingly difficult for them to attend. What should convenors do about this? And is the practical problem a sufficient sole explanation? Work priorities must come into the equation. Yet the GP's contribution may be vital and the presence of the health visitor, reporting for the doctor, is not in all cases sufficient.

b.   It is commonly said by those outside social services that there are too many representatives of social services at the meeting. They may represent different aspects of concern (legal, social work, etc.). But the effect upon others is of 'overweighting', which influences attitudes at the conference.

c.   The role of the health visitor in relation to that of the social worker in actual responsibility for the child at risk under school age is a source of difficulty. Health visitors frequently say that 'they have no power of entry': in fact, neither have social workers, unless the child is in care, or they have obtained special legal powers to remove a child, an exceptional occurrence. Therefore the issue is not primarily legal, it is professional. The health visitor's role in visiting young children generally places her in a good position 'to gain entry', where the social worker may be distrusted. Yet for the health visitor, as the GP, such cases form only a minute proportion of her general duties and can easily take up a disproportionate time. There is role conflict for the health visitor, and the interactions between social workers and health visitors so frequently give rise to tension that the problem must be structural, not personal.

Activity 16.3
Using the three factors below as a starting point, make an analysis of a case conference you have attended. If you have never attended a case conference, apply them to some other committee meeting you have attended. In either case, use any notes and/or minutes you have of the meeting to remind you of what took place.

a.   The role of the chairman, in the light of para. 3.3. above
b.   Any tensions you observed in the group and the possible reasons for them.
c.   Evidence of understanding and misunderstanding of those present of each other's special knowledge and point of view.

Comments

3.6   There will be no 'right or wrong' answer to this activity. If you go back to the preceding section, you will see a number of the matters which you might have discussed. But they are only examples and it is good if you have thought of other dimensions of conference and committee activity which are not included earlier. What about minute taking, for example? This links with the earlier section on recording.

4   Communication within agencies

4.1   Successful communication between agencies is much affected by what goes on internally. A striking example of this is given in the section in the Colwell inquiry dealing with Maria's schools. (Paragraphs 164 to 177 in the Reader, p. 249). This description raises many issues: the use of internal records, the role of the school secretary, relationships up the hierarchy of the school, to name but three.

2 We need to relate that example to the particular organizations within which we work. For social services, a key position is the degree of consensus between field workers and seniors about the management of the case. If there is conflict, this confuses further interprofessional communication. Sometimes the conference is used, inappropriately, to resolve such difficulties.

3 In hospitals, there are often problems of communication between casualty and paediatric departments, some of which require quite sophisticated practical arrangements to ensure a proper information flow.

Activity 16.4
Take an example from your own experience of a serious failure in communication within an organization. It need not be a case of child abuse but, if possible, choose an example where the wellbeing of an individual (client, patient, school pupil, etc.) was involved.

Note down:
a. the circumstances and the outcome;
b. what you suppose to have been the reasons for the failure;
c. what you would need to find out in order to explain it fully.

The Colwell reading (paragraphs 164 to 177) will suggest areas upon which to focus.

Comments

4 Any failure in communication within an organization is likely to be related to some or all of the following:
a. the formal arrangements for passing on information to whom: whether these are adequate and whether they are adhered to;
b. the formal levels of decision making: whether they are clearly understood and adhered to;
c. the extent of anxiety engendered by the situation and its effect upon the participants (for example, precipitate action);

d. extraneous and unpredictable factors (for example, bad weather, telephone breakdown, another crisis at same time, absence of key people);
e. confusing or conflicting messages from outside – both from other professionals, or, in 'welfare problems', from the clients/patients themselves.

There are many other examples. The probability is that, in any serious failures, a complex of factors is involved. It is a useful exercise to analyse the process in a chronological sequence, so that a picture builds up over hours, days or weeks.

Recommended further reading

DEPARTMENT OF HEALTH AND SOCIAL SECURITY (1974) *Report of the Committee of Inquiry into the care and supervision provided in relation to Maria Colwell*, London, HMSO.

Self-assessment questions (Block 4)
Richard Fothergill

1 Which of the two types of court, juvenile (civil) and adult (criminal), is appropriate for the following statements.

   a. Proceedings may be brought by the local authority.
   b. Evidence has to be beyond reasonable doubt.
   c. It can punish an abusing parent.
   d. It can make a care order.

2 Stephen is seven years old, and has a history of minor illnesses. His stepfather was convicted of abusing a child in his previous marriage. The boy is very thin and apparently underweight. His teachers are very concerned by the state of the child who, although apparently bright, is far behind normal levels of achievement. When his class teacher visited a neighbour, she was told that they often heard sounds of beating coming from the house.

Answer the following questions.

   a. How can the teachers get a case before a court?
   b. In the light of the above evidence, which is the appropriate court?
   c. Can the fact of the stepfather's previous abuse of a child be used in evidence?
   d. What should the teachers and neighbours be doing to promote the chances of a successful action?
   e. What outcome should be aimed for?
   f. What further factual evidence should be offered?
   g. If, as a result of criminal proceedings only, the stepfather was sent to prison, what would happen to Stephen?

3 As Stephen's class teacher, you have reported your anxieties but the reaction from other authorities is long delayed while the boy continues to suffer. You decide to visit his home yourself.

From the following list of possible approaches, select those which you think will be most helpful, and note down their letters.

   A. You ask to see the stepfather alone and reprimand him for battering Stephen.
   B. You ask to see Stephen first and show great concern about his injury.
   C You ask for Stephen to be sent away as you want to discuss his school record with both parents.

D. You wait till Stephen leaves the room. Then you tell both parents that action is pending and explain the procedures that will follow.

E. You make clear your concern for the child and warn them that you are keeping a watchful eye on him at school.

F. You ask the parents sympathetically about any difficulties with the child.

G. You tell the parents that Stephen is doing as well as can be expected at school, and suggest things they can do to improve his performance.

4 As the person called upon to prepare a background report for a case conference on Stephen,

   a. list 8 broad headings under which you would write your report.

   b. state who you would expect to be present at the case conference.

5 According to LASSL (74) 13 and LASSL (76) 2,

   a. how often should an area review committee meet?

   b. list 4 functions of an area review committee.

   c. list 4 pieces of information that should be included in a register, other than child and family's names, addresses and occupations.

Answers to self-assessment questions (Block 4)

1 a. Juvenile (civil), if the action is to protect the child. The local authority may bring criminal proceedings against the abuser in the adult (criminal) court.   (1 mark)
   b. Adult (criminal)   (1 mark)
   c. Adult (criminal)   (1 mark)
   d. Juvenile (civil)   (1 mark)

Total: 4 marks (ref: Unit 13)

2 a. Report to NSPCC, police or social services department. Note that the local area review committee has probably issued 'guidelines' on recommended procedures to be adopted, most likely in the possession of the headmaster.   (1 mark)
   b. For immediate protection of Stephen, the juvenile (civil) court is the most appropriate. Proceedings may be taken in the adult (criminal) court against the stepfather if sufficient evidence can be provided.   (1 mark)
   c. Yes, in the juvenile (civil) court.   (1 mark)
   d. Keeping records of 'events'. Watching for evidence of injury. (1 mark)
   e. We favour a care order.   (1 mark)
   f. Medical evidence of boy's physical condition, including comparative height and weight charts, skeletal survey. Educational psychologist's evidence on under-achievement. Statements from the stepfather, mother and child on what has been happening.   (1 mark)
   g. Stephen would remain at home. On the completion of his sentence, the stepfather may return home and start the beatings again. A care order granted by the juvenile court would assist the social services department in acting quickly, should that prove necessary. (1 mark)

Total: 7 marks (ref: Unit 13)

3 The answers to this are arguable. Our decision is that D, E, F, and G are helpful, A, B, and C are unhelpful.   (1 mark for each)

Total: 7 marks (ref: Unit 14)

4 a. (1 mark for each of the following):

   i.   In what ways the child is thought to be abused.
   ii. Past history, medical and social, of the child.

182

iii. The family unit now.
iv. Child's behaviour, compared with siblings.
v. Economic and material circumstances of the family.
vi. Parents; health, intelligence, etc.
vii. Attitudes of parents to their children.
viii. Other important people in the family's life.

Total: 8 marks (ref: Unit 16)

b. Your list should include at least the following 5:

paediatrician, teacher, police, GP, social services department
representative.   (1 mark for each. Add a bonus if you suggested
health visitor as an alternate with the GP)

Total: 5 marks (ref: Unit 16)

a. Once a quarter.   (1 mark)
b. (1 mark each for any 4 of the following):

i. advise on formulation of local practice/procedures.
ii. approve written instructions defining duties of personnel.
iii. review work of case conferences.
iv. provide education/training programmes.
v. collect information about work being done.
vi. collaborate with adjacent area review committees.
vii. advise on need for inquiries.
viii. provide forum for consultation.
ix. devise procedures for ensuring continuity when family moves.
x. consider ways for publicizing channels of communication for general public.
xi. write yearly reports.

c. (1 mark each for any 4 of the following):

i. GP's name, address, telephone number.
ii. Child's school.
iii. Nature of injury/reason.
iv. Date and time of referral.
v. Name of referrer and agency.
vi. Agencies involved.
vii. Action taken.

Total: 9 marks (ref: Unit 15)

Maximum marks: 40

Block 5   Methods and techniques for professionals

This block consists of a double unit followed by two linked units, all with their focus on professional skills. Units 17–18 pick up the theme of communication from Unit 16 and explore it more fully in the context of team work. Unit 19 is an introduction to the principles of behaviour modification, and Unit 20 demonstrates, with illustrations from practice, how the behavioural approach has been used successfully in the treatment of abusing families.

Units 17–18 The team approach
Malcolm H. Hall

Units 17–18 comprise a double unit, intended to be undertaken in two study sessions. The reference numbers in these units refer to the notes on p. 207.

Objectives

When you have completed these units you should be able to:

1. describe the dangers of a single-handed approach to suspected cases of child abuse;
2. describe the difficulties raised by inter-disciplinary team management;
3. list the conditions necessary for satisfactory management by an inter-disciplinary team;
4. explain why one or two individuals are still responsible for the management of non-accidental injury, although acting on behalf of colleagues;
5. explain the necessity for a frank disclosure of information to those closely involved with cases and be able to discuss the potential danger of confidential material being disclosed to persons minimally involved;
6. distinguish between emergency and formal case conferences and describe their respective functions.

1 Introduction

1.1 Some of the dangers associated with a single-handed attempt to manage cases of non-accidental injury have been dealt with in other units. Units 17–18 will examine the advantages as well as some of the problems of a multi-disciplinary approach.

1.2 A minimum of two persons is necessary if communication is to take place. Apart from someone wishing to communicate, there must be a person to whom the communication can be made. The emphasis is on communication at a personal level. Communicating with an amorphous department or service is inappropriate for the management of child abuse and, if messages are not to be lost or distorted in transmission, there must be a clearly laid down channel along which messages can be passed.

Communications within the same service are easier than those which have to be made with persons from other disciplines. At a personal level, talking to colleagues does not present major difficulties but, when one has to discuss matters with members of a different organization, individuals frequently fail to convey their message as clearly as they might have done, because of the invisible barrier that appears to surround a close-knit group of single discipline workers. Apart from a few individuals in every service who have somewhat abrasive personalities, most people welcome involvement and discussion with other services.

Inter-disciplinary management of cases is not a new development; it has been practised for many years in the psychiatric services, where the treatment teams hold regular meetings to discuss the progress and treatment of their patients. The inter-disciplinary management of a case of non-accidental injury differs in an important aspect from the psychiatric type of approach; what this difference is, and any implications that may arise from it, will be discussed later in these units. It will be clear from the units that have already been studied that no one service knows all the facts about a case of child abuse. If the situation is to be handled correctly, it is imperative that all the information about the child and the family should be made available to each of the services involved in the future management. This can only be achieved by a meeting of all the workers at a case conference. It is the single most important step in the management of these cases.

2 The case conference

Activity 17.1
Before studying this section read the editorial from the *Lancet* (1975) in the Reader, p. 220. Write a summary of the article in as few words as possible, trying to pick out the message that the author is conveying.

Comment
Your summary should read something like this:
'Multi-disciplinary case conferences play an important role in the early management of cases of non-accidental injury. They are very time-consuming for the people who take part and care must be taken to avoid spending valuable time discussing trivial or doubtful cases. Although the management of child abuse has greatly improved, there are still many problems, particularly on the legal side, to be solved and the child suffering from

neglect or emotional abuse is often still left to suffer. Self-scrutiny and an ongoing monitoring of the work of the case conference is essential to avoid less important cases taking an excessive proportion of the available resources.'

2.2 Even more briefly, the *Lancet* is saying 'Do not allow an enthusiasm to contain this condition blind you to the presence of other equally important though less spectacular, conditions.'

2.3 This is the background against which to study the process of inter-disciplinary communication at case conference level. The aim is set out clearly in the following extract from the recently published *Report of the Committee on Child Health Services: fit for the future* (Department of Health and Social Security and Department of Education and Science, 1976).

> In the last two or three generations we have come to realize how precious is our inheritance of children and also to recognize their needs as being different from those of adults. At one time children were dressed in adult clothes, scaled down to size, which seemed to reflect an attitude that they were in a sense retarded adults. Childhood was thought of as an inadequate and incomplete form of the adult state. By contrast we have become increasingly aware of childhood as a separate state, as a period of human experience in its own right. And more important still, we have come to realize the extent to which experience in childhood determines the adult outcome. . . .
>
> We have found no better way to raise a child than to reinforce the ability of his parent(s), whether natural or substitute, to do so. Almost all parents want the best opportunities for their children but too many still set low expectations and assume that their child's life will be governed by innate ability and maturation, as though mental, physical and emotional development were things that simply happened up to a determined level by an automatic process. One conviction that informs this report is that parents need to be made more aware of the learning (in the widest sense) that goes on day by day through experience, and of their part in it. Future improvements in the health of children will depend as much on the beliefs and behaviour of parents as on the services provided.
>
> Another of our convictions is that the disadvantages of birth and early life cast long shadows forward. Many parents

have to contend with circumstances which grossly hamper their natural and acquired ability to be good parents and many children are crippled by circumstance. It should be an objective of a civilised community to ameliorate the condition of those affected in this way and always to strive to remove the causes so far as future generations are concerned. We now know that the effects of early disadvantage can be much diluted by the environmental circumstances the child encounters during the middle and later years of childhood; and that it is especially worth making this corrective effort because early disadvantage tends to lead to later disadvantage, so that, unless there is intervention, there develops a compounding of difficulties. It is this train of events which is influential rather than the critical effect of particular circumstances in early life considered in their own right.

Ideally, correction of a disturbance in the family dynamics should start in time to prevent any physical injury to the child. At the present time we have to accept that many cases will be recognized only when they have progressed to a stage where physical injury has been inflicted on a child and it is primarily with this type of case that these units are concerned.

Immediately an injured child is suspected of having sustained a non-accidental injury, steps must be taken to protect him from further injury. This is effected, in the hospital context, by admitting the child to the ward. This may be necessary for the treatment of the injuries; for investigation of the blood in cases of bruising; or to ensure the safety of the child.

If the parents are unco-operative and will not allow the child to be admitted, or if they are likely to remove the child before it is considered advisable by the doctors; or if the child's condition indicates a severe degree of injury; or if the child needs separation from the parents but hospitalization is not appropriate, the doctor will recommend that a place of safety order (see Unit 13) be obtained. It is at this stage that the first type of case conference is held.

3   The emergency case conference

Kempe, in a discussion with the Tunbridge Wells Study Group, indicated that, in an emergency, a case conference could be held between two people. One of the few single-handed decisions in the management of these cases is made by a hospital doctor when he decides to admit a child, suspected of being injured.

Activity 17.2
Make a list of the reasons why a hospital doctor may decide to admit
a child.

Comment

3.2 Your list should include the possibility of a non-accidental injury, the
necessity to treat the injury, medical investigation to exclude any con-
comitant disease, failure to thrive, to give the mother a rest from a
particularly demanding child, to investigate the dynamics of the family
relationships.

3.3 Whatever reasons the doctor may give to the parents it may be felt
necessary that a place of safety order should be obtained. This order,
whilst it can be provided by a police officer, is usually obtained by a social
worker, either from the social services department or the NSPCC.

3.4 The doctor will discuss the situation with a social worker before the order
is obtained. Such a discussion is invaluable. The doctor will have the
clinical state of the child available in some detail, but he may only have
been able to make a short assessment of the parental background. The
family may be well known to the social services or the NSPCC and this
information can be added to the clinical picture. This discussion also
helps avert the possibility of a breakdown in communications occurring.
The preparation of a medical report takes time and, as the relevant social
service unit is aware of the situation and its urgency from the beginning,
investigations and consultations can begin immediately.

3.5 The child may be brought to hospital by a social worker, health visitor,
nursery nurse, school teacher, a relative or a neighbour. A parent may
bring the child if the injuries occurred outside the family circle as, for
example, at a baby minder's. The doctor will take the history from anyone
who can give details and he will then hold a conference with the professional workers who are present.

3.6 The doctor may have decided that the child should be admitted. The
conference cannot question this decision since it is a matter of clinical
judgement, but there is room for discussion as to the necessity or otherwise
of obtaining a place of safety order if the reason for the child's admission
is not primarily for medical treatment. In these circumstances the discussion is similar, though on more informal lines, to the main case conference. If the doctor feels that the child does not need admission, but

should be in a place of safety, then discussion can clarify the position. Admission may be necessary to allow the social services department time to find a suitable foster home.

Infrequently the doctor may be concerned about the well being of a child but unsure as to the best method of dealing with the situation at that time. Discussion with another informed person is of considerable assistance in deciding on the most appropriate immediate action. You will have noted that in the previous sentence the adjective 'informed' was used. When an experienced doctor is in doubt, there is little point in discussing the problem with an inexperienced person. It requires an exchange of views between equally well informed members of senior status from the various services who may be involved with the immediacy of the problem. The emergency case conference is the first contact made between the various disciplines. As soon as the safety of the child has been ensured, the social services, as the agents responsible for organizing the full case conference, can begin the investigations, the collation of information and the considerable amount of work that is necessary before calling a case conference.

4   The case conference

1   Timing of the conference is important. When a child is detained in a place of safety, twenty-eight days from the making of a magistrates order are available for investigation and discussion before it has to be allowed to lapse or an application is made to a juvenile court. If, for various reasons, the local authority or the NSPCC are unable to proceed, they may ask for an interim order, but the formal proceedings in which application for a care or supervision order is made are initiated only when all the information required is available and has been subjected to detailed discussion through the case conference mechanism.

2   The legal aspects of these cases are discussed in Unit 13 but you should realize the limiting factors that the law imposes upon the social services in their management of these cases. Whilst twenty-eight days may appear to be an adequate period, in practice it is found to be minimal and when, for example, psychiatric reports are required on the parents, it may prove to be inadequate. However, a magistrates' place of safety order, lasting for twenty-eight days, is preferable to that provided by a police officer, which is valid only for eight days before juvenile court proceedings are necessary.

3   An ideal time for a conference is about three weeks after a place of safety

order has been obtained.[1] If such an order has not been taken out and the child is in hospital on a voluntary basis and the parents wish to take the child home, a full conference may have to be called at short notice. A decision may be required and, even if all the information is not yet available, it might be necessary to apply for a place of safety order on the child. The position of other children in the family might need consideration: do they need to be received into care? If the parent responsible for injuring the child is in custody and likely to be discharged, what are the appropriate measures needed to protect the children? If the children are members of a single parent family and the parent is exhibiting marked signs of a psychiatric disorder, what are the appropriate steps to take (a) for the child's protection, (b) for the protection of any siblings, and (c) for the well being and care of the parent? These, and similar problems, frequently require an urgent answer. A semi-urgent conference, attended by fewer people than the full conference, may be necessary at short notice, leaving full discussion to a full conference later.

4.4 The responsibility for requesting a conference is left to any of the professional groups involved in managing the case. Junior members of these groups will discuss their concern with their seniors who will, if they consider it appropriate, request the social services department to call the conference. This is one benefit of the emergency case conference: the social services are involved from the beginning of the situation and are thus in a better position to arrange the timing of the meeting.

4.5 Considerable work is involved in this apparently simple undertaking. It is extremely difficult to find a time which suits all the various persons who have to attend and, if necessary, some degree of priority must be given to those whose commitments are more rigidly fixed by appointments which are not amenable to alteration at short notice. The paediatric consultant is in a particularly difficult situation in this respect. With the best will in the world he may be unable to miss a clinic and this must always be taken into consideration when the time is being arranged. The general practitioner is in an even more difficult position in respect of short notice conferences. His surgery and home visits are even more difficult to rearrange than the hospital consultant's. This is one important reason why it is found throughout the country that general practitioners are not good attenders at conferences.

4.6 The choice of a place at which to hold the conference is also dependent on the convenience of essential attenders. Hospital doctors may be able to attend if the conference is held at the hospital; they may not be able to attend if they have to travel to the social services department office some distance away. As in all things, a commonsense approach and a realization of other people's problems does, despite the apparently insurmountable problems, enable the majority of people involved to attend. The individuals concerned will decide on the importance of their presence in each case and will always accept considerable disruption of their work if the matter is of sufficient gravity. The *Lancet* editorial discussed earlier emphasizes this aspect and, when it is realized that a hospital consultant, whose area may cover several local authority areas, may be required at two, three or four conferences in a week, the importance of avoiding unnecessary meetings will be realized. This assessment in no way denegrates the importance of the other services or the difficulty that they may have in attending. Nevertheless, if the primary initiating action is medical, it is desirable that the doctors concerned should be given every opportunity of attending.

7 The preparation of documents for use at the conference, the provision of secretarial assistance during the meeting and the preparation and circulation of minutes of the conference are the responsibility of the social services department. The action of the DHSS in placing these responsibilities on the social services has caused a considerable extra workload which has necessitated a reassessment of priorities. Fortunately for abused children, they are given top priority in management and the cases, which were often seen several years ago presenting with multiple major injuries, are far less common, whereas the more minor types of injuries are being seen with greater frequency.

8 It is usual for the chairman of the case conference to be the area officer of the social services department involved. In practice it matters little who fills this role; the proceedings are not formal and the primary purpose of the chairman is essentially to guide the discussion and prevent it from becoming side-tracked into less important issues.

Activity 17.3
Before proceeding further, check that you have a clear idea of the purpose and aims of a case conference. Make a list of all the factors that a case conference should consider in relation to the child under consideration, the siblings, parents, guardians or other adults having care of the child and the effects of the situation in relation to the members of the case conference. Each section should be considered in relation to the events which have led up to the situation under discussion, the present situation and the manner in which it is hoped that the situation will develop in the future.

Comment

4.9 Check your list with paragraphs 4.1 to 4.8.

4.10 The case conference is concerned with the health and safety of the child and siblings. It must decide how best to support the parents in their present difficulties and how future management may restore the unity of the family in which the well being of the children is assured. It must acquire the information on which to base a psychosocial evaluation of the family as a whole, for which it needs adequate information from many bodies. Communication within, and also across, inter-disciplinary barriers is therefore essential, but at the same time confidentiality must be protected.

5 The dynamics of the case conference

5.1 Many members will have been involved with the family prior to the conference. Some may have been deeply involved for a long period. In many cases a strong bond is in existence between the caring professions and the family. Some degree of personal involvement is inevitable under these conditions, though it will vary, depending on the personality and experience of the professional involved. In general, the younger and less experienced tend to become more involved than the older person. Some members of the conference may see the family as a major nuisance, whereas others may be neutral in their attitude to the parents.

5.2 The conference must knit this group of widely different professionals, all with different attitudes towards the family, into a group which can discuss the matter impartially, giving due weight to the opinions of the other members, whilst taking care not to allow any personal involvement to influence their decisions. The object of the exercise must be kept clearly in mind: it is the present and future well being of the child, and it is imperative that the child is not used as a therapeutic object with which to treat the parents.

5.3 It is common for conference decisions to subject some of the family-professional worker relationships to a major disruptive strain. This is a source of great anxiety, particularly to the case workers, and other members of the conference must accept that this concern and anxiety is fully justified. The conference must support the case workers and allow them to 'talk through' their anxieties. There are occasions when all members of the conference are worried because of an inability to take action which is desirable, and it can be seen, if the group is studied, that the conference is acting as a stress-releasing mechanism for all its members.

6 Constitution of the case conference

Activity 17.4
Make a list of the various persons who might be considered necessary
at a case conference.

Comment

The diagram of the communication problem (Reader, p. 293) and your
notes on Unit 15 should be studied and used as a checklist. Can you think
of any other services that should be represented? The term 'service' is
used here deliberately. Some individuals, for example, the paediatricians,
attend in their own right because of the information they possess. Others,
for example, social workers and health visitors, attend because of the
information they possess and as representatives of their own service. It
would be illogical for the director of social services to attend, but frequently a senior member of the service, for example, an area officer or
community nursing officer, may attend even though they may have no
personal knowledge of the case. Their involvement is necessary to provide
support for their field workers and to assess the situation, in relation to
their discipline, in a broader context than is possible for their junior.
When an immigrant family is the subject of discussion, a community
relations officer should be invited to attend.

Do you consider that the members of the conference are able to make
major decisions about very complex points of law which may arise in some
cases? The answer must be that, while there is a considerable knowledge
of the more usual branches of juvenile law, complex issues and assessments
of the possible results of legal action are primarily matters for lawyers
and, if difficult legal decisions are to be made, a lawyer from the town
clerk's department should be invited to attend. The diagram on the communications problem is an over simplification and the report from which
it is taken points out that the consultant psychiatrist and the hospital
nurses have been omitted.

Obviously it would be impractical to have representatives from every
service present at every conference. Usually attendance is limited to those
persons who are able to make a contribution to the proceedings. The
composition of a typical conference might be: chairman, the area officer
of the social services; the case worker from the social services and,
possibly, an officer from the NSPCC; the general practitioner and/or a

health visitor (if possible attached to his or her practice); a community nursing officer; a representative from the housing department; a paediatrician and a sister from the children's ward; a consultant in charge of an emergency and accident department; the education welfare officer or a teacher; a probation officer; a police officer with decision-making capability. This is an average-sized conference. There are fourteen persons present. Some have expert knowledge of child abuse; others only a limited knowledge and others, whilst having no practical knowledge of the problem, can make a major contribution to the deliberations by virtue of their expertise in their own field.

6.4 It is clear, therefore, that any decision-making process among such a large number of people, many with a differing professional outlook, cannot be easy and might well fail because of a rigidity of outlook and an inability to work across their professional boundaries. (See also Units 7, 8 and 16.)

6.5 When members of a case conference meet for the first time as strangers, or when the majority of members are known to each other and strangers take part, time is necessary to allow the group to adjust itself to the various personalities who are present. Superficial adjustment occurs fairly quickly but full acceptance by each person of the others' skills in their own disciplines may take a considerable time. For this reason it is essential that the senior members of a conference should respect the members of the other services as experts in their own right. In this way the fears and anxieties of the less senior members can be relieved. To accept a decision which appears to cut across one's own inclination and training is far from easy. Such an acceptance can only be based on a respect for the capabilities of those involved in reaching the decision. This in its turn necessitates that previous decisions have been correct and based on a professional expertise that can be appreciated by the other experts involved.

6.6 However important you may consider your own discipline in these cases, others may have just as much, or even more, to contribute. No person, be he hospital consultant or trainee social worker, is more important than another. It is natural that more attention will be paid to the views of the more experienced person; it is essential that respect should be given to the requirements of any professional who has ethical considerations to keep in mind, but it would be totally wrong not to attend to the views expressed by a rather nervous and worried member of a service attending a case conference for the first time. Beware of stereotyping a person, as members of the social services and police force occasionally tend to do. The stereotypes are based on inaccurate press reporting or the television portrayal of, for example, the police force. The officers who attend conferences are not large burly men with size 10 shoes, determined to prosecute everybody, but are well informed, caring adults, whose main desire, apart from ensuring the well being of the child, is to play a constructive part in the resolution of the difficulties that face the family. The role of the police in case conferences is of considerable importance and this will be dealt with in greater detail later.

7 It is the duty of the chairman to guide the conference and prevent it getting bogged down in side issues of no relevance to the matter in hand, to ensure that any decisions reached are properly recorded and that those who are responsible for taking any action are fully aware of what is expected of them. There are three stages involved in reaching a decision. Initially, information is presented to the conference by the various services. This is then discussed until, finally, a decision is reached and responsibilities for action are allocated.

8 Information

The type of information that is needed has been discussed in previous units. Information may be first-hand from, for example, a health visitor or social worker, or it may only be passed on, for example by a health visitor on behalf of a general practitioner who is unable to attend. The information may be minimal. If the family is not known to any services this is a common occurrence. At other times the amount of information may be surprising, each member of the conference having a large file about one or other member of the family.

9 Confidentiality

It is at this stage that matters of confidentiality arise, particularly in relation to the disclosure of medical information about the parents or about family matters which have become known because of a previous involvement with the family. The reply of a paediatrician to questioning during the Auckland Inquiry (Daily Transcript, Day 5, pp. 390–2) is very relevant to this difficulty. She was asked, 'You would tell other people about any fears (of child abuse) you have?' She replied, 'The normal practice is that confidentiality is not broken. One gives information in the course of one's duty to other people who are concerned with patients in the course of their duty. One does not give information to other people except with the permission of the parents.' When asked, 'When you speak of other people being involved with patients, are you thinking of people like health visitors and the social services, for example?', she replied 'Oh, yes, their duties are to deal with patients.' Clearly this senior doctor, who was very concerned about confidentiality, had no doubts that it was her duty, when she was concerned for the well being of a child, to communicate her concern to members of other disciplines who could help. This is a very sound principle on which to base one's approach to this most difficult area, for it is only by realizing that other disciplines have as much concern about confidentiality as one's own that it is possible to ensure that sufficient information is made available to the case conference to enable it to reach a decision.

6.10 If it not felt possible to provide the full details of one's involvement with any of the persons under discussion, then a paraphrase of the essential aspects or, at the very least, an opinion about future possibilities, in certain circumstances is equally acceptable. Discussions about the case conference with persons who are not directly involved should never enable an identification of the family to be made. Casual gossip may rapidly disseminate information around a neighbourhood, producing a disastrous effect on the family and a rapid decline in the relationships between them and any of the services involved.

Section 7 marks the beginning of your second study session.

7   The role of the police

Problems of confidentiality affect every discipline involved in the case conference. In spite of the protestations made on occasions by members of the various services, no one body can claim a monopoly of concern over the disclosure of information gathered under a professional cloak of secrecy in the course of their work. It must be realized that excessive reluctance to share information may prejudice the future well being of the child and, even when the representative feels strongly about disclosing information, he must accept that the other members of the conference have equally stringent ethical rules governing this matter. The police and probation services, apart from ethical and/or professional difficulties, also have legal requirements concerning the non-disclosure of information and it is much to the credit of their personnel that it has been found possible to make relevant information available. It is important to realize that the information required at a conference must be relevant to the matter under discussion. Details of convictions or prosecutions for offences which do not raise the possibility of violence are, in the main, irrelevant.

The functions of the police force are: the protection of life and property, the prevention of crime and the detection of crime. They are thus very much involved in the problem of non-accidental injuries and have a major concern in both the preventative and management aspects of the disorder. Their important role has been recognized in the government circular, LASSL (76) 26, published jointly by the Department of Health and Social Security and the Home Office (DHSS 1976). It emphasizes that, within the limits of confidentiality, oral information should be made available concerning relevant previous convictions and points out that disclosure of convictions 'spent' under the Rehabilitation of Offenders Act, 1974, would be permissible as it would be relevant to assessing the suitability of persons to have the care of children or young persons; and it would not, as pointed out in this circular to the police, constitute an offence under section 9/2 of the Act.[2]

Paragraphs 11 and 12 of LASSL (76) 26 on confidentiality are worth quoting in full as they apply equally to all members of the conference.

> 11.   Records of previous convictions are confidential, and it is important that details of previous convictions which are divulged to the case conference should only be disclosed to professional colleagues involved in the case. Similar

restrictions should apply to any notes which may be taken of such convictions.

12.   Both departments attach great importance to maintaining the strict confidentiality of case conference proceedings. Information given to the case conference, whether by police or by any other person concerned, should not be revealed to a member of the public or to a representative of any service not represented at the case conference without the explicit consent of the person who gave the information.

Activity 18.1
It is worthwhile at this stage to consider in more detail the role of the police in these cases. Read the extract, in the Reader, p. 173, from *Children in danger* by Jean Renvoize, concerning the police. To an extent this has been overtaken by the LASSL circular (which is also designated Home Office Circular 179/76) quoted above, but the discussion in Renvoize is still useful.

7.4   The police are often seen as society's means of obtaining vengeance on the person who has broken society's laws or code of conduct. It is essential to realize that the police have a statutory duty to prevent crime, which is as important as their involvement in the detection process. It may be argued that the physical abuse of children, in the battering situation, is not a crime but a disease arising from social factors, many of which are outside the control of the individuals concerned. This is the view often held by the social worker. The police, on the other hand, hold that to injure a defence-less child is a crime. Both arguments are equally valid, but it is the attitudes resulting from these different ideological positions which produce diffi-culties in reaching an agreed decision. If the police feel that every child abuser should be prosecuted, there is little prospect of reaching a decision. However, the acceptance by the police of the social aspects being of major importance in the management of the case does cut across the philosophy of the force and presents difficulties for many individual officers. It is much to the credit of the chief police officers that they have in general accepted the medical and social service views about the dynamics of child battering and are prepared to allow their subordinates to play their part in the management of cases. This development has not occurred over-night. It is the result of a decade of dialogue, persuasion and demonstration by both medical and social workers that the best results for the child are produced by the avoidance of a hard line prosecution policy.

There are still areas of occasional difficulty with some police forces, which are not necessarily attributable to an ingrained attitude. For example, if the police are deliberately excluded from all or the majority of case conferences in a district, and casework management proceeds with police ignorance that a child has been seriously injured, they are, not surprisingly, likely to pay little attention to any conference decision and may take action which appears to them to be appropriate to protect the child and to prosecute the offender. Such a situation is not unknown and there are recorded incidents where the non-involvement of the police has resulted in the serious injury or death of a child. It is not necessary for a police officer to attend each conference; they may feel unable to help in any way and to attend would only waste the officer's time, but, if their co-operation is to be ensured, then they must be given the opportunity to be present.[3]

The present author, who has worked closely with the police for at least ten years in these cases, agreed, after discussion with senior officers, to involve the police in all cases, provided that they would not unilaterally take legal action against the parents without allowing an opportunity for the opposing point of view to be made. At no time has there been any cause to regret this decision; in many cases they have, admittedly with reluctance, agreed not to prosecute. Fortunately, the decisions taken at case conferences have supported the correctness of the approach and, as a result, there is now mutual respect between the various disciplines based on an acceptance of the professional expertise displayed by the services involved.

8   The role of the case worker

Case workers who have been closely involved with a family for a prolonged period may find themselves exposed to considerable stress and difficulty in discussing the situation. It is inevitable that close identification will be made by the case worker with the family; such identification with a family can be a major factor in establishing a relationship within which assistance can be both offered and accepted.

Whilst information is being presented to the conference, one's unspoken views, which are gradually evolving into an opinion, can vary widely as further information is received. A similar effect is noticeable during the discussion. It is easier for people not deeply involved with the family to consider the problem dispassionately and it is very easy to identify a person with a too close attachment to the family by their responses to suggestions which may, or might be considered to, cause a disturbance to this relationship. This may, rarely, be so marked as to justify a question being asked as to whether the person is aware of such a close identification with the family. Such a question should not be regarded as a criticism; it is a request for the person to consider his attitude and see if he is aware of his position. Usually he will accept this as fair comment and will explain why it has arisen. It is essential that the other members of the conference appreciate their colleague's difficulty and give him every opportunity to comment upon the differing views expressed by other members of the conference. Usually the difficulty is resolved, though not necessarily easily. If, however, the person concerned has a fixed opinion which he is not prepared to moderate in any way, the situation will have to be accepted. A person in a relatively junior position who adopts such an inflexible position might well raise the question of his fitness for further involvement with the case. A too close or a fixed identification with the family might well raise doubts as to the value of any reports that might be submitted later. A case worker who has the responsibility for managing the case must be prepared to see both the good and bad aspects of the family he is involved with and an over-commitment can result in a total inability to recognize the early signs of a critical situation developing. Some of the cases in which an official inquiry has been held have arisen as a result of an over-commitment to the family by the case worker, possibly arising from inexperience, but other factors, such as a determination to manage the case alone or an excessively over-confident attitude to the problem, may also have played a part.

8.3 The Chairman must allow adequate time for all views, comments and suggestions to be put forward. Usually the appropriate course of action becomes apparent during these discussions. A decision about further action and the allocation of a key worker to carry out the decision is then made.

9 Decision

9.1 It is essential that the record of the case conference shows the decision taken, the name of the key worker and others who may be allocated duties, and the name of any persons who may dissent from the case conference decision. It should also indicate when a review conference should be called. Ideally, the decision should be reached by consensus and not by a formal vote. Two situations exist where a decision cannot be made

a. The conference was held too soon. Full information could not be acquired within the available time. In this event the conference will be reconvened when the information has become available.

b.   The conference can become deadlocked. Rarely, the discussion goes round and round. This may develop in cases which are not clear-cut and where there is a total lack of discoverable information about the personality of one or other of the adults involved. If the child's injuries are clearly not of an accidental nature, but the typical background is missing, it may be impossible to reach a consensus decision and a vote decision may be inappropriate. It can be very helpful to reconvene the conference and ask an expert from another area to attend and take part in the discussion. The reconvened conference may follow the same pattern as the original but the presence of an outsider can go far to cut through much of the tangle of opinions in which the conference has enmeshed itself.[4]

2   When the conference reaches a decision that casework management is appropriate, it is relevant to consider the comment made by Mrs Barbara Auckland during the inquiry (Daily Transcript, Day 2, p. 63). She stated, '. . . It had been like Charing Cross Station, our house, there'd been so many people coming and going'. In the context of any decision recommending supervision, it must be realized that too many visits by too many representatives from various services are non-productive: they confuse the client and may not prevent the very situation developing that visits are designed to prevent.

3   Consider three different types of case conference discussion.

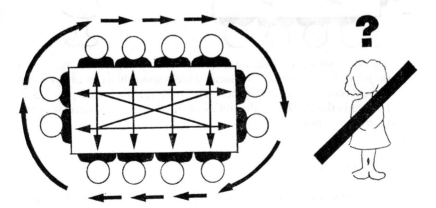

a.   The conference is so busy discussing the matter that it fails to realize the object of the exercise. Any recommendations made are lost in the discussions which operate as an end in themselves. No action follows.

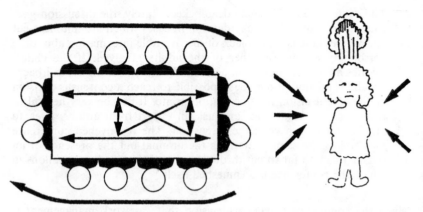

b. The discussion follows a more orderly pattern, but a large number of people are involved in the final action; they all descend on the client and it ends up 'like Charing Cross Station'.

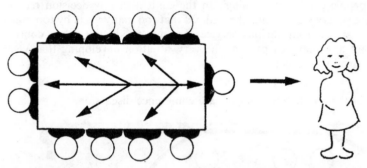

c. The discussion, though informal, is co-ordinated and reaches a decision. A 'key worker' is allocated the responsibility of carrying out the decision of the conference. The only satisfactory type of conference is the third, but the duties of the 'key worker' need studying in greater depth.

10 Key workers

10.1 A key worker can be placed in a position of conflict if he does not support the decision of the conference. The key worker is frequently the person who has previously been involved in casework management with the family and may have identified closely with them and their problems. If it is felt that the conference decision conflicts with the case worker's feelings, it would be inappropriate for him to continue unless he is prepared to

18

support it. A key worker, apart from having his own professional approach to the family, should realize that he is also acting on behalf of the other disciplines involved. These other disciplines have given up their own right to direct involvement for the sake of the extra efficiency that controlled visiting brings and, in the case of the police force, a decision not to prosecute has been made based on the understanding reached at the case conference. It is, therefore, necessary that the worker should not, apart from working within the guidelines formulated by the conference, attempt to conceal any deterioration in the situation or allow personal involvement to colour the reports given to superiors.

.2 There must be a close liaison at personal level between the representatives of the different services. The case conference must lay down the framework within which the various services can function and must stipulate to whom they should report if anything untoward should arise. For example, the failure of a child to appear at a day nursery might be an indication to report to the key worker. The reason might be sickness or it could indicate that the child was bruised and the parents did not want the bruise seen. Similarly, the possibility of eviction would require urgent steps to be taken to provide temporary accommodation for the family. The admission of a parent to hospital, particularly a mental hospital, might also demand urgent action and, unless the information is made available to the key worker, action may fail by default.

.3 The case worker involved should not feel that his actions are constrained in any way by working within a framework produced by the conference. It is important to follow the basic principles of his profession if errors are to be avoided. The inexperienced worker may well feel inadequate when faced with a complex case which has been discussed by many experienced personnel. This is quite normal and any fears or uncertainties should be discussed openly, either at the conference or with a superior in a less open forum.

.4 If an immigrant family has been the subject of the conference, most of the participants are likely to be uncertain of their ground because of the language and cultural differences. In these circumstances, the community liaison officer will have a major role to play and the case workers will have to liaise very closely with him. These cases raise difficulties from the beginning: the cultural characteristics of many of the families make information difficult to acquire, the involvement of the caring services is seen as a slight on their community, the women often occupy an inferior position and, in certain situations, action can result in the family being ostracized by the rest of the community.

10.5 Decisions which have to be made when the law is already involved or may have to be involved, are some of the most difficult that a conference has to deal with. The law will be involved in cases where a place of safety order has been taken out or the police have decided to bring charges against an individual for harming a child. In the former instance, the case conference will have to decide whether a place of safety order should be allowed to lapse or whether proceedings should be brought in a juvenile court to obtain either a care or supervision order.

10.6 In both instances, the case conference will be primarily concerned with the well being of the child, but casework management will nevertheless have to proceed irrespective of any legal involvement. This is a further cause of stress on the key worker, whose role will inevitably be ambivalent in that, on the one hand, her local authority may be responsible for initiating juvenile court proceedings, and yet she will also be expected to continue her normal role with the parents. Under these circumstances the case worker will need the support from both the conference and her superiors in order to deal effectively with both aspects of the situation. Considerable skill is necessary to maintain a working relationship with the adults involved.

10.7 If the police are bringing charges against the parents, the role of the social worker is somewhat eased because the police are seen to be the persons responsible for the circumstances in which they find themselves. The conference may have indicated that the child should remain in the care of the local authority, and it will be the responsibility of the case worker to encourage and maintain the relationship between the child or children and their family.

10.8 Infrequently, the case conference may decide that proceedings in an adult court against a parent may be beneficial to the management of the situation. For example, if the father has a drinking problem and has injured a child when drunk, adult court proceedings can be used in an attempt to ensure that he will receive treatment for his alcoholism. Decisions of this nature may appear, superficially, to cut across the philosophy held by certain workers in the management of the parental situation. It is important, therefore, that any case worker who is involved in a situation of this nature should be fully conversant with the thinking that has led to the decision being taken. Such a decision is not, in fact, incompatible with a caring attitude, particularly when it may offer the only prospects of being able to restore the family unit as a safe and working environment for the children.

10.9 The whole mechanism of the case conference, in both its emergency and formal aspects, may appear to be complex to the uninitiated, and it may be wondered how conferences ever succeed in reaching decisions which, in practice, appear to work very well. In fact, the effectiveness of these processes depends as always on how much effort the individuals concerned are prepared to put in. The ability to reach a consensus decision which is acceptable to all the disciplines involved is based entirely on mutual trust and respect for the other person's point of view. Even though it is recognized that each service is always at liberty to take any action it considers best, it is remarkable how rarely this prerogative is used and, over the years, it has been possible to see an increasing degree of trust and respect developing between the members of the widely different disciplines who hitherto have had very little, if any, contact with each other. The lessons of the case conference have far greater implications than are apparent at first sight. Overall, an approach of this nature would be beneficial in many fields for all the caring professions since it is based on an acceptable evolutionary development. The student might care to consider, in relation to his own discipline, how standards of care for clients could be improved if such an approach, however informal, were regularly adopted.

Notes to Units 17–18

[*These are 'second opinions', contributed by Rhoda Cross, Woman Superintendent, Northumbria Police.*]

1 No consideration is given here to the involvement of the police should the case be one which is serious and needs early investigation. It is important, if it is a case for early police involvement, that the investigating officers should interview the alleged offender before too many other agencies have done so. Police officers find that when an alleged offender has been interviewed by a variety of agencies before the police, it often becomes difficult to arrive at a true explanation of what occurred, the true or untrue having been related to so many people. Also, in calling a case conference, there are many occasions when three weeks is too late for police purposes. It is my experience that in this area a case conference is called, even in cases of a less serious nature, far earlier than this.

2 This circular also permits police officers to release certain other information: 'The police may often have other relevant information about a family which will assist the work of a case conference. Where this is so (for example where they have been called in to deal with matrimonial disputes or violent quarrel with neighbours, or have knowledge of adults in charge of a child when drunk or who leave their children alone in the house) this information should also be communicated to the case conference under the same conditions of confidentiality as set out for criminal convictions' (para. 15).

3 LASSL (76) 26, para. 5, states: 'The Departments consider that area review committees should work towards police attendance at all case conferences concerning

non-accidental injury where this is not already the practice, but consider that this can only be achieved through agreement and mutual confidence. The Departments urge all concerned to do what they can to achieve this'.

4 I feel that it is necessary to clarify the consequences of a police officer's disagreeing at a case conference with the rest of the members. Therefore I quote from LASSL (76) 26, paragraphs 16–18.

'The prosecution of offences is a matter which rests by law within the discretion of the chief officers of police concerned, who may in some serious cases consult the Director of Public Prosecutions. In considering their exercise of discretion in a particular case, chief officers of police will no doubt take into account as far as possible any views expressed by the case conference on the question of prosecution.

'In considering the need for an investigation, the Departments hope that where a case conference has been held, chief officers of police (whilst retaining the capacity to take independent action) will take into account any views expressed by the conference about the effect of an investigation on the welfare of the child. Generally, where an investigation arises from the disclosure of information at a case conference, the person by whom the information is given should be informed that an investigation is to be made.

'Where the police representative attending a case conference dissents from the view of other participants and thinks that it is right to take action (for example by way of investigation or prosecution) contrary to what they recommend, he should suspend further action until a decision has been made by the chief officer of police. Where the chief officer of police decides to take action contrary to the recommendations of a case conference, he should notify the other members of the case conference of the proposed action and of the reasons for it'.

Unit 19   The behavioural approach to child abuse (1)
Vida Carver

Units 19 and 20 are linked units.

Objectives

After completing Units 19 and 20, you should be able to:

1. outline a case for the formulation of professional goals in behavioural terms;
2. define and explain some of the main terms used in behaviour therapy;
3. outline the main principles that govern human learning;
4. outline the planning stages for a treatment programme as identified in Unit 20;
5. explain the significance of the behavioural analysis for the treatment plan;
6. describe some of the techniques used in behaviour modification and quote examples of applications in the field of child abuse.

1   Introduction

.1   In these two units a frankly propagandist case will be made for the wider use of the behavioural approach in the prevention and treatment of child abuse. We shall not attempt of course, in two short units, to train behaviour therapists, but we hope to show how an understanding of the principles of behaviour modification can be of value to all those in contact with abusing families. We hope too that, as a result of their study, students will be ready to seek the advice of practising therapists in the health and education services who can help them to plan suitable programmes of behaviour modification for their clients.

.2   A secondary aim will be to increase awareness of some of the ways in which behaviour may be modified without deliberate intent. We are all of us, even in our everyday social contacts, busily modifying the behaviour of others and when, with all the authority of the 'expert', we intervene at some crisis point in another person's life we can easily by our own behaviour produce unplanned and perhaps unwished for changes in the client's.

.3   A difficulty that students experience in the literature of behaviour therapy is the unfamiliar technical language of the therapist. (We know this because we once experienced it ourselves!) It is not made easier by the fact that many of the terms used are words that have familiar meanings in everyday language but have extended technical connotations for those working in the field. We shall try, therefore, at the risk of over-simplification, for which we hope we may be forgiven by more experienced students, to use everyday language as far as possible, explaining any usages which may be unfamiliar as we come to them.

1.4 Behaviour therapy depends upon the known (but often underestimated) capacity of all human beings to learn new patterns of behaviour. This capacity has been convincingly and repeatedly demonstrated in unborn infants, the very old, and at all levels of intelligence, including the severely mentally handicapped. The scientific study of learning has been a central concern in experimental psychology since the first psychological laboratory was founded in 1879. We now have a good understanding, based upon a very large number of well controlled studies, of the main laws that govern human learning. These laws enable us to make reliable predictions about the outcome of any programme of treatment *provided we have accurately identified the main relevant variables in the case*. Social learning theory provides the framework for the discussions that follow. Every problem is unique and necessitates an extensive behavioural analysis before treatment can be considered. Then, therapist and client together can set precise goals concerning the new behaviour patterns to be achieved and a treatment plan is specified. The therapist has today a wide range of well tested treatment techniques at his disposal but there are no cook-book remedies ready for application in individual cases. As Ullman (1972) has said, 'if a person thinks he can use a procedure in place of his head and heart, he will get the results he deserves'.

1.5 Essential equipment for the would-be therapist's 'head' is a sound working knowledge of the principles of learning, of which only the briefest sketch is possible in these units. For those who will wish to take their studies further there are several basic texts available and Bandura (1970), *Principles of behaviour modification*, though hard going for the beginner, is particularly valuable. In recent years, too, a number of publications have appeared which aim to introduce learning theory and behaviour modification to the caring professions. Jehu's *Learning theory and social work* (1967) and Jehu *et al.* (1972), *Behaviour modification in social work*, are readable and stimulating as well as academically sound. Poteet (1974) has produced a 'practical guide for teachers' on the use of behavioural methods in the classroom; and Peine and Howarth (1975) have addressed themselves directly to parents. Marks, Connolly and Hallam (1973) describe an approved scheme at the Maudsley Hospital, London, for training psychiatric nurses as therapists (a similar scheme is in operation at Graylingwell Hospital, Chichester). One of the cases reported in this last publication concerns the successful treatment of an abusing parent.

In none of these works is the main focus the prevention or treatment of child abuse. There is, however, evidence of a growing awareness of the uses which can be made of behavioural treatment methods with abusing parents. Jeffrey (1976), Polakow and Peabody (1975) and Reavley and Gilbert (1976) among others have reported cases successfully treated by a variety of behavioural methods. An examination of some of the cases reported by these authors will form the basis of our discussion of the practical aspects of behaviour modification.

2 Behavioural objectives

The formulation of objectives in behavioural terms is now recommended routine practice for many professions. It is, for instance, part of the scheme of this course. It is perhaps surprising that in the area of child abuse, where behavioural change is an essential criterion of success, the objectives of intervention only rarely include a detailed statement agreed between professional worker and client of new behaviour patterns that need to be attained. The practice need not be limited to the strictly therapeutic situation. Too often objectives, if formulated at all, are vague statements of good intentions on the part of the intervening worker. The following example preceded an (unpublished) report of suspected child abuse.

Aims and objectives

a. To gain the confidence of the mother and build up a good relationship with her.
b. To support her in times of stress and refer her to the appropriate agencies when necessary.
c. To keep the child's progress under review and advise the mother on child-rearing problems.

The account that follows this statement of aims and objectives covers nine months of regular visiting, during which period the child was repeatedly (and admittedly) abused and the parent was repeatedly referred to general practitioner, social services department and a psychiatrist; but at no point were the objectives reviewed or revised. The account ends with the reception of the child into care.

Activity 19.1

a. Read the following (fictional) account:

Mrs West has been prescribed an anti-depressant by her doctor after telling him that she feels so low that the noise the twins (20 months) make when playing is driving her mad.

A health visitor is asked to visit. Mrs West breaks into a long account of her troubles. She doesn't feel so bad in the morning, but by the time she's cleaned the place up and the kids have followed her round the house turning it into a pigsty again, she could scream. Then she has to put them in the pram, rush to the shops, come back and cook for them, then try to get them to rest, all before she can get a bite for herself. And then she's too tired to eat properly and they are screaming and messing up the place again before she has finished eating. There is usually a row and she slaps them and shuts them in the bedroom to scream it off while she makes the evening meal for her husband. He comes in and asks why she can't keep them in order and she gets mad at him which puts them both off the meal. Then he goes off crossly to the pub and leaves her to get them to bed alone and clear up all over again. So of course she's depressed!

b. Formulate a set of behavioural objectives that the health visitor might suggest to Mrs West.

c. Assuming that Mrs West agrees to trying out the plan, what advantages do you see in having it written down in the form of behavioural objectives?

Comments

2.2 We must begin by saying that if the health visitor had formulated her initial objectives in such general conventional terms as 'gaining confidence, building a good relationship, and offering support in times of stress', she probably would not have elicited such a clear picture of routine behaviours from Mrs West! With the information she has been given, however, she can now prepare a plan to suggest to her client. She might propose an immediate trial change of routine, for three days.

a. Instead of clearing up in the morning, just put the breakfast dishes into the sink and leave the table ready for lunch. Then, while she still feels fresh, do her shopping with the twins in the pushchair.

b. Go straight from shops to the park and allow the children to run about and get physically tired before lunch.

c. A light lunch with the children followed by a rest for both mother and twins.

d. Clean and tidy up once only, just before husband returns . . . etc., etc. (Your plan is probably as good as ours.)

The aims of the exercise should be discussed fully with Mrs West and the detailed objectives worked out and written up in consultation with the worker. They are most likely to be achieved if the mother writes them out herself, with dates and times, pins them up where she can see them and ticks them off as each activity is performed. Most clients fail to grasp the *principles* involved until they have worked at the exercise for some time. The health visitor's part in the agreement might be to pop in from time to time particularly in the early stages and celebrate improvements in a friendly chat, or help modify the plan if parts prove impractical.

3 Among the advantages you may have noted are:

  a. worker and client are immediately united in working together towards an achievable amelioration of the client's conditions;

  b. there is therefore little risk of the developing relationship between worker and client being marred either by dependency or patronage;

  c. progress can be measured precisely against the plan;

  d. new problems can be discussed as they arise and their solutions incorporated in future plans;

  e. from the beginning, the client will be in charge of her own destiny and each improvement in her situation will carry a bonus in increased self-confidence.

3 Behaviour and its determinants

.1 Behaviour can be defined as 'any activity of an organism that is observable, or potentially observable, by another organism'. In these units the 'organisms' under discussion will always be people. This definition is wide enough to incorporate many types of activity not usually included in the lay concept of 'behaviour', from the watering of an eye in response to grit below the eyelid to the beating of a crying child – or the report on her feelings given by Mrs West in Activity 19.1.

.2 Adaptive, maladaptive and deviant behaviour

Behaviour can be classified in several ways. A large part of our everyday behaviour is learned behaviour. As a result of past experience we have learned the ways in which we adapt to our present environment. We handle our knives and forks as we have learned to do, speak the language we have learned, and our social interactions are dependent upon past learning. The term *adaptive behaviour* is usually retained for behaviour which results in effective interpersonal and environmental interactions. When, however, behaviour is ineffective or produces results which have damaging or distressing effects for the person himself, or which get him into trouble with the authorities, the term *maladaptive behaviour* is used.

An important thing to keep in mind is that much maladaptive behaviour is behaviour which, in the context in which it was learned, served an adaptive purpose. The 'frozen watchfulness' of the abused child possibly once saved his life. If it persists after he starts school, where the expectations and opportunities are different, it will be maladaptive behaviour. The term *deviant* is used for behaviour which deviates from some socially sanctioned 'norm'. But, as we saw in Unit 3, 'normal' child-rearing practices vary considerably from one culture to another, so it is impossible to use this term with great precision. Indeed, there is always an evaluative element in the use of any of the terms discussed in this paragraph. Deviant behaviour, because it can often bring the individual into conflict with the authorities, is often also maladaptive behaviour.

Activity 19.2
Most of us exhibit some maladaptive behaviours. Write down one of your own which fits the definition given (are you or have you been, for example, an habitual smoker?). Think back to the situation in which the behaviour was acquired. What adaptive end did it serve? If you are quite sure you have no maladaptive behaviour in your repertoire, think of someone else's – but it will be more difficult to answer the second part of the question. No comments will be given, since we have no inside knowledge of your or your friend's bad habits!

3.3 Respondent behaviour and instrumental behaviour
To understand how behaviour is learned we need to use a different classification. Both respondent and instrumental behaviour can be either adaptive, maladaptive, or deviant.

a. *Respondent behaviour* is behaviour mediated by the *autonomic* nervous system. It includes such automatic reactions as 'eye-watering' and salivation. More importantly, it includes those involuntary emotional responses such as anger, fear, guilt and anxiety discussed in the context of your own reactions to photographs of abused children in Unit 2 (para. 2.1). From the standpoint of the 'behaver' respondent behaviour usually seems more like something that 'happens' to him than something he 'does'.

b. *Instrumental behaviour* (sometimes called *operant behaviour*) is mediated by the *central* nervous system, and includes all that we generally think of as voluntary behaviour, such as walking (or refusing to go for a walk), talking (or deciding to remain silent); striking someone in anger (or restraining an angry impulse). Instrumental behaviour is 'cued' by some stimulus in the environment (for example, dinner on a plate prompts the picking up of a fork). But internal stimuli may also be relevant factors in operant behaviour (the man who hasn't eaten for twenty-four hours will behave differently towards his dinner from the man who had a very heavy lunch).

Stimulus and response

The 'unit' of behaviour is the *response* to a *stimulus*. The stimulus may be internal (for example, some change in body chemistry) or external (for example, a crying child). It is important to note that both stimulus and response may be very complex, with both directly observable and hidden components. The relationship between stimulus and response is at the centre of the learning process.

It is common ground between behaviour therapy and the more traditional approaches that environmental factors – physical and social; past, present and future – are of the first importance in determining patterns of behaviour. They offer differing explanations, however, on how behaviours are learned and on how they may be modified. (For an alternative view see, for example, Unit 6.) In social learning theory all three types of behaviour pattern described in section 3.2 are acquired and maintained on the basis of three regulatory systems.

First, some response patterns are controlled primarily by external stimuli, and these include both respondent and instrumental behaviours.

a.   *Respondent learning.*   Any autonomic response, such as fear, can be learned through the process known as classical conditioning. For example, all young children respond with fear to sudden loud noises. If the family cat approaches a child a moment before his mother drops a dinner plate behind him, then the cat will become for future occasions a fear-eliciting stimulus. Once the cat has acquired the power to arouse fear, this new response may be conditioned to new stimuli. A friendly milkman arriving one day just before the cat may find himself in future greeted with screams of terror. This process is known as higher-level conditioning. Further, the fear response to the cat may 'generalize' to all cats and possibly (though to a lesser degree) to all four-legged animals.

All such conditioned responses become weaker in time if there is no repetition of the original experience until eventually they are extinguished (although even extinguished responses can under certain conditions be revived). We shall see that all these principles have important implications for therapy. By varying the stimulus conditions, new response patterns can be produced.

b.   *Instrumental learning.*   Operant ('doing') behaviours are also controlled by external stimuli. If his mother had not been careless with dinner plates the child in our first example might have reached out and stroked the cat. Had he found the experience rewarding, it is highly probable that cat stroking would become a recurring part of his behavioural repertoire. Each such rewarding experience reinforces the response; that is, makes it more likely that the next time the child sees a cat he will stroke it. This principle of *reinforcement* is cardinal to the understanding of learning and therapy. There is nothing mysterious about it. Our actions are governed by their anticipated consequences. From our child's point of view 'family tabby' has come to signify 'pleasant experience if stroked'. Note that it doesn't matter whether or not he 'thinks' this. What concerns us is that he 'behaves' it. Therefore psychologists prefer the neutral term 'reinforcement' to 'reward'.

Social reinforcers are among the most powerful reinforcers of instrumental behaviour: smiles and affectionate gestures, words of approval, indeed almost any kind of human attention, including self-attention and approval which often work best if spoken aloud.

Now take one more example. Suppose our child goes to stroke the bad-tempered black cat next door and gets scratched. He has been 'punished' for his response, and the black cat has become an 'aversive' stimulus. If, however, his response to tabbies is by now well established the new response will not generalize to the family cat. Only black cats will be avoided in future. This is *discrimination learning*, also used in therapy. Note that the principles of *generalization* and *extinction* apply to operant as well as respondent behaviour.

3.6 The strength and durability of learned responses depend upon the *amount* and the *number of presentations* of the reinforcing stimulus (i.e., the amount of practice) and the *timing* and the *scheduling* of the reinforcement. Quite small quantities of reinforcement are sufficient for learning to take place but performance is increased with greater amounts of reinforcement and more frequent opportunities for practice. Respondent learning is most effective if the new stimulus presents about half a second before the original stimulus. For instrumental responses, immediate 'rewards' or 'punishments' are, generally speaking, most effective. Scheduling refers to the frequency with which a response is reinforced and to the pattern of reinforcing events. This is a complex question which has been widely studied and all the research cannot be reviewed here. Again speaking very generally, it has been found that most responses are acquired more rapidly under *continuous* reinforcement: that is, if in the early stages of learning a 'reward' arrives every time the response is made. However, once acquired, new responses are more stable and persistent if reinforced only *intermittently*. This too, is an important principle which those who are concerned with the modification of behaviour can use to advantage.

The **second** behavioural control system involves *feedback* at the time of the response. From the individual's point of view, what he sees and hears, how he feels, how he evaluates his own behaviour, etc., all affect the probability that he will behave again in the same way. In ordinary life quite small changes in the stimulus conditions (is the sun shining?) may lead to variations in future responses.

The **third**, and probably most important, mechanism operates through *higher-level central mediation processes*. This is the 'thinking' and 'imagining' level, where stimuli are sorted out and evaluated according to probable outcomes – rewarding or punishing. Responses may be tested symbolically in imagination and rules may be developed to guide appropriate behaviour in specific situations. It is at this level that people behave in the way we like to think of as most typically human.

People are known to learn new behaviours (including new skills) rapidly by observing the behaviour (and its consequences) of others, in real life or even in films or pictures. This is particularly effective if the learner immediately joins in and tries the new responses for himself and if the 'teacher' explains the principles involved and corrects initial errors in performance. When used in therapy this technique is called *participant modelling*. It can be assumed that the processes described in paragraphs 3.7 and 3.8 are involved in this type of learning.

In this brief and over-simplified sketch we have tried to overview the main principles of human behaviour and learning, according to social learning theory. It is a conceptual scheme in which, according to Bandura (1969), 'man is neither an internally impelled system nor a passive reactor to external stimuli. Rather, psychological functioning involves a reciprocal interaction between behaviour and its controlling environment. The type of behaviour that a person exhibits partly determines his environmental contingencies, which, in turn, influence his behaviour'. The primary goal of behaviour therapy is, then, to develop behaviour to be under the control of the client, and to increase personal freedom by increasing his options among a range of possible behaviours and giving him the skills to manipulate his environment appropriately and so bring about and maintain change. Therapy is not just devoted to tackling an immediate problem. It works to equip the client to tackle any other problems which may come along in the future. We shall now leave theorizing and turn to practice.

4 Behaviour therapy in practice

4.1 A treatment programme always begins with a full behavioural analysis, and the selection of treatment procedures is made in the light of this analysis. One programme may incorporate the use of several different techniques. In Unit 20 we will examine in some detail two complete programmes with reference to two cases reported by Reavley and Gilbert (1976). In what remains of Unit 19, however, we will look at two procedures, isolated from full treatment programmes, to show how the theoretical position outlined above provides a framework for both the planning of treatment and the explanation of results.

4.2 First, however, let us look quickly at some of the procedures we shall be meeting in the discussions to follow. It should surprise no one that most of these procedures have had parallels in everyday practice ever since parents and teachers began. After all, the theory describes the basic processes of human learning, and the vast majority of human children reach adult life with at least a workable set of adaptive behaviours. Compare the two lists below – which are of course only a selection from the range of techniques employed by therapist or by parent.

Therapists	Parents and teachers
Shaping behaviour by selective reinforcement, non-reinforcement and aversive treatment.	Rewarding 'good' behaviour with sweets, treats and attention; ignoring occasional failures and punishing 'bad' or dangerous actions.
Teaching new skills by participant model.	'Showing how', telling how, helping and correcting mistakes.
Modifying inappropriate emotional responses by training in relaxation for anxiety management.	Soothing fears, diverting anger with humour and settling the child to rest when 'over-excited'.
Setting behavioural objectives and using behavioural change as the criterion of 'improvement'.	Well, isn't that what 'Mum' and 'Sir' do all the time?

4.3 **An example of planned positive reinforcement**
One of Jeffery's (1976) cases demonstrates how a simple reinforcement technique was used to shape new behaviour patterns in an abusive family. Note that the example has been isolated from a wider treatment programme. Like most abusing families, this one (father, mother and six-year-old son) presented more than one problem. The parents are described

as 'simple, noisy, likeable people' who interacted highly but excessively negatively with the child.

> Observations showed a circle of negative interactions.
> Parents are angry, child cries and whines, parents are angrier
> still, and it all ends in the child being hit, or sent to bed,
> or reduced to tears. Sometimes he says or does quite friendly
> things, but these are missed by the parents. Occasionally
> they are quiet or warm and positive to him, but rarely . . .
> Nobody likes . . . the desperate stream of anger and abuse . . .
> Baseline observations showed negative (interactions)
> exceeding positive by 3 to 1.

A therapist joined the family for an hour a day for two weeks. Positive friendly behaviours were rewarded immediately with approval and if at the end of the session positive responses had exceeded negative the parents were rewarded with tokens exchangeable for wall posters. To assist generalization to the rest of the day when the therapist was absent the family agreed to the installation of a taperecorder which switched itself on and off without their knowledge. The tapes were analysed and tokens awarded on the same basis. Results are shown in Figure 1. This inter-

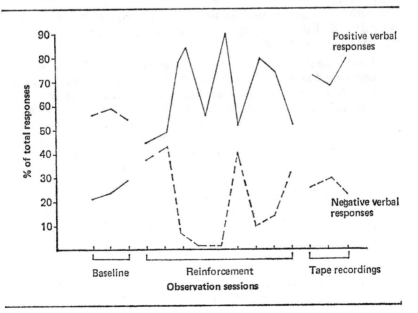

Figure 1
Reinforcement to increase positive verbal responses to a 6 year old boy

vention marked the beginning of change, and further interventions were directed to the relief of other family difficulties. There was no reabuse.

Activity 19.3
Look back at the theoretical discussion in section 3 and make notes on how the principles outlined there are relevant to this procedure.

Comment

4.4 The most relevant paragraphs are: 3.3(b), 3.4, 3.5(b), 3.6, 3.7, 3.8, 3.9 and 3.10.

4.5 **The management of anxiety**
Reavley and Gilbert (1976) trained an abusing mother to reduce anxiety before undertaking certain mothering tasks with her child. The technique illustrates how learned respondent behaviour (anxiety) can be brought under a client's control by procedures which involve all the learning mechanisms discussed in paragraphs 3.5 to 3.10 above.

Activity 19.4
This activity is intended to demonstrate how anxiety can be lowered in every day life. Before carrying out the practical part of the activity (b), it is important to undertake the reading (a).

a. Read Case A in the Reavley and Gilbert paper (Reader, p. 148) to understand how a technique for reducing anxiety was incorporated into the treatment programme. You will see that the mother reported that she was more likely to hit the child when she became anxious and tense. She had therefore taken steps to avoid contact with the child when anxious. The anxiety then had the effect of both endangering and protecting the child, depending upon circumstances. This illustration demonstrates the importance of the full behavioural analysis before starting treatment.

b. Below are the instructions for a simple technique for producing tranquillity and calmness which is based on a standard Yoga exercise and can be learned and used by anyone. Note that it is not the technique taught in the case discussed above, which necessitated the presence of an instructor. Nevertheless, it should not be taught indiscriminately to clients because in such circumstances as those described in (a) it could lead to further abuse. (This principle applies equally to any indiscriminate use of tranquillizing agents, including drugs). However, as you are now possibly feeling a little tense after an evening's hard work on this unit, you can practice it safely on yourself to prepare you for a good night's rest. You will have to learn the instructions before you begin – this exercise must be performed with closed eyes.

Alternate nostril breathing
1. Now (and whenever you feel a need to reduce tension) go alone to a quiet room. Sit in an erect but comfortable position.
2. Close your eyes. Rest the middle finger of your right hand lightly on the bridge of your nose. You are now ready for the first 'round' of the exercise which should be repeated five times. *Control your breathing as well as you can, not allowing the air to rush in and out of your nostrils, and keep your hand relaxed throughout.*
3. *Round 1*
   a. Close right nostril by pressing it lightly with your right thumb and exhale all the air in your lungs. Take eight seconds to do this, counting the seconds silently and rhythmically as you do so.
   b. Now inhale slowly through the same (left) nostril for a *second* count of eight. Try to fill your lungs completely.
   c. Press left nostril with the third finger of your right hand so that both nostrils are closed. Retain the air in your lungs for a *third* rhythmic count of eight. Keep your hand relaxed.
   d. Gently release thumb and exhale completely through right nostril for a *fourth* count of eight.
   e. Without pause and without moving fingers, begin to fill lungs again (this time through right nostril) for a *fifth* count of eight.
   f. Close both nostrils and retain air for the *sixth* count of eight.
4. You have now completed Round 1. Without pause, begin the next round by starting again at 3(a).
5. *Repeat* until you have completed five rounds without a break in your rhythmical counts of eight. The whole exercise (five rounds) should have taken about four minutes. When you have finished lower your hand, which should still be relaxed. Keep your eyes closed and relax completely.

Once you have mastered this technique you can slip away and use it at any time in a busy working day, before or after a stressful job or interview, or at the end of the evening to prepare you for rest.

Comments

6 Goodnight ... sweet dreams ...

Unit 20 The behavioural approach to child abuse (2)

William Reavley, Marie-Therese Gilbert and Vida Carver

1 Introduction

Activity 20.1

Read Reavley and Gilbert (1976) in the Reader, p. 146, in full. Note down any unfamiliar terms as you read and refer back to Unit 19 for clarification if necessary.

1.1 It is our belief, based upon experience at Graylingwell Hospital, Chichester, and upon published accounts of success in a number of apparently intractable cases, that significant improvements in the child-rearing practices of the majority of abusing or potentially abusing families can be made in a relatively short time by well planned programmes of behaviour modification. In the 20 months from September 1974 to April 1976, of twenty-four cases of child abuse or inappropriate child handling referred to the Graylingwell Unit only three were not accepted for treatment. The process is one of ruling out the grossly unsuitable rather than selecting the most suitable. The grounds for rejection were the following.

   a. The abusing parent (father) had a long record of violence and was under a court order restraining access to the child.

   b. Severe alcohol and drug abuse problems were involved.

   c. Blackmail involved: parents separated and the child in care at time of referral. Mother, who frankly disliked the child and all other children, wished to return to her husband but he made her return conditional upon the return of the child as well. Motivation considered inappropriate.

1.2 In all cases where treatment has been completed, marked improvement occurred; some cases are still in progress but there have been no withdrawals from treatment. The hospital is situated in a fairly affluent area and clients from all social classes have been referred for treatment. The length of treatment programmes has varied from three months to one year, with follow-ups at one month, two months, three months and a year. During follow-ups the maintenance of progress is re-assessed or difficulties in maintaining progress are investigated. The number of sessions has varied from 6 to 62, and session length from 1 to 8 hours, with overall therapy time of 15 to 100 hours.

2 The role of the therapist

At Graylingwell, the therapist retains responsibility for the treatment plan at all stages. Planning proceeds in clearly defined steps to be discussed in section 3 of this unit but, within each stage, there is room for considerable flexibility. To be successful, the therapist needs the ability to think on his feet, to take advantage of a chance situation and capitalize upon it. A social worker, health visitor, home-help, spouse, family friend, or even the child himself may at times be enrolled as co-therapist and trained in his or her specific functions. In some situations the parent must be allowed to make some progress very rapidly in order to re-establish some self-control and confidence before the most difficult tasks are tackled. In others progress with caution is necessary.

Reavley and Gilbert (Reader, p. 146) emphasize the importance of establishing an appropriate relationship with the client. The aim of therapy goes beyond the prevention of further abuse. Behaviour therapy is positive, problem-focused and forward-looking, and the parent needs to be enlisted from the beginning as an active collaborator in the further-ance of this aim. Most parents express the wish to succeed. The therapist offers them expert guidance, hope, and a challenge.

The therapist normally works in the family home. Kempe has taught (see, for example, Kempe and Helfer, 1972, Reader, p. 196) that abusing parents very frequently have a need themselves for good mothering. We do not quarrel with this argument, but the objectives of therapy as well as the basis of treatment define the 'client-mothering' role rather differently from Kempe. We have seen that the techniques of behaviour therapy bear resemblances to those employed by the practical, problem-facing parent or teacher. In the client's home the focus of attention is a problem, one common to therapist, parents and children, and working in the home throws up many supplementary problems and day-to-day domestic crises, to be met realistically and incorporated into the treatment as each occurs. This indeed is the environment in which ordinary parents and teachers normally work. The therapist's approach must be open and friendly, but if he is to be fully effective he needs to see himself as an instructor. The client is his pupil, but not a spoonfed pupil, rather a pupil who has to choose whether he or she wants to learn a new bahaviour of not, and if 'yes' has to choose which behaviour it is to be. From the therapist's standpoint this implies that he is not so much 'adopting a role' as doing a job and the relationship he develops with his workmates is a good-humoured, spontaneous but essentially workmanlike one.

2.4 Co-therapists

Again, our position differs from Kempe's on the role of co-therapists. In the Denver scheme, their relationship to the parent is 'characterized by a listening, approving and non-critical point of view. A great deal of dependency is encouraged early and the therapist often shows special affection and concern with a birthday card or small present'. The behaviour therapist seeks helpers who will participate actively in treatment and the qualities he looks for are that they should be intelligent, unflappable, consistent, firm, kind, not shy of being direct, non-judgemental, practical and have a good relationship with the parent. A large part of the treatment programme depends on participant modelling. Although one model is good, it is sometimes difficult for the parent to relate all the time to that model. With two or three modelling co-therapists, each might tackle the same problem slightly differently and this makes the coping situation more flexible, more realistic and more effective. Co-therapists add to the consistency of the programme and promote communication.

Activity 20.2
Consider the discussion above in the light of (a) what you know about social learning theory and (b) Unit 14, section 2, 'The professional dilemma'. Then make notes on the following:

a.　suggest one or two ways in which a well-meaning but uninstructed co-therapist might impede the progress of a treatment;

b.　what kind of instructions might be given to eliminate the risks you have identified?

Comments

2.5 The risks that we think you are most likely to have identified are:

a.　That by over-sympathetic behaviour the untrained person may re-inforce positively dependency responses, self-pitying responses, and some responses to the child (for example, avoidance or excluding responses) which a therapy programme would aim to modify.

b.　Kerr in Unit 14 points out the pressures on the worker in a family in conflict to demonstrate his sympathy by taking 'sides' and so deepening the conflicts by involvement in them.

2.6 These risks (and possibly others you may have identified) could be reduced in behaviour therapy treatment by making the co-therapist fully conversant with all the therapeutic objectives and giving precise instructions on the appropriate responses to each of the client's identified behaviour patterns.

3 Treatment planning

1 Below is the planning schedule used by Reavley and Gilbert in the cases you read about in Activity 20.1. Read this through carefully as it will give you an idea of the systematic approach necessary for successful treatment. In the discussion which follows we will not deal with each item in turn but will focus on certain key procedures, illustrating them by reference to cases treated at Graylingwell.

2 The planning schedule
a. Establish a treatment contract with client.
b. List all problems.
c. Determine priorities.
d. Record concrete examples of selected problem, including targets, antecedents, negative consequences, positive and negative reinforcers, response strength (i.e., frequency, intensity, duration).
e. Formulate short-, mid- and long-term goals, specifying: the desired responses; the antecedents; potential reinforcers; desired response strength (frequency, etc.).
f. Identify resources and barriers to therapy. Build in generalization.
g. Design measurements for use during therapy.
h. Decide upon therapeutic strategies.
i. Clarify contract.
j. Begin therapy.
k. Evaluate effectiveness of therapy (with reference to (e) and (g)).
l. When final stage reached, ensure generalization and maintenance of change.
m. Select next problem and begin at step (d). In practice, this stage is usually moved to before (l) so that several problem areas are being tackled but are at different stages of treatment.
n. If final therapy goal not attained, re-assess the problem.

3 Determining problem priorities for treatment
The criteria usually employed for establishing priorities are that at each stage priority is given to:

a. the problem that is of the most concern to the patient or significant to others (family, friends);

b.   the problem that has extensive negative or aversive consequences for the patient, significant to others or society if it is not handled properly;

c.   the problem that can be handled most quickly considering the resources of the patient and also the resources of the therapist;

d.   the problem that needs to be treated before other problems can be treated.

4 Implementing the plan

4.1 Contracts

The plan begins with a contract which sets down the mid-term targets and long-term aims of therapy and the obligations of each party to the treatment plan. Contracts play an important part in therapy. They can be made with children when appropriate as well as adults. They objectify agreements reached and provide an exact record of objectives. You will notice that the contract is clarified at (i) in the schedule after the details of the treatment programme have been worked out.

4.2 The behavioural analysis is at the heart of the plan. All problems must be identified before priorities can be determined. A referral form is usually the first resource from which information about the parent's presenting problems can be extracted, for example,

a.   frigidity, and disharmony in the client's marriage, and child abuse;

b.   child-handling problems, causally attributed to the client's strong obsessional personality and behaviour.

4.3 Interviews with the parent and direct observation of parental behaviour are the main sources of detailed information. The therapist will need information on the following points.

a.   *The situations in which abuse or handling difficulties have occurred.* For example, Sylvia in Case A identified 'an uncontrollable wish to harm Anna when she cries'.

b.   *What or whom in the person's environment, beside the child, can affect and maintain the parent's behaviour?*

c.   *The contributions of the second parent.* In most of the cases treated at Graylingwell only one parent (almost invariably the mother) had difficulties in relating to the child. But the spouse nearly always contributes to the abusive parent's behaviour, either by taking over the childcare role, or by refusing to recognize that there is a problem, or by continuous, undermining criticism. Often the parents hardly communicate and the mother spends both day and night in effective social isolation.

d.   *The child's contribution, as expressed by the parent.* Was the child
wanted? If not, he may be perceived as 'in the way'. What were her
attitudes to him while pregnant? Is the child the 'right' sex? Whom
does he resemble – the parent, or a spouse or grandparent who has
been a problem in the parent's life? Is he thought to be over-
demanding, or underachieving? Is he physically and mentally 'normal'? Medical referral may be needed. (See also Unit 10).

e.   *Circumstances of the attack.* Obtaining information on this may be
difficult. A parent will emotionally describe her feelings, for example,
of being unwanted or misunderstood, or will angrily shout that the
child annoys her on purpose, but will avoid describing specific
incidents of abuse.

f.   *How the parent copes in difficult situations.* Behaviour might include:
avoidance (leaving childcare to someone else), neglect, drinking,
rushing through mothering tasks, shouting or physical abuse.

g.   *Other relevant factors.* The parent's personality is important. Is she
rational? Forthright? Obsessional? Houseproud? Also, her interests,
if any, and social contacts. Assessing her motivation to change is
essential. Information about circumstances of referral should be
obtained as they throw much light on motivation.

4   The behavioural analysis is the basis for all subsequent steps. Often many
related family problems are revealed, not all of which can be treated at
once, so priorities must be determined. In Case B, for instance, Kathleen's
problems with her daughter were assigned priority over her sexual
difficulties, for which she received treatment later.

5   The selected problem must be closely analysed in concrete terms. In each
of the cases in the Reavley and Gilbert paper in the Reader you will find
a list of target behaviours identified by the parent in consultation with the
therapist as areas of difficulty where change was desirable. These have
been arranged in order of difficulty with the easier tasks first.

Activity 20.3
Read the two lists. Now, for the last behaviour in the Case A list,
identify by referring to the case history:

a.   the immediate antecedent stimulus (pre-treatment) to Sylvia's
maladaptive behaviour.

b.   Sylvia's customary (i) emotional response, and (ii) her alternative
instrumental responses (two).

c.   the reinforcement she received for her instrumental responses
at (b).

Comments

4.6 a. Child cries.
    b. Sylvia responds with
        i. anxiety and tension
        ii. *either* hits *or* avoids the child.
    c. In either case her instrumental behaviour is reinforced by the removal of the crying child by the baby minder or husband.

4.7 Formulating goals

In line with identified priorities short-, mid- and long-term treatment goals are formulated, and here again it is necessary to describe these precisely in behavioural terms. As well as desired responses and their antecedents, the desired response strength should be specified. (Should Sylvia run and catch Anna to her bosom *every* time she whimpers?) The identification of potential reinforcers for the new behaviours, both while they are being learned and for their maintenance and generalization after the completion of therapy to new situations, is particularly important. In Sylvia's case, husband, social worker and baby minder were enlisted as co-therapists. It was necessary that:

a. they should cease to reinforce the undesired responses;
b. they should play an active part in reinforcing the target responses;
c. they should understand their roles in detail after the therapist's withdrawal.

4.8 If you read Case A carefully you will see that many different patterns of reinforcement, positive and negative, were built into the treatment programme. In the earlier stages the therapist retained full responsibility; then the co-therapists took over reinforcement in the therapist's absence; and, finally, as Sylvia became more competent in her handling of the child and began to enjoy their interactions, Anna's responses came to assume reinforcing properties. And throughout treatment Sylvia was trained to reinforce her own adaptive responses, either verbally or by recording on a card the level of pleasure she derived from carrying out specified target tasks. One of the cards used by Sylvia in treatment is reproduced as Table 20.1. You will see that there were 'good' days and less good days in the week of the record but, as the weeks passed and level of enjoyment of all tasks increased, Sylvia was able to monitor her own progress by comparing early results with later – an important step in the restoration of confidence and the building up of self-control to the point where she could not only maintain newly learned behaviours but also formulate general behavioural rules by herself for use in new situations.

Table 20.1 Sylvia and Anna

Tasks	Mon.	Tues.	Wed.	Thur.	Fri.	Sat.	Sun.
Bath	4		10	7	7	7	9
Undress	4		10	7,6	4	5,5	5,5
Dress		8	10	7,6	4	5,5	5
Play		9, 8, 8,	7, 8, 8, 10, 10	6, 6,	8	6,7	8,7, 8,
Feed		9	5, 8	8	6	6	7,7
Cuddle	6	9, 9, 10	9, 9. 10	5	7	8	7,
Comfort when crying			0	1,1	2	1, 1, 2, 1	1,2
Change nappy	4	8	8	3.	2	5	
Potty		8,5	7,6,7	3,4,4	6	5,6	5,8

The numbers represent Sylvia's own estimates of her level of enjoyment while performing each task, on a scale from 0 to 10. Note that at this stage in treatment 'comfort when crying' is still a very difficult task.

5   Treatment

In both the cases we have been studying, complex treatment strategies were adopted to meet complex needs, and a range of techniques were employed. In Case A, nine different types of procedures were employed.

a. Contracting.
b. Anxiety management taught.
c. Progressive introduction to graded problem situations.
d. Prevention of deviant responses (by therapist's presence).
e. Teaching of new skills in adaptive behaviour by participant modelling.
f. Control of own behaviour by self-spoken instructions taught.
g. Withdrawal of therapist supervision and training of husband to take over the role.

h.   Self-control programme taught by participant modelling.
i.   Written self-ratings of satisfaction.

Activity 20.4
The case of Kathleen (Case B in the Reader article) is in some respects similar and in others very different from that of Sylvia. The procedures used in treatment were basically similar.

a.   Identify in behavioural terms the main similarities and differences in the presenting problems (parallel lists will help).
b.   Write down the *common* treatment procedures and make notes on how these were adapted in Kathleen's case to meet her particular problems.
c.   Check your own answers by re-reading.

---

6   Measuring success

6.1   The measurement of success is related to the behavioural analysis and is built into the treatment programme, where target behaviour and precise achievement criteria are specified. Where cue cards are used (as in Table 20.1) there can be continuous monitoring of progress towards a given goal, and minor adjustments in treatment can be made from session to session. Once treatment for a particular problem has begun, attention is focused on the next problem. Problem priorities are decided jointly by client and therapist. As each treatment goal is reached and new behaviours maintained, a new problem is selected for analysis and treatment. If any treatment goal is not attained, the implication is that the problem has been wrongly assessed and a re-assessment is made.

6.2   Follow-ups are important for the evaluation of maintenance and generalization of new behaviours under the client's own control. After both partners are satisfied that the client is meeting the important goals and can generate appropriate solutions to new problems, there will be a period of time (varying according to circumstances) when the therapist will visit at progressively longer intervals to monitor continued success. A rather backhanded reward sometimes arrives for the therapist when the parents tell him politely they'd rather he didn't call again because he reminds them of the bad old days! From that point he must seek validation from social workers, doctors or others still in touch with the family.

7   The children

1   Abused children often present maladaptive behaviour patterns of their own and with older children these may be very well established. Children's problems can usually be incorporated in a home treatment programme. Polakow and Peabody (1975) report an interesting case of a twenty-eight-year-old woman with an extensive history of child abuse and abandonment, placed on probation for holding her seven-year-old son's hand over an open gas flame to stop his incorrigible behaviour which included temper tantrums, stealing and fire-setting. Removal of the child from home and psychiatric treatment for both mother and child had been recommended. Behavioural analysis, however, revealed that Mrs A lacked the discriminatory skill necessary to control her son's behaviour. 'Her inconsistent attention ... functioned as an intermittent reinforcer which maintained the behaviour and in turn provided more occasions for Mrs A to exhibit inappropriate responses. Thus, a vicious circle was established'. The mother expressed a strong desire to be able to control her son without violence. The treatment programme, spread over a year, consisted in training the mother by behavioural methods to act as her son's therapist. Contracts were drawn up between parent and therapist, and parent and son. At the end of the year target behaviours had been achieved and were being maintained. Both clients were controlling their own behaviour successfully, relations had improved and there was no re-abuse. An 18-month follow-up revealed the mother acting as both foster parent and therapist to her fiancé's 'problem' six-year-old, and her own son had been elected president of his class at school!

2   Where, however, parents cannot be treated and a child has to be placed in a new home, there is a case for some instruction of new care-givers in the principles of behaviour therapy. A home which offers entirely new patterns of reinforcement can sometimes of course be spontaneously therapeutic but usually very careful planning, assessment and matching is necessary to achieve this end. If you have time you should now read Koluchova's reports (Reader, p. 204) on a pair of severely deprived and abused twins. No formal behaviour therapy was involved in this case, but you may find it interesting, in the light of Units 19 and 20, to pick out the environmental factors that contributed to the rehabilitation of these children.

Recommended further reading

BANDURA, A. (1970) *Principles of behaviour modification*, London, Holt, Rinehart and Winston.
JEHU, D. (1967) *Learning theory and social work*, London, Routledge and Kegan Paul.

JEHU, D., HARDIKER, P., YELLOLY, M. and SHAW, M. (1972) *Behaviour modification in social work*. London, Wiley.
POTEET, J. A. (1974) *Behaviour modification: a practical guide for teachers*, University of London Press.

Self-assessment questions (Block 5)
Richard Fothergill

1   Patricia Bradley is an unmarried mother with two children, a four-year-old son and a two-year-old daughter. She is behind with the rent of her council flat. The health visitor finds the two-year-old daughter with a suspected fracture of the arm when she makes one of her regular calls on the Bradleys. She accompanies mother and both children to the hospital, and waits with the son while the daughter is examined.

   a.   After talking with the mother, the consultant paediatrician is uncertain whether this is a case of non-accidental injury. What should he do?
   b.   It is decided to obtain a place of safety order. Explain the difference between one provided by a policeman and that obtained through a justice of the peace.
   c.   A full case conference is to be arranged. Who organizes it and what is the ideal time for having it?
   d.   In the intervening period, what should the various workers concerned be doing?
   e.   Who is responsible for secretarial assistance at the conference?
   f.   The investigation reveals that Tom Jenkins is living with Mrs Bradley. Tom is known to the policeman present to have recent convictions for assault. Should this information be given at the conference, and if so, how should it be recorded?
   g.   At the end of the conference, the record of it is prepared. Name the four chief elements that should be in that record.
   h.   The child is released to the mother, but the family will be observed carefully. The rent situation does not improve; the elder son is frequently missing from nursery classes; Tom Jenkins seems to be living permanently at the flat. How do you think the various members of the case conference are monitoring the situation?

2   List 3 advantages of the behavioural approach to therapy.

3   To which behavioural techniques do the following statements by a mother belong? Associate the letters in the first column with the appropriate techniques in the second.

   A.   'Watch me clean my teeth, then do yours the same way.'   a.   shaping behaviour by selective reinforcement.
   B.   'Very good, the way you hold the brush – but you do use a lot of toothpaste.'   b.   Teaching new skills by participant modelling.

234

| C. | 'Practise buttoning that coat by yourself now, to show Granny you can do it perfectly on Sunday.' | c. | Modifying inappropriate emotional responses. |
| D. | To a child who is frightened of a neighbour's cat: 'Sit quiet on my knee and listen how she purrs when I stroke her'. | d. | Setting behavioural objectives. |

Give 2 examples of 'unwanted' learning effects which might result from the intervention of a sympathetic lay helper unversed in behavioural techniques.

a. Before treatment starts, to what questions should a behaviour therapist seek an answer?
b. Having found the answers to these questions, what is the next stage?
c. After treatment has progressed for an appropriate period of time, identify the next 2 stages that should take place.

Answers to self-assessment questions (Block 5)

1 a. Call an emergency case conference (1 mark) with the health visitor.   (1 mark)

Total: 2 marks (ref: Unit 17)

b. The policeman's order lasts eight days, that of the justice of the peace twenty-eight days.   (1 mark)

Total: 1 mark (ref: Unit 17)

c. The social services department. About three weeks after place of safety order has been obtained. This is the time mentioned in Unit 17. However, in serious cases, the time may be very much quicker.   (1 mark for each point)

Total: 2 marks (ref: Unit 17)

d. 1 mark for each of any 3 of the following:

medical attention to the girl; collecting information on the family; helpful concern with Miss Bradley; concern over the elder son.

Total: 3 marks (ref: Unit 17)

e. Social services department.   (1 mark)

Total: 1 mark (ref: Unit 17)

f. Oral evidence of this nature can be given at the conference (1 mark), but written notes are probably unnecessary. If they are made, care should be taken to prevent them passing beyond members of the conference. Note that evidence of 'household disturbance' which does not lead to any conviction, could also be offered by the police at a case conference.   (1 mark)

Total: 2 marks (ref: Unit 17)

g. The decision; name of key worker and others who have duties; names of those dissenting from the decision; timing of a review conference.   (1 mark for each point)

Total: 4 marks (ref: Unit 17)

h. Your answer should contain at least the following points.

The key worker, probably the health visitor or a member of the social services department, is collecting information from the housing department, social services department, nursery teacher

(1 mark), and keeping in close touch with the police (1 mark).
Visits to look at *both* children are taking place (1 mark).

The housing department is concerned with the form of the accommodation arrangements (1 mark). The key worker will be keeping all members of the Conference informed on progress (1 mark), and the new events may encourage an earlier reconvening of the next meeting (1 mark).

Total: 6 marks (ref: Unit 17)

1 mark each for any 3 of the following:

a. worker and client are immediately united in working together for an achievable improvement in the client's conditions;
b. little risk of the relationship between worker and client being marred by dependency or patronage;
c. progress can be measured precisely against the plan;
d. new problems can be discussed as they arise and solutions incorporated;
e. client is always in charge of own situation and will gain satisfaction from each achievement.

Total: 3 marks (ref: Unit 19)

Ab, Ba, Cd, Dc.   (1 mark each)

Total: 4 marks (ref: Unit 19)

a. Dependency responses will be positively reinforced by over-sympathetic behaviour.
b. Taking 'sides' may occur which may deepen any conflict.
   (1 mark each)

Total: 2 marks (ref: Unit 20)

a. 1 mark each for the following questions:

   i. what are the situations in which abuse or handling difficulties have occurred?
   ii. what or whom in the person's environment beside the child, can affect and maintain the parents' behaviour?
   iii. what are the contributions of the second parent?
   iv. what is the child's contribution as expressed by the parent?
   v. what were the circumstances of the attack?
   vi. how does the parent cope in difficult situations?
   vii. what other relevant factors are there?

b. Formulate the goals for the treatment.   (1 mark)
c. i. Evaluate the success of the treatment by noting the goals that have been achieved.
    ii. For all those goals that have not been achieved, re-assess the problem and plan.   (1 mark for each point)

Total: 10 marks (ref: Unit 20)

Maximum marks: 40

Block 6   Longer perspectives

In this last block some of the wider issues raised by the course are explored. Units 21–22 take an overview of treatment, its planning and evaluation, bringing together and developing further a number of themes raised in earlier units. Unit 23 focuses on abused children and reviews recent research on their developmental problems and the effects of professional intervention on their future prospects. Unit 24 raises important questions about how we prepare young people for the difficult and demanding role of parenthood. In the last unit the course team looks back over the course and invites you to assess how well its aims have been fulfilled for you, and looks forward towards possible new developments in preventive and therapeutic practice and research.

Units 21–22 Treating the family
Alfred White Franklin

Units 21–22 comprise a double unit, intended to be undertaken in two study sessions. Their aim is to provide an introduction to treatment needs, treatment planning and methods and the evaluation of the efficacy of treatment. Their introductory nature must be emphasized. No inexperienced student should consider himself in any sense 'qualified' to treat an abusing family without further study and training.

Objectives

When you have finished Units 21–22 you should be able to:

1. identify and distinguish between the crisis and long-term needs of families;
2. describe the 'cycle of abuse' and its implications for treatment;
3. discuss the prognosis for the family and the child;
4. list and discuss some of the main factors which may affect both treatment plan and probable outcome;
5. describe some of the medical problems of treatment planning in the hospital context.
6. outline some of the treatment methods available to the social worker;
7. discuss the contribution that can be made to the treatment of a family by other professional and non-professional workers, lay workers and abusing parents;
8. identify the criteria by which the efficacy of treatment may be assessed.

1 The aims of treatment

1.1 In these units, 'treatment' is used in the narrow sense of the treatment of the abusing family as a family and the treatment of the individuals who compose the family. Attempts at prevention, if any were made, are assumed to have failed and the family has been labelled as vulnerable, or as under grave suspicion for neglecting or abusing the children, or some specific evidence of abuse has been recognized. What is it hoped that treatment will do?

1.2 **Protecting the child**
First comes protection of the child from injury. Both compassion and the law require that a child shall be protected from physical injury as well as

neglect. Because the results of physical injury (battering) are 'obvious' or easily diagnosed and may either be fatal or lead to permanent injury, protection of the child from physical injury has been the priority (see MacKeith, 1975 in the Reader, p. 184).

One result has been that too little attention has sometimes been paid to the evidence of neglect and of emotional deprivation (see Friedman and Morse, 1974 in the Reader, p. 191).

3 **Rehabilitating the family**
The second and longer-term aim has been the so-called *rehabilitation of the family* so that the child can safely be placed once more in the care of those who are acting as mother and father.

4 Another description of the aims of treatment is 'to improve the quality of life for the whole family by giving every member a fresh start and an opportunity for emotional growth and development'. The last applies especially to the abused child. This description forms part of the statement of common agreement formulated by the Ad Hoc Working Group on Child Abuse that met in Bellagio, Italy, in October 1975, under Dr Kempe's chairmanship. We shall return to the work of this group later.

5 No one can dispute the pride of place given in these aims to protection from physical injury with its toll of death, blindness, mental and physical handicap. Nevertheless, fractured bones heal better than damaged personalities. Unfortunately too much emphasis on rehabilitation of the family in the form of restoring the child to the family from which it came has sometimes led to emotional crippling. Abuse may follow in the second generation.

2   Prognosis and treatment for the family

1 A big assumption underlies the validity of the second aim, the rehabilitation of the family. You will notice the words 'acting as mother and father'. These words were used advisedly, The functions of parenthood may be assumed by a woman and a man or a succession of men, and not a married couple. The assumption is that a stable family life is not only possible for but also desired by the individuals concerned. This is not always true.

2 **The 'cycle of abuse'**
For a child, family life should fulfil four basic functions: to ensure growth and physical health, to give the right scope for emotional experience, to

teach by example the art of parenthood and to teach the behaviour needed for satisfactory human relationships. Some adults are unable to provide these necessities and this is especially likely when they have themselves been inadequately parented. This sequence has been called 'the cycle of abuse'. It begins with the grandparents whose failure has made the parents vulnerable and unable to cope with the day-to-day problems and strains of family life so that in their turn the parents fail their own children. For some adults the formation and the maintenance of stable family patterns seem to be beyond reach.

2.3 Not only the management and treatment of child abuse but also its accurate prognosis depends upon a clear and complete recognition of many factors. Among the most important are:

a. the nature of the fundamental problem
b. the parents' willingness to be helped
c. the ability of the professional workers involved to respond appropriately
d. the availability of resources.

3 The nature of the problem

3.1 The whole problem of child abuse would be simplified if families could be categorized into neat pigeon-holes: the psychopaths, those with personality disorders, the immature through age, the inadequate, and so on. The abusing parents often fit into a number of categories and, to make matters worse, many of them are arch-manipulators of other people, are magnificent liars and are able to coax their supporters into a trusting attitude which blinds them to what is really happening before their eyes.

3.2 The *psychopathic parent* who abuses the child is usually regarded as beyond rehabilitation. The expectation is that about ten per cent of the families contain a serious psychopathic member and in these the outlook is hopeless. When such parents have not been recognized earlier, the true state of affairs is usually revealed by an incident or a series of incidents of abuse leading to a crisis. The treatment is of necessity permanent removal of the child once the psychopathic nature of the parent has been established, usually from a psychiatric examination.

3.3 In perhaps another ten per cent of families the outlook cannot be predicted. A trial is justified but many experts suggest that the trial period should not exceed six months. In the remaining eighty per cent of families the risk of fresh physical injury should be negligible given adequate family support. Dr Kempe's group in Denver believes that in about three quarters of the families the non-accidentally injured child should be residing safely at home within one year of the reported injury. For the rest, meaningful therapeutic help may take several months to become established and during that time the child may need to be removed for his own safety.

4 Two jargon words are frequently used in the description of the abusing situation. We speak of '*inadequate*' parents and mean by that parents who are immature either because, although physically able to conceive and bear children, they are not emotionally mature enough to accept the importance of fulfilling the baby's needs when this conflicts with their own. Or they may be of poor mentality with a bad educational record. They may have shown earlier evidence of failure to cope with life by truanting, delinquency, drug-taking and precocious or promiscuous sexual activity. For the child the jargon word is '*scapegoat*'. Often one child in a family seems to attract all the blame and all the punishment. Such a child may have been rejected by the mother from birth.

5 What is by no means certain is the extent to which *parents with personality disorders* can be helped to become good parents. They may be dissuaded successfully from further physical assaults upon their children, but it does not follow that they can be persuaded to 'give the right scope for emotional experience'. The aim of treatment in such cases must be to enable the parents to understand and accept the nature of their problem and to allow themselves to be guided into a new and safer attitude towards family life.

6 **Treating a situation**
Unfortunately, standard guidelines for treatment can never be laid down. It is, in one sense, a situation rather than a person that first needs to be understood. The situation is one where the child is in danger. Although the abusing parents present no standard, easily recognizable pattern, some of the commoner stresses recur. An especially sensitive time is the depression after childbirth when a vulnerable mother may break down. A baby who cries a lot, and crying during the night is the worst or, where feeding is difficult, who vomits and messes with motions, may precipitate a crisis of anger in a mother. Unreal expectations of infant or later childhood behaviour may lie at the root of the trouble. The parents do not understand the normal actions and reactions of their baby and feel that what the child does is aimed against them and that the child is beyond their control. They may, too, be people whose normal method of communication with each other is violence, either by word or deed or by both.

3.7 Full medical, psychological and social assessments are necessary as the basis on which a treatment plan will be formulated by the case conference, which will also nominate the person to take charge of the plan's implementation (see Unit 18).

4 Willingness of parents to accept help

4.1 The success of treatment depends in part on the skill of the professionals, first in making a correct assessment of the family situation and, secondly, in offering help in a way that is acceptable to the parents. A part is also played by the ability of the various professionals to work together as a team. And much depends on the family's ability to gain an insight into the nature of the problem that faces it, as well as on its attitude towards authority in general and in particular the authority which, as the family sees it, is vested in the professional workers. Some families contain many delinquent members and the tradition is to oppose authority. For others the abuse problem may mark the first contact with the professional workers and future reactions and responses may depend upon the character of this first contact. The difficulties that may arise in forming appropriate relations with parents were discussed in Unit 14. Some of them are closely associated with the traditional aims and roles of the workers, as we go on now to discuss.

5 The professional workers and their aims

5.1 Later on in this text and in the reading linked to it, we shall be looking at the varieties of aims and methods required of professional workers who may be involved in the management and treatment of the family. Here we shall consider the professions and what are likely to be their aims. The *doctor* is traditionally most concerned with physical health, the prevention of battering and, when there has been battering, with the relief of symptoms and with the healing of bodily damage. To him, therefore, the key to success is the prevention of rebattering.

5.2 The *social worker's role* is more complex. Because she has statutory responsibilities for the protection of children, her loyalties are divided. She has, of course, to help the family by all means in her power. But she has also to act as a supervisor of the behaviour of the family and as an assessor of the child's progress. The social service departments play a large part in making the decision as to the treatment plans. Inevitably this responsibility biases them against finding fault with the plan when it is put into action. The worker has to act as a friend and also as a critic of the family and at the same time as a servant and a critic of her employing authority. In addition, her personal involvement in the family and her feeling of personal responsibility for the welfare of the child make a cool appraisal of the situation very difficult. For the social worker, the stability of her relationship with the family may be the priority.

3 Neglect and abuse of children bring the parents into the sphere of criminal law. The *police* priority is the prevention and detection of crime and, as the law now stands, the police have the duty to make an enquiry and are empowered to decide whether or not to institute proceedings. The police are also concerned about the wellbeing of the children and the family. Inevitably the two attitudes cannot always be reconciled within the police force and certainly the difference in approach, and in decisions, between police, social workers and doctors is a fruitful source of difficulty. (See also Units 7, 8 and Unit 18). It is fair to add, however, that often now police investigations begin and end at the case conference stage.

4 In the *courts*, fact, opinion and suggested plans are presented. When the prognosis for family rehabilitation is seen to be bad or hopeless, the child can be put into the care of the social service department. Less drastic steps are available when hope is greater. Two fundamental difficulties operate against ideal solutions. It is the outlook for rebattering that dominates the picture. The concepts of emotional deprivation are not yet clear enough for legal argument and interpretation and, furthermore, what is available to the social services as alternative care cannot be guaranteed to fulfil the child's emotional needs. The second difficulty arises because the court, having placed the child in care, has little opportunity to influence or to learn from what happens thereafter. The court's experience of prognosis is limited.

6 Availability of resources

.1 Availability of resources can often be a decisive factor in determining the line of treatment to be adopted. This point is made clear in the following extract from Kempe and Helfer (1972) which presents in a practical way guidelines to the planning of a treatment programme.

> The involvement continuum diagrammed below is based on a 5-point degree-of-involvement scale. These points are very arbitrary and they are not necessarily equal. The '0' level of involvement is defined as no involvement at all. The child is at home and abuse continues. The 1+ level of involvement provides little meaningful intervention. The child is at home

and the social worker, probation officer[1] or nurse visits on occasions and essentially says to the parent, 'Be a good mother and I'll see you next month'.

The 2+ level of involvement is little more as far as the parents are concerned but does provide a rather significant degree of protection for the child. This level assumes that the child is separated from the family on a voluntary basis or by the court. No other meaningful therapeutic intervention is made and the hopes of having the child returned and remain safe upon his arrival are minimal. Separation fails to solve the basic problem and should not be considered as an end in itself unless there truly is no other 'solution'.

The 3+ level of involvement is based on the belief that the home can be made safe (in the large majority of instances) by the early initiation of a practical and feasible community-hospital based treatment programme.

The 4+ level of involvement is probably an unrealistic general goal. Not only is the home made safe and the child returned, but the psychiatric problems of the parents are largely resolved. Although this is not impossible, it is an impractical goal in most situations. There are certainly not enough psychiatrists available to undertake the overwhelming task of establishing a meaningful one-to-one therapeutic relationship with parents who abuse their small children.

0	1+	2+	3+	4+
No involvement; child home	Little meaningful intervention; child home	Child and parents separated	Home made safe; child home	Psychiatric problem resolved; home safe; child home

The worker in the hospital or social agency is often caught up in the trap of not knowing if a particular child has been physically abused, i.e. does the child meet the criteria for 'battering?' All too often, children and their families find themselves without any meaningful treatment programme

---

[1] The functions of the British probation officer differ from those of the USA probation officer described here.

because of the disagreement over whether or not abuse has occurred. The definitive diagnostic study usually is not available, and confessions rarely occur. Our recommendation in this situation is to get off the 'did-it-occur' or 'who-done-it' kick, and get on with helping the child and his troubled family. The implementation of a meaningful therapeutic programme must often occur well before any firm determination of child abuse has been made. We are rapidly moving toward the point when, by early recognition of the potential to abuse small children, a treatment programme can begin even before the child is born – and possibly even before the child is conceived.

Activity 21.1

In any particular case, the level of involvement prescribed should depend primarily upon the assessment made of the needs of all members of the family. To make the correct decision on this basis alone, however, it would be essential to be able to rely upon a wide range of alternative resources (for example, a crisis nursery, psycho-therapeutic services, etc.). Consider carefully the resource implications at each level of involvement and then make lists of the institutions and services which you think would need to be available for a free choice of suitable programme, under the following three headings.

a. Resources for the family.
b. Resources for the children.
c. Resources for the parents.

Comments

2 In para. 1.4 a reference was made to the Ad Hoc Working Group on Child Abuse that met at Bellagio, Italy in 1975. This group produced the following comprehensive list of resources required to meet the aim quoted in para. 1.4. Compare this list with your own to see how closely they agree.

a. *Resources for the family*
   i.   Crisis nursery.
   ii. Residential family treatment.
   iii. Therapeutic day care centre.
   iv. Family therapy.
b. *Resources for the children*
   i.   Paediatric services.
   ii. Lay therapy for children.

   iii. Therapeutic play school.
   iv. Play therapy.
   v. Individual psychotherapy.
   vi. Group psychotherapy.
c. *Resources for the parents*
   i. Crisis 'hot lines'.
   ii. Child-rearing counselling.
   iii. Public health nurse service.
   iv. Lay therapy.
   v. Social casework.
   vi. Individual psychotherapy.
   vii. Marital therapy.
   viii. Group psychotherapy.
   ix. 'Parents anonymous'.

6.3 When comparing the lists (and, if it seems necessary, expanding your own), keep in mind that in the UK (c. iii) would include the health visitor attached to a general practice, and (c. iv) and (v) might be in the hands of one of the NSPCC workers. For (c. vii) both marriage guidance counselling and family planning services could be involved.

7 Treatment

7.1 **A medical perspective.**   The professional worker involved with a given family has a threefold task. The first part concerns the crisis of diagnosis and the decision about ensuring the safety of the child. In the second part, further decisions must be taken about the long-term handling of the family and the actual provision of help. The third part involves the worker in making a cool critical assessment of the success or failure of the methods being used. For the rest of this double unit we shall be examining more closely the second and third parts of the task, largely through the eyes of four writers whose contributions to the discussion are reprinted in the Reader.

Activity 21.2
Before moving on to section 7.2, please read the extract in the Reader (p. 79) from Bentovim (1974), 'Treatment: a medical perspective'.
This paper reviews the problem primarily from the standpoint of the hospital service and contains some important observations on the organization of the hospital team.

Paragraph 7.2 marks the beginning of your second study session.

A social perspective.   Bentovim's paper makes clear the important and often very difficult role that social workers play in the treatment programme for abusive families, and particularly the treatment of the parents. The social worker has a choice of several different approaches and it is useful to review the research which gives some indication of which methods are likely to prove effective in particular cases.

Activity 22.1
Read now the extracts in the Reader (p. 87) from Jones and Jones (1974), 'Treatment: a social perspective'. As you read:

a.   note the name of each project mentioned;
b.   summarize briefly the theoretical basis of the methods employed;
c.   make a note on problems likely to be encountered.

Using which approach would you personally expect to be most effective for which type of case?

Innovative therapeutic approaches.   The social services generally suffer from a chronic shortage of fully trained, experienced professional personnel. This is not the only case, however, for including in the treatment team members of allied professions, non-professional workers, lay helpers and other abusing parents.

Activity 22.2
Read the extracts from Kempe and Helfer (1972), 'Innovative therapeutic approaches' in the Reader, p. 196. Against each type of help scheme described note down the particular contribution each can make. All these schemes have some parallel in the UK. (*Note:* the roles of 'public health nurse' and 'homemaker' in America correspond approximately to those of 'health visitor' and 'home help' in Britain.) What barriers do you see to their extended use in this country? What needs to be done to improve this situation?

8   Evaluating the efficacy of treatment

The evaluation of the efficacy of treatment is easiest when the measure is freedom from further battering. As already indicated, this is of the greatest importance but it is far from the only important measurement. Under ideal circumstances, the child would be given a series of assessment tests at specified periods, the character of which would depend on the child's age. Growth in height and weight are sensitive indices at all ages, as is appropriate behaviour related to age. Intelligence tests and tests of social adjustment are available, but educational progress and school attendance can be useful guides, together with such simple observations as cleanliness, clothing, habitual unpunctuality and attitude to school meals. By making assessment too technical and by listening only to 'experts', many tell-tale evidences that all is not well with the child are missed. Is enough opportunity or encouragement given to teachers to voice their anxieties about the home conditions from which their pupils come? The charts and test reprinted in the Reader (p. 295–309) should be studied by all students. It is not often possible (or desirable) in an informal visit to take detailed accurate measurements of a child but gross deviations can usually be detected by an observant and inventive person aware of normal expectations. You don't have to use a tape measure on a toddler to estimate his height, for example. A 'note' of his height against your own body can be checked after leaving the house. Where there are grounds for real anxiety, of course, a referral for formal assessment is essential.

8.1 Criteria for assessment of the efficacy of treatment

Much of great value is contained in Martin (1976), *The abused child: a multi-disciplinary approach to developmental issues and treatment*. 'This is a book about abused children, it is not a book about child abuse'. What happens to the victim is here the prime consideration, and the literature contains little enough information. This is partly due to the difficulties inherent in making assessments in damaged children. In the context of this Unit, two chapters are of especial importance; that by Martha Rodeheffer and Harold Martin on special problems in developmental assessment (Chapter 10), and that by Martin again on factors influencing the development of the abused child (Chapter 12). The serious student would be well advised to read the whole book.

8.2 Developmental assessment is made in actual practice by interview with parents, casual observation, periodic screening examination and complete detailed evaluation. The inadequacy of the first three is amply and often revealed by the tragedies which occur while the family is under supervision. Even the complete evaluation which requires considerable expertise is beset with difficulty because the reactions of the abused child may be distorted as the result of the bad experiences from which the child has suffered. The bases should be a developmental history; a physical examination, especially neurological, of the child; and a formal developmental test. The parent's account of the history needs as many crosschecks from hospital and social service records as can be made available and both this and the neurological examination have as their main value the interpretation of the developmental test data.

Six forms of behaviour, according to Martin, are likely to prevent the child from performing up to his potential level in the test situations and there are, of course, characteristics which will influence his responses to situations in real life. The six are hypervigilance, fear of failure, difficulty in attending to instructions, verbal inhibition, failure to scan, and passive-aggressiveness and resistance.

Hypervigilance is interpreted as preoccupation with the examiner and what the examiner may be feeling and thinking at the expense of concentration on the task in hand. 'He behaves as if extremely vulnerable and must be in constant readiness for unexpected events'.

Fear of failure reflects the amount of punishment meted out to him by parents because of previous failure to measure up to their standards. It shows itself in the child's unwillingness to tackle difficult problems at all or to keep seeking reassurances from the examiner that he is on the right track. Without such reassurance 'some abused children will change correct answers and become quite disoriented, anxious and uncooperative'.

Difficulty in attending to instructions, especially for the pre-school child, is for some the result of an irresistible impulse to touch and manipulate the test materials without seeming to appreciate the instructions. At the other extreme, the child may be afraid to touch without express permission. Because in the abused child's life parental actions have spoken louder than words, verbal communication is in some way less available.

Verbal inhibition reflects the abused child's difficulty with word finding and organization of thoughts in response to questions. His verbal output may be reduced because he has learned the dangers of talking. Verbalization is an important step in cognitive development and learning this important developmental skill 'requires practice and feedback from others. Such experience is often not part of the abused child's history'.

Failure to scan the alternatives when discrimination between events is called for shows itself in an impulsive selection of the first possible solution without perception of a better one. It reflects the child's method of coping with anxiety.

8.9 Finally passive-aggressiveness and resistance describe the child's subtle, and for the examiner frustrating, obstruction to the examiner's wishes. The child is disagreeing, opposing and refusing the adult, but has learnt that this cannot be done openly with safety.

8.10 Tests need, therefore, to be presented by an examiner who appreciates the viewpoint of the abused child. The scale must be the developmental rather than chronological age, since social and emotional retardation are to be expected. The examiner must make allowance for the child's readiness to feel threatened, his need for encouragement and the need to protect him from any distraction and to reduce to the minimum his sense of failure.

8.11 In interpreting the results of developmental tests, the two important tasks are, first, to enquire whether performance reflects retardation, anxiety, inadequate environmental experiences or sensory deficit. Secondly, the evaluator should be in a position to suggest forms of treatment which could help the growth and development of the child.

8.12 **Learning and intelligence**
For most abused children, the development of intelligence is severely compromised and distorted. Mental retardation may result from injury to the brain of the child. Neurologic handicaps compromise learning. In addition to structural central nervous system damage, the development of various ego functions of the child are also affected by the home environment in which he lives. Learning, competency, exploration, initiative, autonomy are not valued in most abusive homes; indeed, they may be the basis for physical assault by the parents. The fear of failure for most abused children is commented on. A variety of adaptive mechanisms of the child (such as hypervigilance and attention to various sensory input) which may have high survival value are quite handicapping to the child's learning. There is a small subset of abused children who demonstrate superior abilities on intelligence tests. Experience with such children is the basis for several hypothetical explanations for this seeming paradox.

8.13 Intelligence is not just what is measured on intelligence tests. The child who has successfully survived in an abusive home has evidenced intelligence through his adaptive mechanisms, albeit they may be quite handicapping to him in more formal learning. Still, it is important to appreciate the ego's facility to adapt to an abusive home. This ability is not measured on formal tests of intelligence. This ability to adapt may be seen primarily in terms of psychopathology. Nonetheless, it bespeaks a valued ability of the organism to survive and adapt. These adaptive modes most often do require a large price be paid by the child. His learning regarding himself, other people and inanimate objects is severely limited.

The energy of the child is consumed with survival manoeuvres and dealing with his anxiety, fear of assault, loss of parent and loss of love from the parent. There is little energy then available to learn about himself and his world. It is yet to be learned how specific treatment programmes interrupt this process and help the child be more available for learning.

14 Personality of abused children
Martin has set forth five general maxims or conclusions regarding the abused child's personality.

a. The child's personality is affected and shaped by the total environment in which he lives. The specific incidents of physical assault are a psychic trauma.
b. There is no one classical or typical personality profile for abused children.
c. Abused children are chameleons in their adaption to various people and settings.
d. The abusive environment does have impact and influence on the developing child's personality.
e. A most difficult dilemma arises as we try to categorize the effects of the abusive environment on a child's personality. Any particular personality trait can be seen as a symptom, a distortion, a problem, or an adaption of the child to his environment. When we consider the poor self-concept of the abused child, we tend to think of this as a developmental problem. His hypervigilance may be seen as an adaption to a dangerous environment. Opposition or acted-out anger are viewed as symptoms. His object-relations are considered a distortion or a delay in development. And yet this seems not only too simplistic a categorization but also misleading in its implications.

15 These are complex questions, some of which are considered further in Unit 23. Martin's final statement, however, is worth quoting now: 'We truly feel that insofar as it may be possible to understand how the abusive environment affects children's development, one may make a major contribution to understanding the development of all children'.

Recommended further reading

FRIEDMAN, S. B. and MORSE, C. W. (1974), 'Child abuse: a five year follow-up of early case finding in the emergency department', *Pediatrics*, **54**, 4.
MACKEITH, R. (1975) 'Speculations on some possible long-term effects', in White Franklin, A. (ed.) *Concerning child abuse*, Edinburgh, Churchill Livingstone.
MARTIN, H. P. (ed.) (1976) *The abused child: a multi-disciplinary approach to developmental issues and treatment*, Cambridge, Mass., Ballinger.

Unit 23   The predicament of the child
Vida Carver and Carolyn Okell Jones

Objectives

When you have completed this unit you should be able to:

1. describe some of the stresses of life on a child growing up in an abusing environment;
2. suggest explanations for the low level of child-centred research and treatment planning in the field of child abuse in the 1960's and early 1970's;
3. summarize the findings from some important follow-up research studies on abused children and discuss critically their limitations and implications;
4. make suggestions for improving the quality of treatment planning for the child.

1   Introduction

1.1   This unit is a guide to the study of the Reader article by Jones (1977b), 'The predicament of abused children' (Reader, p. 96), which was specially revised for this course from an earlier paper (Jones, 1977a).

1.2   In this course we have looked at the problems of child abuse mainly in the context of family dysfunction. We have tended to follow a well-established tradition in the literature with the parent(s) cast in the leading role as chief protagonist(s) (with problems) and the child as a relatively passive victim (with symptoms).

1.3   The DHSS Circular on non-accidental injury to children (1976a) (discussed in Unit 15) states that 'the safety of the child must in all circumstances be of paramount importance' and offers a blueprint for a national rescue service. In this document the child's role may be compared with that of the cliff-hanging heroine in an old-time movie serial, whose prime function is to be rescued in the nick of time. The authorities have a statutory obligation to try to save the lives of threatened children. They have no obligation in law to ensure that the lives so saved are then rendered worth living, and indeed it would be virtually impossible to formulate a legally enforcible mandate of this kind. This does mean, however, that a moral obligation – and one to which we have in the past all too frequently been blind – devolves upon us all.

In this unit the focus of attention is the child, the whole child and nothing but the child. The intention is not, of course, to deny the needs of the family as a whole, including the parents, but simply to assist us to look clearly and squarely at the child, seeing him less as a life to be saved and more as a person with complex needs of his own and a whole lifetime ahead of him.

The human infant is arguably the most dependent, least self-sufficient of all living creatures. For the satisfaction of all his needs and for protection against all environmental hazards he must for many years rely wholly upon the whims of the self-motivating giants into whose home he chances to be born. If by good luck he happens to please them he is 'good' and they reward him; if he displeases, by relieving himself in the 'wrong' place or signalling loudly that he is hungry at the 'wrong' time, he is 'naughty' and eligible for punishment. Fortunately (since this is the fate of all human infants), he has an inborn propensity to learn.

Provided:

    a. that the standards he is expected to achieve are within his capacity biologically,

    b. that the rewards are consistently related to behaviours that he can distinguish as different from those that bring punishment, and

    c. that the punishments are not so harsh nor so frequent as to damage his learning capacity,

he will quite quickly develop patterns of behaviour that bring him more rewards than punishments.

But what happens if these three conditions are not met? If the criteria for 'badness' include looking exactly like 'that interfering old dragon of a mother-in-law', or being unable (at three months) to cheer up a deeply depressed mother; or still wetting the bed (at six months)? If smiling on demand at one parent evokes jealous anger in the other? Or if punishment takes the form of blows, burns or violent shakings, or by the refusal to satisfy hunger, or the withdrawal of warmth and comfort? Adults cope with an intolerable human situation in one of three ways. They come to terms with it and seek appeasement, or they fight back, or they run away. A baby or toddler, if only because he is less than a quarter the size of his tormentors and has no power to escape, is hopelessly trapped.

It is difficult for an adult to imagine himself back in the position of a baby or toddler, but we suggest that you stop reading for a minute, close your eyes, and try. What courses are open to the child? He can scream for help that never comes, try like an immature adult to meet emotional demands he cannot understand, avenge himself spitefully on the new baby, try to be a baby again to win back attention, or give up and withdraw stupidly into himself. Other solutions may occur to you – but not many. The important thing to remember, however, is that whatever makeshift solution a child may hit upon it is likely to establish a pattern of behaviour that could persist indefinitely – and certainly will unless the environment changes so radically that all these mechanisms become wholly inappropriate and learning to be a person can begin all over again. The rest of this unit is concerned with follow-up studies of children at some time identified as 'abused'.

Activity 23.1
Read now the Introduction to Jones (1976b) in the Reader, p. 96. Pick out and summarize the main reasons offered for the delay in recognizing fully the needs of the child.

Now look back at the analysis of reactions (including your own) to 'contact' with abused children (Unit 2). Make some notes on the part that initial reactions to parent-inflicted injuries may have played in diverting the attention of professional and research workers from the total needs of the child.

Comments

1.9 To most people, first exposure to parent-inflicted injury is a traumatically painful experience (Unit 2). You may have considered that the need to 'escape into action' played some part in (a) the intense preoccupation with the 'technology of saving', (b) priority responding to the dependency demands of the parents, and (c) 'professional theorizing' at the expense of facing up to the actual pain and damage suffered by individual children. Although some change in direction in both thinking and research is now taking place, these escape routes may long continue to tempt workers in the field.

2 Developmental problems of abused children

Activity 23.2
Read now the second section of the Reader article. The following

questions are not 'compulsory' but if you are not used to reading reviews of research findings you may find it an aid to study if you check your comprehension by trying to answer them when you have finished reading. Then check your answers against the text. The relevant passages will be indicated in the 'comments'.

a. The article isolates three factors which may all play an important part in determining an abused child's subsequent development. What are they?
b. List six reasons why it is difficult to evaluate the reliability of the picture that emerges from the research findings.
c. Research findings do concur in finding abused children at high risk for two major types of damage. What are they?
d. List the seven most frequently reported consequences of this damage.
e. Can we yet answer *with certainty* the question: Are handicapped children more likely than others to be abused, or are subsequent deviations more likely to be the effects of the abuse?
f. Neurologic dysfunction is reported frequently in the follow-up studies. List *four* possible causes which may operate singly, or may interact.
g. What is pain dependent behaviour?
h. List the *nine* most common characteristics in the 50 children studied by Martin and Beezley (1976). Suggest against each of these characteristics an example of how it might manifest itself in a school-age child in the classroom.
i. Give three reasons for always paying attention to all siblings of a child identified as abused.

Comments

The answers to the questions will be found in the following paragraphs:
a. 2.1,   b. 2.2, 2.3,   c. 2.4 (first sentence),   d. 2.4,   e. 2.4,   f. 2.5, 2.6,
g. 2.7,   h. 2.7,   i. 2.8.

3 The effects of professional intervention and treatment planning

Section 3 of the Reader article analyses the findings from four important studies which have attempted to relate various patterns of intervention with the prognosis for the child. Look at Activity 23.3 *before you begin to read this section.*

Activity 23.3

Before reading section 3, try to make a few predictions about the ways in which intervention has affected the child's future by answering the following questions. Head a fresh page of your notebook with each question and write your answer immediately below. Then divide the rest of the page into two columns headed respectively 'Evidence for the prediction' and 'Evidence against'. Count as evidence only *reported research findings* and put the author's name and date after each entry as you jot down each item in the appropriate column as you come across it.

Questions
1. Approximately what proportion (as a percentage) of abused children achieve a fully satisfactory adjustment in their own homes, following intervention and treatment planning?
2. What proportion are re-abused (in the technical or legal sense)?
3. What proportion continue to experience emotional abuse, harshness or rejection?
4. What approach to treatment planning carries the highest hope of success *for the child*?
5. What approach to treatment planning seems likely to be least helpful to children?
6. How is length of treatment of a family likely to relate to success in treatment?

When you have finished this activity you will have to make your own summing up by referring back to the article where necessary.

4 Implications for future therapeutic intervention on behalf of abused children

4.1 Section 4 contains proposals for improving the quality of intervention and treatment planning for the child.

Activity 23.4

Read section 4 of the Jones article. As you read, list the recommendations made. Supplement these with any conclusions you have reached either from your study of this course or from direct experience, and then jot down headings for a new set of guidelines on planning for the abused child's future.

Comments

Many people think that the time has come when the government should indeed issue guidelines for long-term treatment planning for the children to supplement those on 'saving'. You will find it helpful to compare your own suggestions with those of Martin (1976). Martin proposes seven questions which should be answered in detail by 'whatever person(s), agency(ies) or team is responsible for the abused child . . . at the time of referral and at every point thereafter when treatment planning is being considered or reviewed'. They are the following.

1. *What is the developmental status of the child?* Under this heading he calls for a detailed assessment covering intelligence and learning; motor skills and coordination; speech and language; socialization; personality, coping styles and interests.
2. *What are the child's reactions to recent events in his life?* Each crisis event to be considered separately.
3. *What other factors in the child's home, besides physical abuse, are deleteriously affecting his growth and development?*
4. *What are the treatment needs of the child?* Headings for consideration include: paediatric care; therapy (speech, physio-, occupational, psychiatric and/or educational); continuation of previous meaningful relationships with relatives, neighbours, peers and teachers; and crisis help for immediate stresses.
5. *What effect will the treatment recommendations for the whole family have on the child?*
6. *Who will be assigned to monitor the child's subsequent course and progress?*
7. *Has the parent-child interaction changed?* Consider parents' (a) attitudes and (b) behaviour towards child; child's reactions to parents.

All these questions, he adds, should also be addressed to all of the abused child's siblings.

Such a programme may sound idealistic in the context of present restricted resources. What it calls for, however, is a concentration of resources on systematic thinking and planning which, if linked to a programme of realistic goal setting, should immeasurably reduce the amount of effort and energy squandered in frequently repeated (and hence negatively effective) crisis intervention which can occur when the child's interests have been inadequately protected. Dr Cooper (in a personal communication) has described a child who was re-fostered ten times in the first twenty months of his life. This well illustrates the point.

4.4 The section also raises important questions about who can and should befriend the child. One finding on which much of the research concurs is his need for continuing stable relationships. A succession of therapists each treating a 'problem' cannot compensate for (indeed, could even aggravate) a lack of such relationships. Yet relationships, professional and lay, outside the home are often fleeting. Even a teacher usually has direct contact with an older child for one year only. Only too often knowledge of the child's background may be kept from her (in the name of 'confidentiality') and she may add to his problems by regarding him as simply troublesome. Alternatively, in one year she can become an effective mother-substitute and behaviour model to a child who has experienced unsatisfactory home relations. If she follows this course, at the end of the year she faces a new conflict: the child may be 'orphaned' into another class. How should a teacher with no training or experience in child-abuse problems resolve such conflicts? There is need for a well publicized alerting and counselling service for people likely to come into regular contact with an older child from an abusing home background.

Further recommended reading

MARTIN, H. P. (ed.) (1976) *The Abused Child: a multi-disciplinary approach to developmental issues and treatment.* Cambridge, Mass., Ballinger.
CLARKE, A. M. and CLARKE, A. D. B. (eds.) (1976) *Early experience: myth and evidence,* London, Open Books.
and in particular
KOLUCHOVA, J. (1972) 'Severe deprivation in twins: a case study', *Journal of Child Psychology and Psychiatry,* **13**, 103–6. Reprinted in Clarke and Clarke (1976). (Extract reprinted in the Reader, p. 212.)

Unit 24　Education and preparation for parenthood
Maurice Chazan

Objectives

When you have finished this unit you should be able to:

1. define what is meant by 'parent education' and give the arguments for and against specific education for parenthood;
2. describe the main skills involved in parenthood;
3. outline and evaluate the variety of approaches which have been adopted in parent education.

1　The nature of parent education

Activity 24.1
Read 'The nature of parent education' from Orville G. Brim, Jr. (1965) in the Reader, p. 32.

Comments

The chapter by Brim which you have been asked to read provides a useful starting-point for a consideration of parent education. It is concerned with developments in the United States of America, where systematic efforts in parent education began over ninety years ago and have continued vigorously ever since. In Britain, parent education has been approached more cautiously (Stern, 1960). Although advice and information are available to parents from a variety of sources, particularly in cases of handicap or other problems relating to family life, parent education does not exist here in a highly organized form, nor is there a widespread demand for it. As Brim says, social changes affecting the family as an institution are forcing parents into greater consciousness of their child-rearing practices, but, even so, attitudes towards education for parenthood are still rather casual in this country. In the past, advice has been sought by parents predominantly over the physical care of children and in times of crisis rather than over wider aspects of the parental role.

However, more interest is now being taken in Britain in developing a systematic approach to parent education, reaching not only adults at the time when they are concerned with their role as parents but adolescents still at school. A growing number of parents would like to share in the knowledge of child development that has been gained over the years through research and practice, and wish to be better informed about current educational methods. Recently, the importance of the home in promoting satisfactory emotional and social adjustment and in encouraging success at school has been increasingly underlined and the parental role, particularly in the early years, is seen by many as crucial in a child's development. Many professional workers concerned with child and family welfare, therefore, consider that parent education can contribute much to the prevention of maladjustment and school failure.

1.3 Parent education is defined by Brim as 'an activity using educational techniques in order to effect change in parent role performance' and, in its narrower sense, by Stern (1960) as 'any educational aid for parents which contributes to the physical and mental care and guidance of children'. The term has been used to cover a large variety of activities, including formal and informal courses, workshops, practical demonstrations, home visiting and group discussions, as well as more impersonal and general approaches through books and the mass media. All aspects of parenthood are encompassed, including preparation for marriage, home management, family life and the development of the child and adolescent. As Brim states, parent education pursues a variety of ends rather than aims at a single goal, but its main purpose is usually to ensure that the child is not only protected from neglect and abuse at home, but is helped to develop his full potential physically, intellectually, socially and emotionally. Although Brim's distinction between parent education and therapy (such as may be involved in casework) is often blurred in practice, it is a useful one to bear in mind, since parent education may, in some respects at least, be seen as wider than the provision of guidance for those parents requiring help in the case of difficulties which they are actually facing. The same agencies may, of course, be involved in both education and therapy.

1.4 Another distinction which Brim makes is between preparation for parenthood ('preparental' education) and educational activities designed for those who are already parents. While it is useful to regard these aspects of parent education as separate to some extent, since different approaches may be necessary at different stages, preparental and parent education are best viewed as part of a continuing process and of an integrated approach, involving many disciplines.

2 The case for parent education

2.1 Although there is now support from many quarters for systematic parent education, strong resistance to specific parent education programmes is still being shown by some professionals and lay-people.

Activity 24.2
Before reading further, note down briefly what you consider to be the reasons for this resistance. How far do you agree with them?

Comments

2 The dissemination of knowledge among parents of the principles and practice of the physical care of children has undoubtedly contributed to the promotion of higher standards of child health. Today the case for parent education is based predominantly on the need for parents to play a full part in providing cognitive and linguistic stimulation for their children as well as giving them a secure foundation for healthy social and emotional development. It is argued that child-rearing is a highly skilled occupation and cannot be successfully undertaken without adequate preparation and knowledge. We have considerable evidence to show that many children, living in unfavourable conditions at home, fail to realize their educational potential or to adjust satisfactorily to the demands of life. Many of the parents who do not provide adequate support or stimulation could be helped to function better in their parental role. Nor is the demand or need for parent education confined only to socially disadvantaged families. Parents enjoying advantageous living conditions are often uncertain about how they should bring up their children and how best to support their efforts at school. Many would welcome expert guidance.

3 In spite of the increasing support from many quarters for a more systematic approach to parent education, resistance to this is still to be met. There are several reasons for this resistance, some of which you may have already listed. First, many people consider that bringing up children is an 'instinctive' function which is best carried out naturally without interference from 'experts': increasing professional instruction may lead parents to become more knowledgeable, perhaps, but less warm and spontaneous in their relationships with their children, and even more anxious and prone to guilt feelings over 'doing the wrong thing'. Secondly, it is argued by some that merely telling or even showing parents what ought to be done does not mean that they will alter their practices effectively. Thirdly, parents may receive conflicting advice from different sources and become confused; or they may misunderstand or distort the

implications of certain viewpoints. They may get the impression, too, through systematic courses in parenthood, that there is one right way of bringing up children.

2.4 None of these arguments, in the writer's opinion, is sufficiently powerful to invalidate the case for parent education. It is important, however, that they should be carefully considered and taken into account in preparing parent education programmes. While there is general agreement about some of the fundamental principles of child development, controversial issues need to be presented as such rather than in an authoritarian way, and theoretical discussions must be firmly related to practice. The personal and emotional involvement of parents is a consideration which should not be overlooked. Now review Activity 24.2 in the light of these comments.

3 The parental role

Activity 24.3
Before reading further, list three major skills involved in being an effective parent.

Comments

3.1 Parent education needs to be based on a deep understanding of the parental role, and of the knowledge, skills and attitudes involved in effective parenthood. Many aspects of the parental role have been discussed in preceding units, but it will be useful to provide an overview at this stage. Cooper (1974, p. 12), in a comprehensive summary, lists the main functions of the family home which:

> offers adequate shelter, space, food, income and the basic amenities which enable the adults to perform their marital, child-rearing and citizenship roles without incurring so much stress that anxiety inhibits a confident and positive performance;

> secures the physical care, safety and healthy development of children either through its own resources or through the competent use of specialized help and services;

> acknowledges its task of socializing children, encouraging their personal development and abilities, guiding their behaviour and interests and informing their attitudes and values;

offers the experience of warm, loving, intimate and consistently dependable relationships;

assures the mother of support and understanding, particularly during the early child-rearing period, and provides the child with a male/father/husband model which continues to remain important through adolescence;

offers children an experience (2–6 years) of group life, so extending their social relationships, their awareness of others and intellectual development;

responds to children's curiosity with affection and reasoned explanations, and respects children through all developmental stages as persons in their own right, so securing affection and respect for others within the family circle and wider social network;

co-operates with school, values educational and learning opportunities, and encourages exploration and a widening of experience;

supports adolescents physically and emotionally while they are achieving relative independence of the family, personal identity, sexual maturity, a work role, relationships within society and the testing out of values and ideologies;

provides a fall-back supportive system for the young marrieds during their child-bearing period.

Most progress in parent education has been made in relation to the *physical care* of children. Mothers during pregnancy and the early years of life are particularly ready to seek and accept advice, and it is not surprising that health visitors and maternity and child health clinics have made a substantial contribution to parent education. This contribution has not been entirely confined to physical aspects of child care, but much less progress has been made in educating parents in other aspects of parenthood.

Many children suffer deprivation because of family poverty, but some are inadequately cared for not so much as a result of low income as because their parents are unable to manage their budgets effectively. There is a need, therefore, for more education in *home management*. Some social agencies give advice on this, and secondary schools are giving increasing attention to the subject, but overall little systematic instruction in home management is as yet available.

Although the part played by early experience in child development is still a controversial issue (Clarke and Clarke, 1976; Pringle, 1974), the evidence suggests that the *cognitive and linguistic stimulation* provided by parents in their one-to-one relationship with the child in early childhood are very important as a basis for development, and difficult to compensate for if lacking. It is true that many parents do provide adequate stimulation without having received any specific instruction on parenthood but, as previously pointed out, a considerable number of children are ill prepared during the early years for later school life. Often this is not only because parents do not know how to provide appropriate experiences for their children but because they are not fully aware of the part that they can play in promoting development. Further, some of the recent research, for example, on language development, has practical implications of relevance to parents as well as teachers (Tough, 1973; Chazan and Cox, 1976).

3.5 Throughout childhood and adolescence, parental attitudes and behaviour influence *emotional and social development*. The high prevalence of emotional maladjustment during the school years, often related to problems at home, suggests that discussions about children's emotional development should be given an important place in parent education programmes.

3.6 Even when the child commences school, parents still have a vital role to play in the educational process. Parental attitudes to, and interest in, education have been found to exercise a profound influence on children's school progress. This needs to be fully recognized by schools and education authorities, who can do much, from the nursery stage onwards, to encourage *home-school co-operation* and to provide parents with relevant knowledge about the school system and educational methods.

4 Approaches to parent education

Activity 24.4
Before reading further, study the table on the opposite page (based on Stern, 1960, pp. 26–7).

Now briefly answer the following questions.

a. Which approaches are likely to be most effective:
   i. impersonal/general *or* personal/specific?
   ii. aimed at future parents *or* for parents now?
b. Is there a need for 'specially created' agencies for parent education?
c. Do you think that any groups of parents particularly need 'education for parenthood'?

You may like to look at your answers again after reading paragraphs 4.1 to 4.5.

Approaches and methods

Parent education may be:

1	*impersonal and general* talk book press radio television cinema	or	*personal and specific* interview correspondence home visits (by specialist home visitor, health visitor, teacher, social worker, etc.) casework toy libraries practical workshops
2	*informative and advisory* book pamphlet lecture letter	or	*evocative ('non-directive')* discussion group interview self-organization of parents
3	*for future parents* parentcraft teaching family life education home management civics moral and religious instruction sex education voluntary courses, etc., by youth and religious organizations visits to nursery/infant schools, etc.	or	*for parents now* maternity and child health courses schools for parents schools for mothers family clubs family associations parents' circles and discussion groups parents' associations/parent/teacher associations participation in preschool playgroups
4	*direct* i.e., all forms of parent education mentioned under 1—3	or	*indirect* through training of persons in contact with parents (in particular, teachers, social workers, doctors, nurses and psychologists)
5	*provided through specially created agencies* parent education service schools for mothers schools for parents	or	*provided by existing agencies* schools medical services churches social and psychological services industrial and voluntary organizations
6	*concerned with all aspects of parenthood*	or	*limited to certain aspects* physical care psychological development of the child psychological aspects of parenthood social, moral or religious questions school questions

267

Comments

4.1 The table in the activity gives a comprehensive picture of the different approaches and methods used in parent education. We do not know to what extent any particular approach is better than any other and a broadly based programme of education for parenthood, using a variety of techniques, is desirable. The mass media have already made a valuable contribution: newspapers and magazines publish many useful articles on bringing up children, and in recent years both radio and television have been responsible for imaginative programmes for parents. However, research on attitude change suggests that approaches stressing personal and active participation are likely to be more effective than impersonal and general approaches. Auerbach (1968) advocates personal involvement in small groups, and her book gives detailed guidance on the use of group techniques and skills in parent education, emphasizing that the leader of groups of parents needs to be highly trained in these skills. In Britain as well as in the USA home-visiting programmes have been designed, in particular, to help parents of disadvantaged or handicapped children to take a more active part in promoting satisfactory development. For example, a home-visiting project was undertaken in the West Riding of Yorkshire as part of the national Educational Priority Areas Project in the early 70s (Armstrong, 1975). The homes of 25 children aged between 18 months and 2 years were visited once every week for a year by the same person, an important aim of the visits being, apart from directly stimulating the children's play, to encourage the mothers to examine their own role and to demonstrate their skills and abilities. Not only did the children make significant progress in their intellectual, linguistic and social development, but the mothers, who at first had not seen themselves as playing a vital role in their children's intellectual development, became very involved and wanted to find out more about the learning process and how they could help. Fathers, too, showed interest and often asked for visits to be arranged at a time when they could take part in the play sessions. Donachy (1976) reports similar results from an investigation of the effects of a four-month programme focusing on the involvement of a sample of parents of children aged three or four years in Renfrewshire. The mothers attended weekly group meetings, when they were given practical advice on the selection and use of play materials and on language stimulation. A significant feature of the project was that the meetings were organized through local primary or nursery schools, thus encouraging home-school co-operation from the outset. It was found that the discussion at group meetings often ranged over wider aspects of education and child rearing, and the mothers appeared to be sufficiently reinforced by the meetings to persist in the programme.

The Open University, too, has recently entered the field of direct parent education with two short, eight-week courses to be presented for the first time in the autumn of 1977 and then twice yearly until 1981. *The first years of life*, made with the help of the Health Education Council, covers the period from pregnancy to the child's second birthday, and *The pre-school child*, made with the Pre-School Playgroup Association, deals with the child from two to five years. Both courses deal with the child's physical, cognitive and emotional development, and the correspondence material consists of lively, highly illustrated booklets which teach largely through planned activities to be carried out with the child. There is a resource pack including record cards, leaflets, posters, etc., and backing from radio and television programmes and a link system to put students in touch with one another. Each course is expected to reach some 6,000 families a year and a further course on parenting five- to ten-year-olds is projected. It is too early to evaluate success but results are being closely monitored.

The timing of parent education has been the subject of much discussion. Parents are likely to be most highly motivated to participate in parent-education activities when they are facing the daily realities of bringing up children, but, as previously stressed, much can be done with adolescents at the secondary school stage, who are normally interested in young children and are beginning to think about their own future role as parents. Many schools are devising challenging courses on preparation for the responsibilities of family life: theoretical instruction and simulation of real-life experiences are in some cases supported by regular visits to help in nursery schools or other institutions dealing with children (see Department of Health and Social Security, 1974b, pp. 46–57). School pupils usually enjoy these courses and find them of considerable relevance.

Given adequate resources, our well established but hard pressed health, education, social and psychological services could contribute a great deal more than they have done already to developing parent education. Some local authorities have, in the past few years, appointed educational visitors or encouraged schemes of preparation for parenthood, but most of the programmes hitherto undertaken in this country have been a part of the work of voluntary organizations (for example, the Pre-School Playgroups Association and the various parent groups concerned with handicapped children), or else of a short-term nature, often set up by an ad hoc research project such as those described in paragraph 4.1. This work has been very valuable, but we need a more coherent policy toward parent education, with greater professional involvement and specialized training for those assuming leadership in this field.

If opportunities for parent education were more widely available, there would be less need to consider the question of priorities and the problems involved in giving special attention ('positive discrimination') to some parents rather than others. In present circumstances, while we await a general expansion of parent education, a case can be made out for devising programmes aimed predominantly at parents of children who are educationally 'at risk' from their early years, whether because of social disadvantage, physical or mental handicap or emotional disturbance. The dangers of stigmatizing parents selected to participate in a programme of parent education are real enough, even if the parents readily agree to being involved. However, the lessons learnt from work with parents of children 'at risk' should prove valuable if parent education is extended.

Self-assessment questions (Block 6, Units 21–24)
Richard Fothergill

Ben Willis is the seven-year-old son of Miriam and Jack Willis. He has a sister, Janice, aged five. Miriam, who was herself abused by her own parents, has neglected Ben and battered him by shaking and striking his head on numerous occasions over the past three years. Her husband Jack is on shift work and sees little of his children, and Miriam works part-time in a local shop. Her home life revolves around Janice, and she describes Ben as a constant irritant and interference to her normal life.

1 What phenomenon is described by Miriam's and her parents' approach to their children?

2 Cooper (1974) lists ten functions of the family home. Which of these are not happening as far as Ben is concerned?

3 Many factors may affect the treatment plan. State 4 important ones.

4 The effects on Ben are only just coming to light. Name 4 kinds of measurement that may be made to monitor his progress and the attempts at therapy that are started.

5 Martin (1967) is quoted as giving 6 behavioural characteristics which could prevent Ben from performing up to his potential level in such measurement situations. Name the 4 most likely to be apparent in Ben's case.

6 There are two aspects to giving help to the Willises; protecting Ben and rehabilitating the family.

    a.   Describe 2 approaches to coping with the protection of Ben.

    b.   To rehabilitate the family, it may be necessary to introduce Jack and Miriam to parent education. Describe briefly the approaches to this that are most suitable for them.

7 From the brief description of the abuse to Ben, state 6 likely types of damage (other than fractures and bruises) which may be evident from testing.

8 Concern must be expressed over Janice. Describe 2 factors which you would be looking for in observing her.

After treatment, it is proposed to return Ben to his home. H. P. Martin has suggested some questions that should be asked before such action takes place. Such questions, he states, should also be asked concerning Janice. List these questions.

Answers to self-assessment questions (Block 6)

1 Cycle of abuse. (1 mark)

Total: 1 mark (ref: Unit 21)

2 Offers adequate space and amenities; secures physical care and development of children; task of socializing children; offers consistently dependable relationships; assures mother of support and understanding; offers children experience of group life; responds to children's curiosity with affection and respects children through their development. (1 mark for each)

Total: 6 marks (ref: Unit 24)

3 Nature of the fundamental problem; parents' willingness to be helped; abilities of professional workers to respond; availability of resources. (1 mark for each)

Total: 4 marks (ref: Unit 21)

4 1 mark for each of any 4 of the following:

growth in height and weight; appropriate behaviour for age; intelligence tests; social adjustment tests; educational progress; school attendance; personal appearance at school.

Total: 4 marks (ref: Unit 22)

5 We think the 4 most likely are:

hypervigilance; fear of failure; verbal inhibition; passive-aggressiveness and resistance. (1 mark for each)

Total: 4 marks (ref: Unit 22)

6 a. 1 mark each for any 2 points from the following list:

place of safety order; court order (care order or supervision order); medical care; individual psychotherapy.

Total: 2 marks (ref: Unit 21)

b. Your answer should include the following 4 points. (1 mark for each)

Personal and active participation is favoured; regular visits to the home setting; group sessions are likely to prove useful; timing should be arranged so that both parents are present together.

Total: 4 marks (ref: Unit 24)

1 mark each for any 6 of the following:

impaired capacity to enjoy life; psychiatric problems; low self-esteem; school learning problems; withdrawal; opposition; pseudo-mature behaviour; hypervigilance; general neurologic dysfunction; growth failure.

Total: 6 marks (ref: Unit 23)

Research indicates that siblings are:

Likely to be abused also; often as deviant in behaviour as the abused child.   (1 mark for each point)

Total: 2 marks (ref: Unit 23)

a. What is the developmental state of the child?
b. What are the child's reactions to recent events in his life?
c. What other factors in the child's home have deleteriously affected his growth and development?
d. What are the treatment needs of the child?
e. What effect will the treatments being undertaken by the family have on the child?
f. Who will be assigned to monitor the child's subsequent course and progress?
g. Has the parent-child interaction changed?   (1 mark for each)

Total: 7 marks (ref: Unit 23)

It is worth noting that Miriam should have undergone treatment. The repeated abuse of Ben indicates a serious situation. If Miriam proved unwilling to accept voluntary treatment, it may be necessary to enforce it through an order from a criminal court.

Maximum marks: 40

Unit 25 Looking backward and looking forward
Bill Roberts and the course team

Objectives

During the course of this unit you will be able to:

1. assess your achievement of the course aims by reviewing your own progress;
2. revise the main themes which run through the course;
3. prepare yourself for assimilating new information and arguments which will occur after you have completed this course.

1 Introduction

1.1 Most of us at the end of a course, whether it is two years full-time, six weekly night school sessions, or anything in between, tend to be more conscious of how much there is to be learned (and, perhaps, how many opportunities we never quite used) than of how much we have mastered. The course team wishes to correct that tendency, and, in finishing with a review, intends that you will demonstrate to yourself that you have a sound grasp of what is relevant and useful to you in the preceding twenty-four units, and that you can use this for future learning and practice. The structure of this unit is simple, a section being devoted to each objective in the order written above.

2 Assessing the achievement of aims

Activity 25.1
Turn back to the aims of the course, immediately preceding Unit 1. Place a bookmark in the page so that you can refer to the aims whilst carrying out this activity. Below you will find a short exercise for each of the aims. Take plenty of time, and write your comments from what you can remember, without referring to your notes or the text. Before beginning each exercise, read the aim to which it refers.

a. *Aim 1*   Make a list of types of child abuse, distinguishing between non-accidental injury and deprivation.

b. *Aim 2*   Note three characteristic attitudes of parents (towards self or child) associated with child abuse. Write brief notes on the total predicament of the abused child.

c. *Aim 3*   Note the positive features and functions of the three groups of professionals least known to you when you began this course. Note three goals of intervention which you would set out to achieve when working, directly or indirectly, with an abusing parent.

d. *Aim 4*   Make notes to distinguish between a 'low risk', 'high risk', and 'emergency' situation. What action would you take, in your locality, in each of the above situations?

e. *Aim 5*   Describe the symptoms of minor injuries which are possible indicators of physical abuse. What are the most significant indicators of deprivation? Below are three pairs of management activities. Make brief notes comparing the purpose and effectiveness of the activities in each pair (A i. compared with A ii. and so on).

A. i. 'Preventive' visiting
   ii. Providing a lifeline

B. i. Care order
   ii. Registering the family as 'at risk'

C. i. Intensive visiting to give support
   ii. Contract work with planned goals.

f. *Aim 6*   Given six one hour sessions to teach preparation for parenthood in a youth club, what would you consider as essential to include in your curriculum. (Be realistic about what you can do in six hours.)

When you have completed the exercises, check your answers against the text, your answers to self-assessment questions, and your notes. To help you to do this, following are the main unit references relevant to the exercises above:

a. Units   1, 5, 6
b. Units   4, 6, 9, 10, 11, 23
c. Units   7, 8, 19, 20, 21, 22
d. Units   7, 8, 15, 16, 17, 18
e. Units   4, 5, 6, 19, 20, 21, 22
f. Units   24.

Comments

2.1 Unless you are unusually confident in your own abilities, you have probably found that you know more than you thought you did, and can assess to what extent you have achieved the course aims. Remember, however, that this sort of exercise tests recall, which is not all that there is to 'knowing'. If you have kicked yourself for turning up something in your notes which you knew all the time, but forgot when doing the exercises, give yourself the benefit of the doubt. If you are dissatisfied with your achievement of any of the aims, you can go back over the relevant part of the course, or do some further reading afterwards. There is recommended further reading at the end of most units, and in the reader.

3 Revision

3.1 This section is the third element of that advice to teachers which runs, 'Say what you are going to say; then say it; then say what you have said'. In reminding you of what has been said, we have adopted a different framework from that within which the content has been presented in the course. Deliberately so, for in using different links between units of information you will be provided with more 'hooks' to hang it from. This section, then, is concerned with a very brief review of the course under four headings: *prediction, prevention, diagnosis,* and *management*.

3.2 Prediction

Prediction is the active outcome of understanding behaviour. If we know that A always causes B (i.e., we undersatnd why B occurs), then we also know that when A exists, B will follow (i.e., we predict B from the existence of A). This statement, 'A always causes B', will be referred to again later. Prediction is the activity upon which the other three activities depend – even diagnosis, when what we are diagnosing are predisposing or precipitating factors. The course units concerned with parenting, the family, and predisposing factors (Units 4, 9, 10 and 11 respectively) all have something to say about prediction in their different ways. Although, for example, Cooper discusses abnormal parental behaviour descriptively, the information can be used, with caution, as predictive of a child-abuse situation. In Unit 9 Peckham discusses the family in predictive terms, and Lynch and Roberts are much more specific about past as well as current events in the lives of the adults as predictors (Units 10 and 11).

3.3 Although the difficulties of prediction, and the research which underpins it, have been discussed in the text, it is worth repeating that since prediction comes from understanding, and understanding can come only after the behaviour has occurred, then the whole process is retrospective and selective. For example, we do not know how many families having all the

278

characteristics described in the units mentioned have reared their children adequately. Nor do we know whether there are numbers of undetected abused children where the causes or associated factors might be quite different. The NSPCC, for example, has been conducting research, still unpublished at the time of going to press, into the incidence of abuse of older children – hitherto under-researched – and the associated factors.

Prevention

Prevention has been dealt with in a number of units of the text, but Lee's examination of official inquiries (Unit 12) and Chazan's consideration of the desirability and practicability of education for parenthood (Unit 24) are what one may term 'long-range' prevention. 'Short-range' prevention should be one of the effects of obtaining good information, as described by Stevenson (Unit 16), and of working towards achieving realistic goals in the way suggested by Carver *et al.* (Units 19 and 20). It should be obvious, too, that much of the content of the units which is noted below under *Management* is clearly concerned with prevention in the sense of minimizing the effects of what has already occurred. In terms of the 'A always causes B' statement, this form of prevention is concerned with ensuring that, if 'A' exists, 'B' will not follow. The major intention of many official inquiries, for example, is to ensure that in general, and in future, 'B' can be prevented from following 'A'. Chazan's thesis, on the other hand, is that 'A' need never exist in the first place.

5 If you are now observing that the four point review framework is coming apart at the seams, this is all to the good. Any learning that is not purely an academic exercise (and some that is), especially in the field of human behaviour, usually refuses to be confined to watertight compartments. Compartments are useful only for presenting and assimilating blocks of information. But understanding and using it is an integrative and eclectic activity.

6 Government guidelines (dealt with in Unit 15) are clearly preventive in intent, since they seek to establish systems which encourage co-operation and the flow of information between co-workers so that identification of risk situations occurs earlier.

7 The earlier and the more long-range preventive action is, the more difficult it is to monitor its effects. If a potential child abuse situation is identified, services are provided, and abuse does not occur, there is no means of knowing whether the child would have been well treated without intervention. The effects of long-range prevention are susceptible to monitoring in general terms, but only over a long period. If education and preparation for parenthood proved effective, for example, it might take a generation

to be sure. We shall have something more to add on prevention at the end of this unit.

3.8 Diagnosis

Three aspects of diagnosis were studied early in the course. Cooper, in comparing normal and abnormal parental behaviour (Unit 4) offers aid in diagnosing the possible 'abusive environment', and continues (Unit 5) by describing the typical signs and symptoms of physical abuse and deprivation. Of particular importance here are the minor and apparently insignificant injuries which can be diagnostic of abuse. Kolvin (Unit 6) draws attention to the emotional and social development of the child, the abnormal interrelationships which are found in the abusive environment, and the typical effects these can have on the child. The emphasis on diagnosis has been to provide the knowledge to enable people to recognize the symptoms of early and minor abuse.

3.9 Management

The contributors to this course intended that it should be of practical benefit. It will come as no surprise, then, to discover that twelve units are concerned, in part or in whole, with management. The following overview is offered as an alternative means of making sense of this mass of information from that which was adopted when presenting it during the course.

3.10 Jobling reminds us that child abuse is nothing new and invites us to consider it as a social phenomenon, providing a cultural and historical context (Unit 3). In contrast to the 'sympathetic horror' response (noted as a common attitude in Unit 2), Jones and Carver (Unit 23) are concerned with the whole child, its predicament and its future, and focus attention on development rather than rescue. White Franklin (Units 21 and 22) is similarly concerned with long-term and whole development in examining the goals and effects of treatment. Having the whole child firmly in mind (and for a child to be 'whole' we must think of him in the context of a 'whole' family), it is useful to consider next what the law requires and allows. Cavenagh not only explains the law's provisions, but discusses the conflicts of interests which can arise in legal proceedings, and gives practical help on such matters as the presentation of evidence (Unit 13). Similarly, Lee and Roberts (Units 7 and 8) discuss misunderstandings between professionals, in addition to providing a basic description of who does what. The ways in which professionals and others involved in managing child abuse can pool their expertise and co-operate to provide an effective service are considered by Desborough, who explains and discusses how government attempts to influence and guide practice (Unit 15). Also, both Stevenson (Unit 16) and Hall (Units 17–18), use the case conference as the context for describing good communication and co-operation. Finally, at the 'sharp end', Kerr takes us through the typical reactions of parents and professionals to the crisis of becoming aware of child abuse (Unit 14), and Carver, Reavley and Gilbert (Units 19 and 20) make the case for operational and realizable objectives, and goal-orientated methods, in treatment.

11 This review has been concerned to remind you of what you already know. If you have been nodding in agreement, finding yourself saying 'of course', or 'not again', then all is well. If, on the other hand, you have found that you are unsure of anything, do refresh your memory from the text or your notes before continuing.

4 Preparation for new information

In this section you will be given some information not previously discussed, and invited to consider what effect this has on your present understanding.

1 Consideration is being given to mounting an action research project which would use, for prevention, what is already known about family circumstances and factors which are associated with the risk of non-accidental injury. (You are familiar with some of these from your reading of Units 10 and 11.) Such a project would seek to identify, at antenatal clinics, families possessing 'risk factors', who would be given extra care and services before, during, and after the birth of the baby. Monitoring of the actual incidence of non-accidental injury, compared with the incidence prior to the project and in control groups, would establish whether or not screening and extra services had had any preventive effect.

Activity 25.2
Imagine that in six months from now the results of the project described above are published. Imagine further that the results are generally accepted as showing that non-accidental injury to children has been dramatically reduced by providing services to families identified as potentially at risk by detailed enquiry at antenatal clinics.

Write some notes on how this information might affect your understanding of the whole question of child abuse; and on whether, and how, you think the emphasis on *dealing* with this problem should change.

Comments

4.2 It is not possible to make any specific comment about your notes on the first half of this activity since your present understanding is not known to the writers. In general, however, some people will find that the aspects they understand best become of less value in the light of this new information, and that this is irritating. Others may find that their professional expertise or function is more, or less, important. Might this make a difference to how acceptable this new information is?

On the question of changing emphasis, you might have included any or all of the following.

a. The major part of effort and resources should be directed towards setting up screening and services at antenatal clinics.
b. The key workers in preventing child abuse would now be midwives, health visitors and obstetricians.
c. Research should concentrate on identifying further causative and precipitative factors so that screening can become even more effective.
d. To enable c. to be carried out, child abuse should be made a 'notifiable disease'. In this way, every known case would be subject to systematic analysis.
e. Much of the present emphasis on case conferences, special units, should be shifted to meeting the same ends at an earlier stage – the six months before and after birth, for example.

NB The 'findings' used in this activity are hypothetical.

4.3 Other developments which have taken place in the last two years are the increasing provision of twenty-four hour 'lifelines', an increasing number of self referrals by abusing or potentially abusing parents, and 'self help' groups, the most recent of which, 'Parents Anonymous', has been formed in the London area in July, 1977. The Select Committee's First Report on Violence to Children (House of Commons, 1977) includes amongst its recommendations the following: '51. In planning for the future, D.H.S.S. should regard the imposition of a statutory duty on local authorities to provide a 24 hour stand-by service as a priority.' The Select Committee (1977) has a further recommendation to make about procedures in managing registers of children at risk. It is that, 'Parents should normally be informed when notification is made to the register. The responsibility for informing parents should rest with the agency making the notification.' (Part of recommendation 31).

Activity 25.3
Consider the information given in paragraph 4.3 above. Make some brief notes in answer to the following.

a. What sort of attitude to abusing or potentially abusing parents does this information imply?

b. What are the implications of this attitude in working with abusing or potentially abusing parents?

Comments

a. Those who advocate and/or provide a twenty-four hour stand-by service must envisage that people will use it. This implies that a significant number of abusing or potentially abusing parents are considered to have the insight to be aware that they are in difficulties, and to have the sense of responsibility and autonomy to avail themselves of a service if it is provided. It also implies that child abuse is 'normal' enough to require a national emergency service. Thus, like the police, fire, and ambulance services, although we hope we shall never have to use them, we are aware that if we did there would not be anything grossly abnormal in our predicament. The attitude that these parents are, for the most part, responsible, autonomous, and normal, is further confirmed by the suggestion that a worker who registers a child as 'at risk' should tell the parent what is being done.

b. In Activity 14.2 in Unit 14 you were asked to imagine your reactions to being suspected of child abuse. For those parents whose reactions include fear, anger, hostility and the like, the attitude commented on above may have some effect in creating more positive reactions. For the worker, then, intervention would be more likely to be constructive at an earlier stage; obstacles to useful initial intervention would be likely to be smaller and more easily overcome. On the other hand, some workers in all professions might find the different approach so unfamiliar as to be very difficult. *Some* police officers, trained to investigate for the purpose of discovering a crime which the criminal is at pains to hide, would need to find ways of questioning with a view to offering help. *Some* doctors, used to patients treating them with reverence, would need to help patients to retain some respect whilst admitting to their doctor that they had abused their child. *Some* social workers, used to thinking of casework as a mystique, would need to promote an open relationship within which the worker's assessment could be discussed frankly.

5 **Summary**
If you have found yourself struggling a little in the activities in this section, you have been prepared, to some extent, for some of the effects that new knowledge can have on us. It can happen that the more knowledge we have (and the more experience), the more is our vested interest in not

having either challenged by something new. However, if you have followed this course with satisfaction so far, you will already have recognized that to be truly knowledgeable and experienced is to have the ability to process and use new information positively, neither dismissing it out of hand, nor jumping on the latest 'bandwagon'.

5 Looking forward

At the beginning we quoted White Franklin from 'The nature of the task' thus: 'We have to begin somewhere . . . the obvious place of departure is medical'. In concluding this unit, and the course, we return to medicine, but to the delivery room rather than the casualty department.

Activity 25.4

In the Reader, p. 4, read the article, 'Parent-infant bonding', (Kennell *et al.*, 1976) from the section headed 'Early post partum period – maternal-sensitive period' to the end of the article. The investigations discussed are concerned with understanding how the mother becomes attached to her infant. (The note 'p < .05' on the figure in this article means that there is less than 1 chance in 20 that the results are accidental or coincidental.)

5.1 Comments

The article was chosen for the conclusion of the course because it shows how something positive could be done in the way of fundamental prevention of child abuse. The authors claim that, 'When the bonds are solidly established, parents are motivated to learn about their baby's individual requirements and to adapt to meet his needs; . . . Fully developed specific ties keep parents from striking their baby who has cried for hours night after night – even when they are exhausted and alone'.

5.2 It is also heartening to know that the results of research in this field are being heeded. The Select Committee (1977) referred to earlier has placed a good deal of emphasis on preventive work, and the theme which runs through its proposals in this area is the reduction of stress. On the matter of parent-infant bonding, it has this to say in Recommendation 37. 'D.H.S.S. should pay more attention to the remarkably consistent evidence of "early bonding" between mothers and their children immediately after birth, and the need to ensure that the whole birth experience is handled in hospitals with greater sympathy and sensitivity than has been the case in the past'. In the body of the report, at paragraph 126, they comment that 'We do not share their (D.H.S.S.) view that "research in this whole field is, at present, at too early a stage to give reliable guidance for action". We are pleased, however, to note that "the importance of identifying the child who is or may be injured, and of preventing handicap of both physical and emotional origin will be stressed in a consultative paper on Services Relating to Pregnancy and Childbirth to be issued by the Department" in 1977'. By the time you are reading this, the next step in reducing child abuse through prevention should have been taken.

References

Extracts from those entries marked * are reprinted in the Reader (see under LEE, C. M. *for full reference).*

APPLETON, P. L. (1976) 'Ethological methods studying the behaviour and development of young children from abusing families', in Martin, P. H. (ed.) *The abused child*, Cambridge, Mass., Ballinger.

*AN ANONYMOUS BATTERING PARENT (1976) 'Consumer's viewpoint', *Social Work Today*, **7**, 3.

ARIES, P. (1973) *Centuries of childhood*, Harmondsworth, Penguin.

ARMSTRONG, G. (1975) 'An experiment in early learning', *Concern* (National Children's Bureau), **18**, 20.

AUERBACH, A. B. (1968) *Parents learn through discussion: principles and practices of parent group education*, New York, Wiley.

*BAHER, E., HYMAN, C., JONES, C., JONES, R., KERR, A. and MITCHELL, R. (eds.) (1976) *At risk: an account of the work of the Battered Child Research Department*, London, NSPCC.

BAKAN, D. (1971) *Slaughter of the innocents*, San Francisco, Jossey-Bass.

BALDWIN, J. A. and OLIVER, J. E. (1975) 'Epidemiology and family characteristics of severely abused children', *British Journal of Preventive and Social Medicine*, **29**, (4), 205–21.

BANDURA, A. (1970) *Principles of behaviour modification*, London, Holt, Rinehart and Winston.

*BENTOVIM, A. (1974) 'Treatment: a medical perspective', in Carter, J. (ed.) *The maltreated child*, Priory Press.

BERRY, J. *et al.* (1975) 'Reflections on the Auckland Inquiry', *Social Work Today*, **6**, 18, 570–9.

BOWLBY, J. (1969) *Attachment and loss*, vol. 1, Harmondsworth, Penguin.

*BRIM, O. G. (1965) *Education for child rearing*, New York, Free Press.

BRITISH ASSOCIATION OF SOCIAL WORKERS (1975) *British Association of Social Workers News*, 4/9/75, p. 345.

BROWN, G. W., BHROLCHAIN, M. N. and HARRIS, T. (1975) 'Social class, and psychiatric disturbance among women in an urban population', *Sociology*, **9** (2), 225–54.

CAMERON, J. M. *et al.* (1966) 'The battered child syndrome', *Medical Society and the Law*, **6**, 2–21.

CANNON, W. B. (1945) *The way of an investigator: a scientist's experiences in medical research*, New York, Norton.

*CAVENAGH, W. E. (1975) 'A view from the courts', *Royal Society of Health Journal*, **95**, 3, 153–5.

CHAZAN, M. and COX, T. (1976) 'Language programmes for disadvantaged children', in Varma, V. P. and Williams, P. (eds.) *Piaget, psychology and education*, London, Hodder and Stoughton.

*CLARKE, A. M. and CLARKE, A. D. B. (eds.) (1976) *Early experience: myth and evidence*, London, Open Books.

COOPER, J. D. (1974) 'Dimensions of parenthood', in Department of Health and Social Security (1974b).

*COVENTRY AREA REVIEW COMMITTEE (1976) *A professional guide on the detection and treatment of child abuse*, City of Coventry.

DEFOE, D. (1728) *A plan of the English commerce*, Fairfield, N. J., Kelley.

*DEPARTMENT OF HEALTH AND SOCIAL SECURITY (1974a) *Non-accidental injury to children*, Circular, LASSL (74) 13, CMO (74) 8.

DEPARTMENT OF HEALTH AND SOCIAL SECURITY (1974b) *The family in society: preparation for parenthood*, London, HMSO.

*DEPARTMENT OF HEALTH AND SOCIAL SECURITY (1974c) *Report of the Committee of Inquiry into the care and supervision provided in relation to Maria Colwell*, London, HMSO.

DEPARTMENT OF HEALTH AND SOCIAL SECURITY (1975a) *Non-accidental injury to children*, Circular, LASSL (75) 30, December.

*DEPARTMENT OF HEALTH AND SOCIAL SECURITY (1975b) *Report of the Committee of Inquiry into the provision and co-ordination of services to the family of John George Auckland*, London, HMSO.

*DEPARTMENT OF HEALTH AND SOCIAL SECURITY (1976a) *Non-accidental injury to children: area review committees*, Circular, LASSL (76) 2, CMO (76) 2, CNO (76) 3.

DEPARTMENT OF HEALTH AND SOCIAL SECURITY (1976b) *Non-accidental injury to children: the police and case conferences*, Circular, LASSL (76) 26 HC (76) 50, HO (179/76).

DEPARTMENT OF HEALTH AND SOCIAL SECURITY AND DEPARTMENT OF EDUCATION AND SCIENCE (1976) *Fit for the future. The report of the Committee on Child Health Services*, (Chairman: S. D. M. Court), Cmnd. 6654, London, HMSO.

DONACHY, W. (1976) 'Parent participation in pre-school education', *British Journal of Educational Psychology*, **46**, 31–9.

DRAKE, F. (1975) 'The position of the local authority', in White Franklin, A. (ed.) *Concerning child abuse*, Edinburgh, Churchill Livingstone.

*ERIKSON, E. H. (1959) 'Growth and crises of the healthy personality', *Psychological Issues*, **1**, 50–100. Reprinted in Lazarus and Opton (1967), pp. 167–96.

ERIKSON, E. H. (1963) *Childhood and society*, 2nd edn., New York, Norton.

FACTORIES AND WORKSHOPS COMMISSION (1876) Report P.P., Volume XXIX.

FREUD, A. (1970) 'The concept of the rejecting mother', in Anthony, E. J. and Benedek, T. (eds.) *Parenthood*, Boston, Little, Brown.

*FRIEDMAN, S. B. and MORSE, C. W. (1974) 'Child abuse: a five year follow-up of early case finding in the emergency department', *Pediatrics*, **54**, 4.

FRY, A. (1976) 'NAI: Danger of over-reaction', *Community Care*, July 14.

287

GAIRDNER, J. (ed.) (1900) *The Paston Letters* 1422–1509, Letter 71, London, Constable.

*GIL, D. (1970) 'Violence against children', in Dreitzel, H. P. (ed.) (1973) *Childhood and socialisation*, London, Macmillan.

GOODE, W. J. (1970) *World revolution and family patterns*, London, Macmillan.

GREENBERG, M., ROSENBERG, I. and LIND, J. (1973) 'First mothers rooming-in with their newborns: its impact upon the mother', *American Journal of Orthopsychiatry*, **43**, 783–8.

GRIFFITHS, D. L. and MOYNIHAN, F. J. (1963) 'Multiple epiphyseal injuries in babies (battered baby syndrome)', *British Medical Journal*, No. 5372, 1558–61.

HELFER, H. E., MCKINNEY, J. and KEMPE, R. (1976) 'Arresting or freezing the developmental process', in Helfer, R. E. and Kempe, C. H. (eds.) *Child abuse and neglect*, Cambridge, Mass., Ballinger.

HOME, HEALTH AND EDUCATION DEPARTMENTS (1945, reprinted 1969) *Report of the Care of Children Committee*, (Chairman: Myra Curtis), Cmd. 6922, London, HMSO.

HOME OFFICE (1945) *Report by Sir Walter Monkton on the circumstances which led to the boarding out of Denis and Terence O'Neill*, Cmd. 6636, London, HMSO.

HOUSE OF COMMONS (1977) *Violence to children*, vol. 1 (329–i), First report from the Select Committee on Violence in the Family, session 1976–77, London, HMSO.

HUBERT, J. (1974) 'Social factors in pregnancy and childbirth', in Richards, M. P. M. (ed.) *The integration of a child into a social world*, Cambridge University Press.

*HULL, D. (1974) 'The medical diagnosis', in Carter, J. (ed.) *The maltreated child*, London, Priory Press.

*JACKSON, A. (1975) 'Court procedure in child abuse', *Midwife, Health Visitor and Community Nurse*, **11**, 329–32.

JEFFERY, M. (1976) 'Practical ways to change parent-child interaction in families of children at risk', in Helfer, R. E. and Kempe, C. H. (eds.) *Child abuse and neglect*, Cambridge, Mass., Ballinger.

JEHU, D. (1967) *Learning theory and social work*, London, Routledge and Kegan Paul.

JEHU, D., HARDIKERS, P., YELLOLY, M. and SHAW, M. (1972) *Behaviour modification in social work*, London, Wiley.

JOBLING, M. (1976) *The abused child: an annotated bibliography*, National Children's Bureau.

JONES, C. O. (1977a) 'The fate of abused children', in White Franklin, A. (ed.) *The challenge of child abuse*, London, Academic Press.

*JONES, C. O. (1977b) 'The predicament of abused children', in Lee, C. M. (ed.) (1978). *Child abuse: a reader and sourcebook*, Milton Keynes, The Open University Press.

*JONES, R. and JONES, C. (1974) 'Treatment: a social perspective', in Carter, J. (ed.) *The maltreated child*, London, Priory Press.

KEMPE, H. *et al.* (1962) 'The battered child syndrome', *Journal of the American Medical Association*, **181** (1), 17–22.

*KEMPE, C. H. (1971) 'Paediatric implications of the battered baby syndrome', *Archives of Disease in Childhood*, **46**, 245, 28–37.

*KEMPE, C. H. and HELFER, R. E. (1972) 'Innovative therapeutic approaches', in Kempe, C. H. and Helfer, R. E. (eds.) *Helping the battered child and his family*, Philadelphia, Lippincott.

KENNELL, J. H., JERAULD, R., WOLFE, H., CHESLER, D., KREGER, N. C., MCALPINE, W., STEFFA, M., and KLAUS, M. H. (1974) 'Maternal behaviour one year after early and extended post-partum contact', *Developmental Medicine and Child Neurology*, **16**, 1972–9.

*KENNELL, J. H., VOOS, D. and KLAUS, M. (1976) 'Parent-infant bonding', in Helfer, R. E. and Kempe, C. H. (eds.) *Child abuse and neglect*, Cambridge, Mass., Ballinger.

*KOLUCHOVA, J. (1976) 'Severe deprivation in twins' and 'A report on further development of twins', in Clarke and Clarke (eds.) (1976). *Early experience, myth and evidence*, London, Open Books.

KOLVIN, I. and SCOTT, D. MCI. (1977) 'The multidisciplinary approach in child psychiatry', *General Practitioner*, February 4, p. 18.

LAMBERT, W. W. (1971) 'Cross cultural backgrounds to personality development and the socialisation of aggression', in Lambert, W. W. and Weisbrod, R. (eds.) *Comparative perspectives in social psychology*, Boston, Little, Brown.

*LAMBETH, SOUTHWARK AND LEWISHAM AREA HEALTH AUTHORITY (teaching) (1975) *Report of the Joint Committee of Inquiry into non-accidental injury to children, with particular reference to the case of Lisa Godfrey*, Lambeth, Southwark and Lewisham.

*THE LANCET (1975) 'The battered . . .', The *Lancet*, May 31, pp. 1228–9.

LAZARUS, R. S. and OPTON, E. M. (1967) *Personality: selected readings*, Harmondsworth, Penguin.

LEE, C. M. (ed.) (1978) *Child abuse: a reader and sourcebook*, Milton Keynes, The Open University Press (Reader).

*LYNCH, M. A. (1976) 'Child abuse: the critical path', in *Journal of Maternal and Child Health*, **1**, 3, 25–9.

*MACKEITH, R. (1975) 'Speculations on some possible long-term effects', in White Franklin, A. (ed.) *Concerning child abuse*, Edinburgh, Churchill Livingstone.

MARKS, I. M., CONNOLLY, J. and HALLAM, R. S. (1973) 'Psychiatric nurse as therapist', *British Medical Journal* 509/73, 156–60.

MARTIN, H. P. (1972) 'The child and his development', in Kempe, C. H. and Helfer, R. E. (eds.) *Helping the battered child and his family*, Philadelphia, Lippincott.

MARTIN, H. P. and RODEHEFFER, M. (1976) 'Learning and intelligence', in Martin (ed.) (1976).

MARTIN, H. P. (ed.) (1976) *The abused child: a multi-disciplinary approach to developmental issues and treatment*, Cambridge, Mass., Ballinger.

MARTIN, H. P. and BEEZLEY, P. (1976) 'The emotional development of abused children', accepted for publication in *Developmental Medicine and Child Neurology*.

MORRIS, P. (1975) 'The question the Auckland Inquiry dodged', *Community Care*, **89**, 18–19.

NEWSON, J. and E. (1968) *'Four years old in an urban community'*, London, Allen and Unwin.

THE OPEN UNIVERSITY (1977) P911, *The first years of life*, Milton Keynes, The Open University Press.

THE OPEN UNIVERSITY (1977) P912, *The pre-school child*, Milton Keynes, The Open University Press.

OUNSTED, C. (1972) 'Essay on developmental medicine', in Mandelbrote, B. and Gelder, M. G. (eds.) *Psychiatric aspects of medical practice*, London, Staples Press.

*OUNSTED, C., OPPENHEIMER, R., and LINDSAY, J. (1974) 'Aspects of bonding failure: the psychopathology and psychotherapeutic treatment of families of battered children', *Developmental Medicine and Child Neurology*, **16**, 4, 447–56.

*PECKHAM, C. (1974) 'The dimensions of child abuse', in Carter, J. (ed.) *The maltreated child*, London, Priory Press.

PEINE, H. A. and HOWARTH, R. (1975) *Children and parents: everyday problems of behaviour*, Harmondsworth, Penguin.

PERSONAL SOCIAL SERVICES COUNCIL (1976) *Complaints procedures in the personal social services*, London.

PETERSON, K. (1973) 'Contribution to an abused child's unlovability; failure in the developmental tasks and in the mastery of trauma', MSW Thesis, *Smith College Studies in Social Work* **44** (1), 24–5.

POLAKOW, R. L. and PEABODY, D. L. (1975) 'Behavioural treatment of child abuse', *International Journal of Offender Therapy and Comparative Criminology*, **19**, 1, 100–3.

*PRINGLE, M. L. K. (1974) *The needs of children*, London, Hutchinson.

*REAVLEY, W. and GILBERT, M. T. (1976) 'The behavioural treatment approach to potential child abuse – two illustrative cases', *Social Work Today*, **7**, 6, 166–8.

*RENVOIZE, J. (1974) *Children in danger*, London, Routledge and Kegan Paul.

RICHMAN, N. (1974) 'The effects of housing on pre-school children and their mothers', *Developmental Medicine and Child Neurology*, **16**, 53–8.

SILVERMAN, F. (1953) 'The roentgen manifestations of unrecognised skeletal trauma in infants', *American Journal of Roentgenology*, **69** (3), 413–27.

SMITH, S. M., HANSON, R. and NOBLE, S. (1974) 'Social aspects of the battered baby syndrome', *British Journal of Psychiatry*, **125**, 568.

*STEELE, B. F. and POLLOCK, C. B. (1968) 'A psychiatric study of parents who abuse infants and small children', in Kempe, C. H. and Helfer, R. E. (eds.) *The battered child*, University of Chicago Press.

STERN, H. H. (1960) *Parent education: an international survey*, University of Hull, with UNESCO, Hamburg.

THOMAS, A., CHESS, S. and BIRCH, H. G. (1968) *Temperament and behaviour disorders in children*. New York University Press.

TOUGH, J. (1973) *Focus on meaning: talking to some purpose with young children*, London, Allen and Unwin.

ULLMAN, L. P. (1972) 'Presidential address: who are we?', in *Advances in behaviour therapy*, London, Academic Press.

WESLEY, J. (1872) *The works of John Wesley*, Wesleyan Conference Office.

WEST, S. (1888) 'Acute periosteal swellings in several young infants of the same family, probably rachitic in nature', *British Medical Journal*, **1**, 856.

*WHITE FRANKLIN, A. (ed.) (1975) 'The nature of the task', in White Franklin, A. (ed.) *Concerning child abuse*, Edinburgh, Churchill Livingstone.

WOOLLEY, P. V. and EVANS, W. A. (1955) 'The significance of skeletal lesions in infants resembling those of traumatic origin', *Journal of the American Medical Association*, **158** (7), 539–43.